MW01204804

THIS BOOK BELONGS TO _____

LIKE THE
Leaves

TO EVERY LITTLE LEAF
NEAR AND FAR,
REMEMBER HOW YOU WERE MADE
AND WHOSE YOU ARE!

-JH

2022

Hello little one
like a leaf new and green,

you just started growing
but oh the things you will see!

Birds flying high
squirrels passing by,

raindrops and snowflakes
and buzzing beehives.

Sunshine and nighttime
cold days and warm,

each new season
with so much in store.

On days when you're up
way high in the sky

and days when you're down
just wondering why.

may you always remember
you were made with such care

and the Maker who made you
gave you so much to share.

To my parents, Robert and Patricia Schreter,
for your wisdom, inspiration and encouragement

To Eric, Dan, Harrison and Michael,
for enjoying our adventures together

Preface

A few years ago, I experienced an "aha!" moment that changed how I mentor startup entrepreneurs and business owners. As a guest speaker at a workshop for "seed-stage" and "early-stage" entrepreneurs, my job was to help the audience understand the fine points of debt and equity funding for "high growth potential" businesses.

During a coffee break, one entrepreneur approached me to talk about his no-fail strategy to get his communication technology adopted by the U.S. military. Clearly the guy was bright but a little naive about the realities of getting new technologies certified by the military. From my experience, the process usually takes one or more years–not a few months. This type of sales miscalculation can wreak havoc on a startup because the founder's financial projections of revenue growth will be grossly overstated. When success doesn't come as fast as entrepreneurs expect, investors and first board members may lose confidence and not give them another chance to succeed.

This entrepreneur mentioned something else that increased my uneasiness: he had already borrowed $100,000 from family members in the U.S. and India to fund his startup. It's not an uncommon story. As I listened to him talk about the sacrifices made by his parents, I thought that the odds were good that this well-intentioned entrepreneur could lose his family's entire savings. Actually, the majority of entrepreneurs in the room that day were going to struggle. The question was when.

After the break, the entrepreneur's family situation still weighed on my mind. Most of the time, head-strong entrepreneurs don't want to hear about what might go wrong because they are so convinced that everything will go right.

With my ambitious audience back in their seats, I asked, "Raise your hands if you are highly confident that your business idea will be super successful?" Of course, all hands shot up without hesitation. Then I asked how many entrepreneurs in the room were first-time entrepreneurs. Again, all hands went up. Yikes, I thought. The grim reaper of disappointment would be on its way because first-time entrepreneurs make a lot of beginner's mistakes, which is normal when anyone tries anything for the first time without much help or knowledgeable guidance.

Then I said something along the lines of, "I wish everyone in this room could read some of the gut-wrenching letters I receive from desperate, near-bankrupt business owners. It might change your perspective about the fine line between success and failure." The audience looked at me blankly. Someone in the back of the room called out, "Not us!"

"Oh yeah?" I thought to myself. And just as I was about to rattle off the statistics of business failures, it hit me. There was a way I could make the realities of startup entrepreneurship a little more real to these first-time entrepreneurs. Here's how I did it.

I asked ten volunteers to come to the front of the room with their chairs. The group represented a good mix of interests: software, e-commerce, clean tech, bio-fabrics, health care services, etc. With all ten uber-confident volunteers standing up, I said to the audience in an exaggerated way, "Let's look into the future. Today, ten out of ten entrepreneurs visualize success. Two years from now, odds are that surprise problems and delays will force at least three of these businesses to close. I tapped the shoulders of three guys and said, "You're done–you're done–and you too are done. Please sit down."

One of the fallen entrepreneurs rebelled and said, "No, no, pick someone else. I don't want to be done." I replied with a smile, "No entrepreneur ever wants to be done, but you are done anyway. Take your seat!"

Then I walked behind two more entrepreneurs and said, "Another two years has passed—more unexpected problems, cash losses and disappointment. It's time for both of you to enter the dead business graveyard." Then I tapped two more shoulders to illustrate that by Year Seven, about seven out of every ten startups will turn to dust.

I said to the audience, "Look closely at this group of seven. Their savings–gone. Their optimism–gone. Their confidence–gone. Their good credit rating–gone. Their friends and family members' money–gone. Their investors' money-gone." The room had grown quiet. At last, I had the audience's attention. Their faces no longer exuded confidence but a little fear. Good!

Of course, I'm used to getting push-back from feisty entrepreneurs. One entrepreneur questioned whether my statistics accurately reflected the likely future experiences of this particular audience. He reasoned that because their business plans were good candidates to attract venture capital and expansion funding, they could commercialize their ideas with fewer capital constraints. Plus, since they were highly educated they would have better odds of success than the average new business owner in America.

Was he right? Are the performance rates of companies that raise equity funding through venture capital funds so much better than average startups? I asked the original ten volunteers to stand up again. Relying mostly on venture capital fund performance data I proceeded to tap the shoulders of three volunteers. "You, you and you–you're out of quarters!" Ouch! These entrepreneurs represented venture-backed businesses that lost all or part of investor funds. For added emphasis, I talked about several well-known companies that had received millions of venture capital funding only to land in the dead business graveyard.

Then I asked three more volunteers to sit down. Their businesses just "broke even" which meant that the VCs got their money back. But because VCs usually own preferred stock, they get paid back in full before all other common shareholders. This means that the founders, family members, and some angel investors get next to nothing on break-even deal performance. This information hit the audience especially hard.

Now only four entrepreneurs remained standing. Their successful businesses provided a healthy return to their investors and most likely to the founding entrepreneurs too. So again, despite the luxury of early funding support and venture community networking advantages, the majority of elite entrepreneurs fail to live out their entrepreneurial dreams.

At last the audience understood that entrepreneurial success required more than a good idea and a confident founder. Other things matter more.

My ten volunteers stayed in their front-row seats throughout the workshop, which lasted much longer than planned. It was great. All key discussion topics and proposed strategies were presented in the lively context of membership in the doomed, "faster-to-disaster" group of seven or the prosperous group of three. No longer did business failure just happen to other people. Unless the entrepreneurs were willing to reinvent their approach to business building, the odds were that only about 20 of the 60 workshop attendees would persevere.

That day, they "got it" and so did I. I'm far more effective teaching about what seven out of ten train wreck-bound entrepreneurs do wrong, than what three successful entrepreneurs do right.

And that's what *Start On Purpose* is all about—giving you the action steps and wisdom to lead your company to greatness, with the least amount of beginner's mistakes and needless money-loss along the way.

Introduction

How to Transform Your Purpose
Into Productive Action

What is your purpose in starting a business? Is it to make so much money that you will never have to worry about money again? Is it to commercialize an invention or really awesome idea? Is it to replace a job that you lost during the recession? Is it to do something "more entrepreneurial" with a close friend or family member?

Well my purpose is to help you achieve your purpose. I want you to experience the joy of building a thriving company—something meaningful that you will name and nurture with pride.

Start On Purpose is not like other resources for startup entrepreneurs. That's a good thing too because despite easy access to free online content and the publication of hundreds of business books each year, the survival rate of startup businesses remains stubbornly low. Why? Why aren't America's hardest working innovators—entrepreneurs just like you—more successful?

I became obsessed with this question when I started writing a weekly Q and A format column on venture capital and small business management in the Seattle Post-Intelligencer. From the first day the column ran, my email inbox was hit hard with questions—not just from technologists but a wide range of self-employed individuals and business owners. Since then, and with the addition of other print and online resources like MSN, Yahoo!, and Fox Business, my inbox brings me in touch with a nationwide audience of enthusiastic business builders. It's been a lot of fun.

"I Wish I Had Known Better"

What I didn't expect when I started writing was the amount of mail I would receive from struggling business owners and, occasionally, their relatives. Some letter writers knew what they needed to do, but reached out for reassurance. Others were paralyzed by problems that they "just didn't see coming" and couldn't see "any way out." Given the magnitude of their pain, an email wasn't sufficient. I had to call.

1

The more business owners I spoke to, the more my interest grew into a mission. I wanted to identify the specific issues, attitudes and missteps that cause the most damage to fledgling businesses. After all, when businesses close, employees lose jobs, investors and lenders lose money, vendors lose customers, and business owners lose their savings and their self-confidence. But when new businesses succeed, they can do amazing things.

Over the past several years, in addition to academic research, I've interviewed struggling and bankrupt business owners all over the country. I've asked about their biggest regrets, surprises, problems, beginner's mistakes, and areas of money loss. What I heard in all of these stories of big dreams and big disappointments was one sentence: "I wish I had known better." They needed access to the right information, at the right time from a knowledgeable source. Had they just "known better," they wouldn't have spent the money, signed the deal, ordered the inventory, leased the office space, or hired the blowhard. Things would have been much different had they only known better.

Fortunately, "knowing better" doesn't mean that you have to be an expert in everything. You don't. But you have to know certain things about startup finance and priority setting, which are ongoing themes of this book. Without knowing what's "worth" your time and cash, it's easy to waste your time and cash—big time.

Translating Your Dream into Action Steps

Start On Purpose is a big book—it has to be a rich, empowering resource if it is going to make it easier for you to succeed. Entrepreneurs always demand, "Susan, just tell me what to do—first, second and third." And that's what I've done: prioritized information and startup business strategies into easy-to-understand, easy-to-implement action steps. Every action step in this book has a purpose—to help you become a highly effective, well-respected leader of a valuable company.

Not every action step in this book will be relevant to your situation today, but it could be relevant tomorrow. For example, when you are ready to select the name of your company, check out Chapter 5 to learn more about trademarks, DBA's, and other nasty gotchas that may force you to start all over again with another company name. And when you are ready to divide up shares of your company with first business partners, check out Chapter 8. There you will find extra information about partnership agreements, vesting, valuation issues, and how to avoid problems from the IRS and future investors.

Sure some action steps in *Start On Purpose* may seem too obvious or not worth your time. But, think again! There's a good chance that a specific action step was included just to call attention to a subject or situation that in one way or another tripped up enough business owners to warrant a place in *Start On Purpose*.

Extra Startup Intelligence

I don't promise that your new company will become an overnight sensation or that you can work just a few hours a day and become a millionaire. But what I do promise is that you will become a better startup CEO.

As the boss of your new business, you will make a lot of decisions every day. The time to buy this book is before you make your first decisions about your company's corporate structure, product line, pricing strategies, brand identity, employee selection, patents and trademarks, target customers, board members, funding sources, sales commissions, and so much more.

There is another aspect of startup decision-making that is not emphasized enough in the venture building community. If you want to make consistently good decisions for your company, you must recognize when it's a bad time (perhaps an impossible time) to make a good decision. You also will have to boldly stand up for your company and your better judgment, even when you are pressured to do otherwise. This is how you will become an awesome and awe-inspiring leader of your new business.

Extra Financial Empowerment

One thing is clear from my research; it will be easier for you to achieve your dreams as a business owner, if you are smart about building the equity value of your business. And you can!

Here's how *Start On Purpose* can help you become more sophisticated about startup finance and equity building:

- **Understand value**

  Entrepreneurial dreams are great to achieve, provided that you don't overpay for your dream. Whatever amount of savings you decide to invest in your business, you have to make sure that your company will eventually be worth more. Unfortunately, too many incredibly dedicated business owners today are operating businesses that are "underwater." This means they invested more hard cash in their beloved companies than the companies are worth today. They worked really hard, but at the wrong things.

  If you are going to all the trouble of starting a company, why not do the things that can make it worth two, four or ten times your cash investment? *Start On Purpose* will introduce you to some of the "fundamentals" of business value that will help you make more rewarding decisions about your products, services, customers, employees and technologies. If you want a fast peek, skip to Chapter 3!

- **Prepare for future fundraising**

  "I can't raise money for my business!" This is the most common remark I get in emails from entrepreneurs who are trying to raise money to start or expand their business. By the time they reach out to me for help, they're exasperated, bewildered, angry or demoralized.

  Start On Purpose is your prerequisite resource if you want to raise extra working capital from investors and lenders. You'll know more about the expectations of financial partners, the business strategies that excite them, and the attitudes of entrepreneurs that repel them. Pay extra attention to the first three chapters plus any action step that is marked with a **$$** sign code.

- **Embrace financial and legal terms**

  Start On Purpose doesn't dumb down important financial and legal concepts or ignore them altogether. A common regret of struggling business owners—including business owners with advanced educations—is they didn't speak up about financial and legal terms that were unfamiliar to them. They didn't ask questions because they didn't want to seem "stupid" or unqualified to run a business.

  An important objective of *Start On Purpose* is to give you enough baseline information so you can talk to prospective business partners, lawyers, accountants, business valuation experts, domain experts and investors with confidence. You'll be empowered to ask smart questions and collaborate with experts to help propel your company to "the next level."

All of the concepts, strategies and action steps in this book have been tested and tweaked through workshops at Small Business Administration offices, incubators, micro-loan centers, angel investment club events, personal coaching sessions and MBA classes. My attitude as a teacher is that it's my job to create "aha!" moments. There's nothing more satisfying and fun than working with an entrepreneur who suddenly "gets" something that used to be intimidating. So dig in.

I hope *Start On Purpose* will expand your horizons and inspire you to think bigger and smarter about your company's possibilities. Whatever you want to accomplish in business, you will be able to do it faster and easier provided that you *Start On Purpose*.

Invest It!

How to Make Big Money Through Business Ownership

Making money is a leading reason why Americans start their own businesses. Yet, when I ask startup entrepreneurs in coaching sessions about their specific money-making goals, they usually have only vague notions about what they want to achieve as a business owner. Even if money-making is not your primary motivation, my strong recommendation is to spend some time thinking through your personal financial goals before investing your heart, soul and savings in a new endeavor.

There are two primary ways you can make money as an entrepreneur. The first is income in the form of a salary and possibly a bonus at year end. The second form of reward—and the one that creates millionaires and billionaires—is the growing value or net worth of the business itself. This is called "equity."

Equity ownership of a valuable business helps create personal wealth. It funds bigger houses, sports cars, vacation homes, college educations, philanthropy and a more secure retirement. It's easy to get excited about equity. Think of equity as the fast track to enjoyment, empowerment and earnings—all with a capital E. And that's what this chapter is about—thinking bigger and smarter about equity.

Build Worth and Wealth

Entrepreneurs are well represented in *Forbes* magazine's annual list of the 400 wealthiest individuals in the U.S. They did not inherit their immense wealth or win it in a state lottery. They earned their fortunes through the growth in value of their businesses, not the steady growth of their salaries.

For example, everyone seems to know Mark Cuban. He's the feisty owner of the Dallas Mavericks basketball team, Shark Tank television show investor, and member of the Forbes 400. But Cuban is also a master of building the equity value of businesses. Cuban started MicroSolutions in the 1980's just as the demand for personal computers was growing. Seven years later, Cuban sold MicroSolutions to CompuServe for $6 million, netting Cuban a cool $2 million. Then in 1995, Cuban and his partner Todd Wagner started what would become Broadcast.com. Four years later, at the height of the dot com boom, Broadcast.com was sold to Yahoo! for over $5 billion in Yahoo! stock. I bet at some point Cuban said "Yahoo!" after he signed off on this well-timed company sale.

And then there is Oprah Winfrey—another member of the Forbes 400. While other popular talk show hosts, newscasters and actors were content to take a steady pay check and report to others, Oprah believed in her vision and founded her own production studio in 1986. When you own the studio that produces a top daytime talk show for 25 years, you are going to make some serious money. Ownership also means that no one can fire you for taking chances. I think it is wonderful that Oprah co-founded a new network called "OWN." Perhaps Oprah's entrepreneurial success reminds us that one way to lead your best life is to *own* the rewards of your hard work.

When I speak to unemployed individuals about reinventing their professional careers through business ownership, I usually point to Forbes 400 members Michael Bloomberg, Bernard Marcus, Arthur Blank and Steve Jobs—each one was blindsided by a high-profile corporate firing. As Jobs said in a speech to Stanford's 2005 graduation class, "I didn't see it then, but it turned out that getting fired from Apple was the best thing that could have ever happened to me. The heaviness of being successful was replaced by the lightness of being a beginner again." Jobs focused his attention on creating wonderful films through Pixar Animation Studios. Several years later he enjoyed a great payday when he sold Pixar to Disney for over $7 billion. Then he turned his full attention again to reinventing Apple.

Bernard Marcus and Arthur Blank co-founded Home Depot in 1978, right after they were fired from the Handy Dan Home Improvement Centers. Marcus and Blank didn't let the bitterness of a public firing get the best of them. Instead, they channeled all of their creative energy and experience into creating something better. Today, Home Depot is the world's largest home improvement retailer with over 2,000 stores. The Handy Dan chain went out of business in the late 1980's.

Entrepreneurs don't have to be groundbreaking technology wizards with advanced educations to build valuable businesses. Sometimes the magic comes from finding a smarter, faster, cheaper way to succeed.

Do you have a few Beanie Babies around your house? At a time when all other toy and novelty gift manufacturers sought success through a few big retailers, Ty Warner targeted thousands of "mom and pop" stores to sell his little stuffed animals. In small shops, Beanie Babies could get immediate shelf space; in large retail toy chains, a low retail value product like Beanie Babies could sit in storeroom boxes for weeks. In small shops, Warner could get his asking price; in large retail chains, Warner would have to juggle to manage all the extra costs associated with selling to large chains.

Warner's distribution alliances with small neighborhood retail shops also gave Ty Inc. the flexibility to change out or "retire" Beanie Baby styles frequently, creating a highly effective "buy it now" customer frenzy. Ironically, Ty, Inc. became billion-dollar big by thinking small.

I'm passionate about teaching entrepreneurship—especially in areas of the country with high rates of unemployment—because I know that business ownership can be life changing to entrepreneurs and their families. Right now, you can start a company that can grow in value to be worth $50,000, $500,000, $5 million or $5 billion. It's all doable in America, provided that building equity remains one of your top priorities for as long as you own your business.

Invest with Purpose

Prosperous entrepreneurs are very much like farmers in that they plant and sow seeds for a lucrative harvest. So what constitutes a successful harvest? And what is the right amount of savings to plant in a new business?

When I first started conducting entrepreneurship workshops, I was surprised by the number of questions entrepreneurs asked whenever I talked about the investment performance of small businesses. Audience members would call out "talk slower," "talk louder," or "say that again." And even though these workshops were primarily focused on other subjects, any reference to protecting the investment value of a founder's cash contributions to a new business would send the workshop discussion seriously off track.

It took me a long time to realize that startup entrepreneurs, especially first-time entrepreneurs don't think of themselves as "investors." Because I come from a Wall Street background, it's natural for me to think about any kind of business funding in terms of future investment value. But that's not natural for most first-time entrepreneurs. They could put all their savings into a startup enterprise and still not think much about generating a positive financial return on their invested cash. Why not?

A Russian immigrant helped me appreciate that the investment decisions of first-time entrepreneurs are driven more by their passion instead of their purpose. The distinctions are subtle but meaningful. He said that up until my class, he always thought that investors had to be "other people." If a neighbor put $50,000 into his new tech company, the neighbor was an investor. If he put the same amount of money into his company, then he was just "a determined entrepreneur pursuing a dream."

When I asked the technologist how he determined the right amount of money to put into his startup, he said that he always assumed that he would fund his company for as much as he was able. Whether or not the added cash contribution was a "smart move" or a "wise investment" was not ever, as he said, "on his radar screen." His funding decisions were based entirely on one simple factor. He said, "If my company needs it, then I will supply it—whatever it takes."

Aha! "Whatever it takes!" Who would think that this phrase would be the source of so much pain and money loss in the small business community! On the surface, the expression represents the single-minded determination of startup entrepreneurs to follow through on their ideas and do something really special in the marketplace. But over time, and as entrepreneurs invest more of their heart, soul and savings in their young companies, their passion to do "whatever it takes" becomes a decision-making liability.

When a company needs another $2,000 to pay a bill, the urgent need overshadows more purposeful questions such as, "Will my company advance or become more valuable by investing another $2,000?" Because entrepreneurs rarely ask thoughtful questions before investing their savings, they tend to "over-invest" in their companies. The insanity stops only when they run out of cash, credit lines, or supportive family members.

No business owner should ever say "I put everything into my company." It's how business owners lose their homes, their savings, and their self-worth—all because they continue to invest beyond what they can afford to lose. It doesn't have to be.

You don't need a college education or an MBA from a prestigious university to invest your savings with purpose. From the moment you transfer funds from a personal bank account into a business bank account you are a business investor. When you start to think and act more like a business investor, you'll find that your actions become more thoughtful, strategic, and smart. Fewer situations will scare you and you will be empowered to solve problems with less angst and mind-numbing indecision. And I bet you will stand taller as you talk about your new company to lenders and investors all because you understand the fine points of earning a positive financial return on your invested time and savings. You can do it!

Your next action steps:

☐ Go for the gain

I would rather earn $1 million in a capital gain from the sale of an asset like a business than $1 million in salary all because I don't like paying more to the IRS than the law requires. Wealthy "angel" investors, who may be a source of seed or expansion capital for your new company, think the same way too.

The top personal income tax bracket—for individuals who report over $400,000 in income—is 39.6%. In contrast, the top bracket federal tax rate on the profits earned from the sale of most assets (like art, stock or a business) that are held more than one year is 20%—not including the Medicare surtax for individuals making over $200,000 a year. As such, the tax rate on capital gains is about half as much as the top income tax rate for big earners, like you in the future.

☐ **Cap your savings investment**

Over the years of coaching a broad range of entrepreneurs, I've learned that when they set a fixed "investment ceiling" prior to starting their companies, they are less impulsive about writing personal checks to cover emergency business needs and much more proactive about seeking outside sources of funding long before they ever need it.

So, what amount of non-retirement savings can you comfortably afford to invest in your new business—not just at the time of startup but over the entire course of business ownership? Your answer should not involve raiding your family's emergency fund. While you might be desperate to start a new income-generating career, investing hard cash in a new business in my book doesn't qualify as an emergency.

The table at the right can serve as a useful guide to help you set your investment ceiling. In coaching sessions, I give extra investment ceiling credit to entrepreneurs who are starting businesses in their primary line of work because they are less likely to make many beginner's mistakes.

Investment Ceiling Guide

50+ age first-time entrepreneurs: 10% to 20% of non-retirement household savings

30- to 40-something first-time entrepreneurs: 25% to 35% of non-retirement savings

20-something first-time entrepreneurs: Go for it!

Startup entrepreneurs who live in two-income households also have more flexibility to invest more of their personal savings in a new enterprise, provided the spouse's income is predictable and comes with affordable family healthcare coverage. Entrepreneurs who have paid off their primary home mortgage and have a significant retirement nest egg in place can be more aggressive startup investors too.

When you think you have a good working number for your investment ceiling in mind, test the reasonableness of your number by answering the following questions:

- How many months or years did it take to save this number? How many years of salaried employment would it take for you to earn back this same amount of money again if you lost it all?

- If your investment advisor lost this amount of your money, would you fire the advisor?

- Would you ever gamble this amount of money during a single trip to Las Vegas or Atlantic City?

- Does this number represent more than 50% of your total non-retirement savings?

$$ ☐ **Invest low**

Now that you have set your investment ceiling, you can have some fun projecting what kind of long-term business valuation growth will provide a lucrative return on your upcoming cash investment. This is not an exercise in wishful thinking. Rather, this action step is one of the most effective ways to encourage entrepreneurs to invest LESS (buy-in low) in their companies in order to make MORE (sell high).

Most startup entrepreneurs assume that buying low is just a reference to the price paid for an asset or a share of company stock. In my workshops, invest low means keeping the amount of capital you have at risk in your company as low as possible. Here's why. The more hard cash you invest in your company, the more your company has to perform to deliver a fat and happy return on your invested cash. Simply stated, it will be easier for you to double or quadruple the value of a $10,000 investment than a $100,000 investment.

Set up a financial spread sheet similar to the table at right. Multiply the amount of savings you plan to invest in your business (your investment ceiling) by several factors: two, four and ten. The result shows you how much you would have to sell your business for in order to earn a robust return on your total invested capital.

For simple illustrative purposes, an entrepreneur invests $35,000 in her new business. Because she builds her company without selling stock to investors, she still owns 100% of her company at the time of business sale. Without considering the time value of money, the entrepreneur certainly succeeded in generating a positive return on invested cash. If she sold her company at a price that was four times her $35,000 investment, she would earn a pre-tax profit of $105,000 ($140,000-$35,000).

Of course, Uncle Sam is the tagalong business partner to every successful entrepreneur. Depending on the entrepreneur's tax bracket, the IRS will take up to 20% of the net profit at the time of business sale. Applicable state taxes may also reduce the owner's take-home profit.

What would happen to the entrepreneur's financial return if the company received one or more rounds of capital from investors? Clearly, every time entrepreneurs sell shares of stock to friends, family members or independent investors, the percentage of their ownership stake declines. In the second simple example, the entrepreneur's equity stake has dropped from 100% to 51%. Assuming that all investors own the same class of stock, the founding entrepreneur will only receive 51% of the proceeds from the sale of her company.

Example 1: Entrepreneur Owns 100% at Sale!

Entrepreneur's Total Cash Investment: **$35,000**	Gross Sale Proceeds	Pre-Tax Profit	Profit After 20% Capital Gains Tax
Sells @ **2 times** invested cash	$ 70,000	$ 35,000	$ 28,000
Sells @ **4 times** invested cash	$ 140,000	$ 105,000	$ 84,000
Sells @ **10 times** invested cash	$ 350,000	$ 315,000	$ 252,000

You can see from the table below that selling a company at a respectable two times the founder's invested capital doesn't produce much of a financial return after paying taxes—just $560. The founder would probably have earned a higher financial return by simply investing the $35,000 in a FDIC-insured certificate of deposit. That's a sobering result indeed given all the hard work associated with starting and building a business!

The purpose of these simplistic examples is to highlight the value of investing LESS in order to make MORE at the time of business sale. The more hard cash you invest in your business, the more you will have to build the salable value of your business (the subject of Chapter 3) in order to earn a generous profit on your invested cash. Most entrepreneurs assume that the opposite is true—that investing more savings in a business will automatically lead to a bigger investment return. Now you know better.

Example 2: Entrepreneur Owns 51% at Sale!

Entrepreneur's Total Cash Investment: **$35,000**	Gross Sale Proceeds	Pre-Tax Profit	Profit After 20% Capital Gains Tax
Sells @ **2 times** invested cash	$ 35,700	$ 700	$ 560
Sells @ **4 times** invested cash	$ 71,400	$ 36,400	$ 29,120
Sells @ **10 times** invested cash	$ 178,500	$143,500	$ 114,800

NOTE: If you have trouble reading any of the charts in this book on small screen e-readers or tablets, visit www.StartOnPurpose.com for easy-to-read versions.

☐ **Balance risk and return**

Angel and venture capital fund investors seek investment returns that are proportional to historical risk. This means that investors in startup companies (including you) should expect an extra reward or a "risk premium" for writing checks to a company that is not yet producing revenues or profits. If you don't bother to set any quantitative performance expectations for your cash investments or merely hope to just "get your money back," then your goals are not high enough for the risk you are about to take as a startup entrepreneur.

☐ **Aim to beat the S&P**

Most professional stock market investors define success as beating the S&P 500, which is a broad based index that includes publicly-traded utilities, energy companies, banks, health care companies, technology companies and consumer product companies with a minimum market capitalization of $4 billion.

Typically, investors in S&P 500 stocks generate financial returns through the growth in share price plus dividend payments. Of course some years are better than others. During the 1990's the S&P 500 returned roughly 18% to investors. During the 2000's, the S&P 500 returned a negative 1%. Overall, however, from 1950 to 2009, the index returned about 11% to shareholders.

To the extent that you pull savings from your non-retirement funds to invest in your new company, you should seek a financial return that at least exceeds the average S&P return. Wealthy angel investors who invest in startup companies think the same way too.

☐ **Get compensated for time**

Another insightful way to think about your upcoming investment in your new company is to factor "investment liquidity" and the time value of money into your decision-making.

"Liquidity" is a financial concept that measures how fast an investor can convert an asset into cash without heavy discounting. Investments in publicly-traded companies like IBM or Proctor & Gamble are considered highly liquid investments because their securities can be converted into cash on short notice.

In contrast, investments in startup companies are considered "illiquid investments" because it's likely that you will have your funds tied up for a good five to ten years before a "liquidity event." This is the happy time when you can sell all or a part of your ownership stake to corporations, local competitors, investor groups, employees or another individual. In rare cases, entrepreneurs can cash out their equity by "going public" on a public stock exchange too.

Savvy investors routinely discount an entrepreneur's projections for the period of time funds are invested in a company. Here's how the thinking goes—in simplified terms, if you triple the value of an investment in three years, you will earn a robust return of roughly 44%. If you triple the value of the same investment in five years, your time-adjusted return drops to roughly 38%.

Considerations related to the time value of money help explain why angel investors and venture capital funds expect such high returns on their investment dollar. Not only are they being asked to invest in a riskier type of investment, but they have little ability to get their money out of the deal on a moment's notice. This will be true for your upcoming investment too.

☐ Diversify your investment dollar

Investing in privately-held companies typically represents a small portion of an angel investor's total net worth–usually less than 10%. In contrast, entrepreneurs can end up investing everything they have in their beloved companies. Most personal finance experts preach the benefits of investment diversification to minimize investment risk. Unless you have income from other reliable sources, investing 100% of your savings in a startup is not the smartest way to capitalize your new business.

☐ Transfer investment risk to others

$$

If you can't afford to invest hard cash in your startup, don't. You can reduce your company's dependence on your personal savings by seeking capital from other investors. The majority of entrepreneurs who are represented on the Forbes list of 400 wealthiest Americans got help from seed-stage and early-stage investors to pursue their business idea. Just ask Jeff Bezos from Amazon.com, Bill Gates and Paul Allen from Microsoft, Larry Page and Sergey Brin from Google, Fred Smith from Federal Express, Steve Case from AOL, Pierre Omidyar from eBay, Marc Benioff from SalesForce.com, Larry Ellison from Oracle and many others.

While asking strangers for money may seem intimidating, you can raise capital for a promising business provided you don't wait until you are out of funds to make a first appeal. In fact, all the action steps in this book are designed to help you raise capital from investors and lenders on the best terms possible, if and when you need to.

Of course, I am used to receiving considerable push back from entrepreneurs who have "heard" about nasty problems associated with raising capital from investors. They assume that it is "expensive" mostly because they don't put a high value on their own savings. If entrepreneurs assume there is no cost to their own savings, then raising funds from independent sources is always going to be perceived as "more risky" and "expensive."

So what's the bottom line? Now you know that your cash is worth something. Your ongoing priority is to make sure that your business is always worth more than the hard cash you put into it. Every dollar you invest in your business today should ideally grow in value to be worth two, four or ten dollars tomorrow. The next chapter will show you how to do it!

FAQs

Q. **I have two different business ideas that can be huge. I'd like to pursue both businesses at the same time. Will investors allow this?**

A. My strong recommendation is to pick one opportunity and pursue it with gusto. If you insist on pursuing both opportunities at the same time, you will struggle to find investors. Investors want to back entrepreneurs who commit 100% of their time to a startup initiative rather than 50% or less.

Q. **What investment returns do venture capitalists expect?**

A. "Private equity" is an important term to know. It refers to investments in privately-held companies as opposed to publicly-traded companies. There are different sectors within the private equity industry, ranging from investments in seed-stage businesses like yours all the way up to investments to acquire large companies, turnaround bankrupt companies, or help publicly-traded companies "go private" again. The term "venture capital" usually refers to investments in seed-stage, early-stage and expansion-stage businesses.

During the last twenty years, the Venture Capital Index returned roughly 25% to venture capital fund investors. But this industry performance significantly understates the investment goals of most VCs. VCs don't write checks to startup companies that might deliver a mere 25% investment return—they look for companies that have the potential to deliver far more. Here's why.

Within every venture capital fund portfolio are massive investment winners and massive investment losers. In order to achieve a blended portfolio financial return of over 25%, one or two portfolio company investments have to deliver grand slam home run returns in order to make up for the larger number of money-losing VC investments that strike out. This is why VCs always seek to invest in seed-stage and early-stage companies that have home run potential and can likely deliver investment returns well over 40%. Another way VCs talk about financial returns is by the multiple of invested capital. Larger funds are happy to earn 10 times or more on their invested capital.

Individual angel investors usually don't have specific rate of return performance objectives to guide their investing activities, though members of angel investment clubs tend to have higher expectations for investment performance. While angel investing is difficult to track, different studies report similar results to VC investing: a few investments that return at least 10 times invested capital help offset the majority of angel investments that lose money. Here's a good guideline to know as you develop your company's financial projections. Average angel investment performance is approximately 2.5 to 3 times invested capital in about 4 years with ballpark returns of 25%.

Q. **Don't investors expect entrepreneurs to invest everything they own in a business to receive funding?**

A. Investors do give entrepreneurs a check mark in their favor for investing their savings in their new companies. It's called "having skin in the game." Angels and VCs like the amount to be meaningful but not so much that the entrepreneur can't sleep at night. My recommendation is to set your investment ceiling and stick to it. When you reach the investment ceiling, simply tell investors that "that's all I have." Unlike commercial lenders, most investors don't ask to review an entrepreneur's personal financial statement before making a decision to invest in a company.

Q. **You always talk about "worth"—is it really worth it for me to start a business?**

A. This is a popular question—and here's my answer. It's worth exploring the possibilities. You may not startup now, but there is a good chance you may need to earn extra income during your career, especially after a layoff or birth of children. There is upside through business ownership too. Salaries for 90% of Americans have been stagnant or trending downward for two decades. According to the IRS, the average taxpayer's annual income is about $33,400. In contrast, the average small business owner in America is likely to enjoy higher annual incomes and three times the net worth of his or her salaried counterparts. Clearly, business ownership can be worthwhile provided you build your company's "worth." There is added upside for women and minority entrepreneurs. Today the gender wage gap—or the difference between a man's pay and woman's pay for the same job—stands at approximately 77 to 80 cents for every dollar men earn. For African American and Hispanic women the wage gap is even greater. Minority women earn just 58 cents to 70 cents for every dollar men earn. In contrast, when women and minority entrepreneurs own the results of their hard work as a business owner, there is no limit to their earnings potential.

Q. **I've been thinking of selling cosmetics through a network marketing company to earn some money. The company's regional sales manager says that being a sales rep is like being a business owner. So what should I focus on most to help me succeed?**

A. I hope after you read more chapters of this book that you'll want to own a business outright and not work as a sales agent for a network marketing or "multi-level marketing" organization. It seems to me that the harder you work selling someone else's products, the more you build the value of the network marketing company's worth—not yours. As an independent sales rep, you bear all the risk, expenses and payroll tax obligations associated with product sales without the upside benefits of real business ownership. You don't own the brand you are promoting and you will never experience the glory of selling your company for thousands or millions of dollars. While you think about your decision, visit Chapter 11 for tips on how to develop lasting relationships with customers. The guidance can help you in any kind of career involving sales.

Aim It!

How to Reduce the Risks of Going Out of Business Before Going into Business

When I meet with new business owners, participants in business plan competitions, "venture-backed" technology entrepreneurs, MBA students, and nonprofit social entrepreneurs, one of the first questions I ask is this:

"As the founder and CEO of your new company, what do you think will be your most important management priority during your first years in business?"

Your #1 Responsibility

It's funny how this seemingly easy question can stump so many entrepreneurs. At first, audience participants think it is a trick question and that a startup entrepreneur's top job is "to do every job." If this is your expectation too, your company is likely going to join the doomed group of seven because you will burn out from the needless stress.

Startup entrepreneurs can't do it all and shouldn't ever try. Trust me, after years of working with struggling business owners, I know that there is nothing productive about acting like an octopus and multitasking through an endless list of work items. That approach lacks leadership focus and will take all the fun out of running your new business. You deserve better!

So what responsibility should rise to the top of your priority list? Is it to design your company's products or services? Is it to set strategy or manage your company's investors and board of directors? Is it to sell and serve customers well? Younger entrepreneurs often say it is their job to be aggressive about social media and promoting their company's big potential. Responses from older entrepreneurs tend to favor leadership values and mission. Technologists usually point to patent filings and domain dominance as top management priorities.

Certainly designing products, setting strategy, and pursuing customers are important activities. But none of these operating priorities rate highest on my list of business founders' top responsibilities.

Are you stumped? If so, you are in good company because not a single university student or startup entrepreneur has ever guessed my preferred answer on the first try.

Here's the real deal on how to succeed as a startup entrepreneur: **don't run out of cash!** Yup, that's it. Don't run out of cash. This is priority #1. There's no great mystery to business viability: businesses close when they run out of cash. As gamers would say, it's kill screen, dead-in-blood or out-of-quarters. In Yogi Berra-speak, when there is nothing left, there is nothing left.

As the CEO of your startup enterprise your top priority is to make sure your company always has enough cash to operate. The concept is so simple and obvious that it's easily overlooked as an operating priority. Companies can manage without mission statements, but they can't operate without cash. They continually have to "fuel up" with cash or fail.

I am somewhat of a renegade educator in my hyper-emphasis on cash, not just for for-profit companies but non-profit social enterprises too. Cash is the fuel that will power your company's growth. Entrepreneurs who are passionate about earning, collecting and protecting their cash are going to stay in business longer than entrepreneurs who don't appreciate its almighty significance to sustainable business operations—that is until it's too late.

It doesn't matter if you want to produce a film, open a restaurant, market an app, or create a hot fashion label, cash availability will fuel your company's success. Cash helps make the dream a reality; lack of cash turns the dream into a nightmare.

Fuel Up or Fail

In 2005, Danica Patrick was the first woman to lead the famous Indianapolis 500 Memorial Day weekend race. At a time when everything seemed to be going so right for the talented rookie, Danica and her team of advisors made a critical error in estimating fuel consumption. While other racers took time out to fuel up, Danica bet she had enough fuel to finish the race in a winning way. She didn't. And so with just six more laps to victory, Danica's competitors passed her by.

Unfortunately safeguarding cash has somehow lost its cache. Perhaps the subject is not provocative enough to warrant "secrets of success" media attention. Sure it's fun to read about how the founders of Amazon, Google and Facebook "broke all the rules" to succeed.

$$ **But if you look closely at the histories of these pioneering companies you will find that each founder fueled up before every major product development or expansion initiative. They didn't bring their companies to the brink of disaster by piling on extra inventory, payroll, office space and other obligations before they had the cash in hand to pay for them. They also didn't bank on someone out of nowhere saving the day before the big bills came due. This is the leadership mindset of highly successful entrepreneurs that is worth mimicking.**

RISK is a Four-Letter Word

Are you looking forward to finally going out on your own and "taking some big risks"? Do you think of risk-taking as one of the fun perks of entrepreneurship? Well, I don't. Actually, in my book (literally), RISK is a four-letter word. Entering into needlessly risky situations or gambling a company's precious cash on untested ideas can create a lot of pain, money loss and embarrassment for an entrepreneur. In the end, there is nothing fun about it.

Is there more inherent risk in a startup than more established businesses? Of course there is! Big companies can more easily absorb unexpected problems than little ones. They have more cash on hand to hire extra help to rework product or service problems or reimburse customers for missteps. Cash-rich companies like Toyota and BP have the resources to recover from the legal liabilities and bad publicity associated with surging car engines and catastrophic leaks from offshore drilling operations. Startups and smaller companies just don't have the same deep pockets to survive too many unexpected problems.

Here's an example of how higher risk "bet the farm" strategies work against startup entrepreneurs. Years ago a business plan landed on my desk from a woman who wanted to start an all-natural line of baby food. When I met the founder, she laid out a point-by-point plan detailing how she was going to challenge Gerber on the major chain grocery store shelves. Her product branding was terrific and consumer purchasing trends in her category matched her business plan beautifully. Still, I thought her first rollout plans were unnecessarily risky and cash-intensive for a startup company. By targeting the largest retail chains in the cut-throat Northeast market she would have to fund larger inventory runs and pay hefty upfront cash "slotting" fees to each grocery chain. If sales did not meet the grocery chain's weekly sales expectations, unsold product could be shipped back to the company for cash reimbursement—putting even more strain on the young company's limited cash resources.

A more risk-adverse rollout strategy for her new baby food business would have favored producing, testing and selling smaller batches of product to local and regional specialty retailers. Once the company "created some traction" and cash flow from first customers, then it could more easily manage manufacturing and product distribution to larger chains in a risk-adverse way.

Whatever happened to this company? The good news is the founder was successful in raising funds from other investors. The bad news is the company "bet the farm" on big chains and lost. Its first batch of fruit-based baby food spoiled, leaving the company without any cash, credibility or hope for a rebound.

$$ No single event or initiative should have the power to completely decimate your new company. All or nothing odds are just not good odds for startup entrepreneurs. There are more productive ways to build your company that will give you a better chance of rejoicing in the prosperous group of three versus the faster-to-disaster group of seven. Plus, the hard cash investment you are about to make in your new company is more likely to get you somewhere rather than nowhere.

Aim for More Purposeful Goals

Entrepreneurs have a lot of terrific ideas about the kinds of products, marketing initiatives, website features and customers they want to pursue in their new companies. Too often they chase after too many ideas and opportunities all at once making their first years in business needlessly cost-intensive and chaotic.

I like easy versus hard. I also like setting clear operating priorities to help take as much aimless indecision and second-guessing out of an entrepreneur's workday as possible.

Your path to achieving your entrepreneurial purpose will get a whole lot easier if you direct all your energy and company resources to reaching four clear-cut targets: The 4 Key Milestones of Financial Safety. If you and your team aim to achieve these milestones—as quickly as you can—here's what you can expect:

- You will be less likely to go out of business

- You will be less likely to lose all or a part of your savings investment

- You will be better equipped to survive unexpected, freak-of-nature business surprises

- You will be more decisive in directing employees and making strategic choices

- You will approach each work day with greater pride, self-confidence and an enthusiasm to achieve your next goals

- You will be more likely to attract investors and qualify for increasing levels of credit from lenders

- You will be less dependent on your personal savings, lenders or investors to meet payroll and other business obligations

- You will be better positioned to sell your business when it suits you best

I've been teaching my milestone model for several years through small business workshops, angel investment clubs, technology incubators, micro-finance organizations, and business school classes. The milestone method works because it is simple and adaptable to any kind of company.

One business owner called my milestones "the magic milestones." In a way they are magical because when entrepreneurs know exactly what they want to accomplish they become more decisive. They don't procrastinate or duck phone calls. They take charge with determination. Best of all they are enthusiastic and happy and so am I.

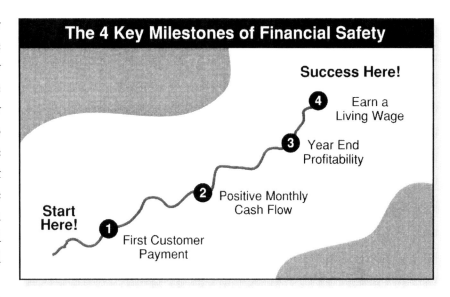

Now it's your turn to use the 4 Milestones of Financial Safety as your road map to business prosperity.

Milestone #1: *First Customer Payment* $$

The large majority of startups in America are dependent on the founder's personal savings to fund startup costs. From the moment entrepreneurs leave a salaried position to start a new business, their personal savings have to do double duty—continue to pay personal living expenses plus fund startup business costs.

Of course, entrepreneurs can raise funds from lenders or investors to help reduce the pressure on their personal savings to pay business expenses. But this is only a temporary solution. Eventually the business has to thrive on its own without help from fickle investors and lenders who can change their minds without warning.

The only sure way to create a financially sustainable company is to generate cash from bill-paying customers. Every dollar of revenue from these sources will reduce the intense pressure on you to keep writing checks from your personal savings or to find investors to support your company's ongoing expenses.

Here's one more benefit of securing a first paying customer as fast as you can. It will be easier for you to raise money from investors on more favorable deal terms. Smart investors know that there is more risk and money loss in pre-revenue companies than businesses that are generating revenues. You'll negotiate better deal terms with investors to the extent you can present some early evidence of repeat business from satisfied customers too.

Despite all the upside from first customer revenue generation, it's amazing to me how many startup entrepreneurs needlessly delay the glory of soliciting, serving and invoicing first customers. It makes me nuts! When I ask why, entrepreneurs, especially in service-related businesses, say that they are not yet "ready." They say they have to learn more about social media, write a newsletter, get a better logo, upgrade their website, create stronger marketing materials, join industry organizations, plan out their sales talking points, etc. These startup entrepreneurs are not productive perfectionists but time-wasting procrastinators. As my Dad says, "they are thinking about beginning to get ready to start."

There is another way entrepreneurs slow down revenue generation. I call them "give away" entrepreneurs because they hand out too many freebies to friends, family members and business colleagues. Free is not ever free to startup entrepreneurs. It costs money to giveaway free products or services. Even worse, prospective customers become conditioned to ask "Do you have any more free samples?" instead of saying "I'm out of your product and would like to buy more."

The best way to start generating revenues is to start asking for orders. Borrowing from Nike's marketing slogan, there is a time when you just have to do it. Put all your excuses aside, and just start contacting customers. This is the only way—the proven fast track—to building the business of your dreams.

Your next action steps:

☐ **Choose the path of least resistance**
If you have two different product ideas that you want to develop and don't have ready access to investment capital from outside sources to launch both products, then favor the product that can be commercialized quickly or does not require extensive capital for research, development or market entry.

☐ **Focus on one**
Direct your attention to securing your first paying customer rather than your first 1,000 customers. Remember that all it takes to achieve your first Milestone of Financial Safety is one customer. This means that if you want to create a successful fashion label, your first objective is to design and produce a first garment for a first paying customer.

Behavioral scientists have long recognized that making any amount of progress in one's work, hobby or sporting endeavor builds confidence. Once you have the first paying customer in hand, it's easier to pursue the second, third and fourth customer. And those first customers can lead to even more business through repeat orders and referrals making the entire sales generating process incredibly satisfying, productive and fun.

☐ **Develop a target solicitation list**
Focus on creating two solicitation or "call" lists: a list of target customers and a list of referral sources. Your list of target customers should include individuals

or businesses that are good candidates to buy your company's products or services. This list can also include businesses that can boost the distribution of your products, services or online presence. As you develop your target customer list, include all contact information so it will be easy for you to contact each target customer—one after another without interruption.

Your referral list should include individuals who may be able to brainstorm with you or refer you to names of individuals or businesses to add to your growing target customer list. Again, as you develop your referral list include all contact information.

Always try to have about 20 names on your target customer list and at least 10 names on your referral list to call, email or meet for coffee for a brainstorming session. Schedule a specific day every week that you will do nothing else but list building. If you don't do this basic contact development on a routine basis, your road to success will be extra long and hard.

☐ Solicit five every day   **$$**

It's very common for startup entrepreneurs to complain that they "have no customers" or "business is dead." When I drill down into the details of their work day, I usually find that they are not making a serious effort to obtain a first customer. Marketing is not the same as sales. To earn a customer, you have to take purposeful steps to meet decision makers and ask for orders.

There is only one way to start each work day. It's not by visiting Facebook, checking sports scores or attending to administrative chores. None of these activities generate revenue in a direct way. You should start by contacting at least five targeted customers plus five other individuals who can help refer you to new customers.

Startup entrepreneurs, who succeed in securing first customers quickly, let the odds of success work to their advantage. The entrepreneur who actively solicits five target customers per day (100 per month) will have more customers at the end of the month than an entrepreneur who contacts just one target customer per day or less. The difference in first year results is significant: Assuming a 5% solicitation-to-closure rate, the active solicitor will serve 60 customers. The startup lollygagger will serve just 12 customers. Repeat business and referrals from first customers will exponentially increase the difference in revenue results with each passing year.

The more calls you make, the better your solicitation pitch and opportunities to receive purchase orders. The more purchase orders you receive, the more cash that will ultimately find its way into your business bank account. That's success!

☐ **Solicit local customers first**

It's cheaper to drive across town than across the country to solicit and serve your company's first customers. Even for e-commerce companies that can potentially appeal to a worldwide audience, your company is likely to generate more buzz in your home town through your personal networking, word-of-mouth referrals, and local public relations than national advertising. Popular consumer-oriented websites like craigslist and Groupon perfected their services for a regional audience before expanding to other cities.

☐ **Balance customer targets**

It can take a long time for large corporate customers—what I call "home run" customers—to say "yes" to new vendor proposals. The long lead times associated with soliciting and meeting with multi-layers of management to gain approval can be deadly to startup companies that are desperate for first revenue generation. Plus, isn't it always true in baseball and in life that swinging for the fences leads to more strikeouts? I think so. Sure, you can include a home run account or two in your target customer list, provided that your solicitation list includes many more easier-to-hit "singles" and "doubles" accounts too.

☐ **Solicit small jobs**

It's often easier and faster to get a first customer to commit to a $25,000 project than to a $250,000 project. If the scope of a work project is sizable, consider dividing the project into two or more smaller, well-defined phases to speed customer acceptance.

☐ **Overcome insecurity**

Don't discount your company's products and services just because you are a new competitor. If your product or service is the same or better quality than your competitors, then set your prices accordingly. You don't want potential customers to make incorrect assumptions about the quality of your company's products or services.

☐ **Celebrate**

When you receive full payment from your first customer, celebrate. If you are a company of one, invite friends and family members to your milestone soiree. Your risk of personal money loss and business failure has gone down all because cash is coming into your company from sources other than YOU!

☐ **Leverage first customers**

A first customer who is "delighted" with your work can lead to more revenue generation provided you practice and perfect "the ask." Consider the following questions. "Who else can use my services?" "When is a good time to reach you to discuss your next order?" Notice that these questions are cleverly phrased to avoid quick "yes" or "no" answers. After you ask a question, stop talking! Give your customers a chance to help you build your company's revenue base.

Milestone #2: *Positive Monthly Cash Flow* $$

When I meet with startup entrepreneurs to review projections, one of the first questions I ask is, "When will your company reach positive monthly cash flow?" It's a revealing question too. If an entrepreneur really doesn't know how to answer this question, then I know more work has to be done to transform their big idea into dollars and good sense.

The first time you can breathe a sigh of relief is when your company reaches positive cash flow, ideally every month. This is the momentous milestone in which your company's monthly income consistently matches or exceeds its monthly expenses.

There are several reasons why I put positive cash flow ahead of business profitability in the 4 Milestones of Financial Safety. Companies can use various accounting tricks to show a quarterly or annual profit for income statement presentation purposes but not have much cash in the bank to pay interim expenses. This situation can be magnified for companies that are experiencing growing customer demand for their great products and services. Imagine the cash flow strain associated with buying offshore goods in the spring in order to ship customers during the summer, only to be paid in the winter. Yikes! Unless a young company has a neat cushion of cash to pay interim bills, it will have to sacrifice some of its remaining cash or equity to pay lenders or investors for basic business survival.

Healthy, forward-moving companies take in more cash each month than they pay out. That's the goal of the second Milestone of Financial Safety. In contrast, entrepreneurs who are weighed down by chronic cash flow troubles can't think too much about the future because their time is consumed by bill collection calls and digging up enough cash to pay next week's payroll. It's a joyless business existence. You and your company deserve better.

Your next action steps:

☐ **Learn about cash flow basics**

Cash flow will become an important consideration in every major decision you make as the founder and CEO of your company. High purpose entrepreneurs know that paying attention to their company's cash flow can help reduce their company's dependence on expensive credit cards, lenders and investors. They also learn to appreciate the timing issues and cash flow impact of payroll, taxes, inventory purchases, equipment obligations, customer payments, product returns, secured commercial loans, and other real world cash consuming transaction scenarios.

For extra help buy one or two accounting books that focus on everyday cash flow management issues. You don't have to read the books cover to cover but it is worth reading paragraphs or chapters that can help empower your management fire power.

Extra Financial Empowerment ··

Financial statements include a profit and loss statement (also referred to as a "P & L" or "income statement"); a balance sheet; a cash flow statement; and in more advanced companies, a statement of stockholder's equity. Most entrepreneurs are very familiar with the components of a profit and loss statement, but not a cash flow statement.

In simple terms, a company's cash flow statement summarizes where it gets its funds to operate and how it spends those funds. For example, a company can accept a $1,000 check from a customer as well as a $1,000 check from an investor. Each check is reported differently on the company's cash flow statement—one comes from "operating activities" and the other comes from "financing activities." I like it best when a business creates most of its cash flow from customer sales, royalties and interest payments. It's the high prize of entrepreneurial life. Lenders, board members, insurance underwriters and investors prefer it too.

··

☐ Collect fast

There are two types of customers you don't want to serve—the ultra slow-payer and the no-payer. It's foolish to think all of your customers will pay your bill on time if at all. The longer you have to wait to collect customer payments, the more money and time you lose in the chase. While accountants might quibble with me about definitions, in my view, sales only count when you collect a check—that doesn't bounce. Check out Chapter 6 for tips on how to deal with deadbeat accounts with confidence.

☐ Minimize fixed costs and overhead mistakes

Some businesses really do need to lease office or retail space to operate, while others can operate from their homes in a cost-saving way. To the extent that you have to secure office, retail or production space, explore low-cost ways to create an initial presence for your company without making long-term financial commitments you might regret just a few months later. It's easier to reach positive cash flow when you keep down big ticket, hard-to-unwind overhead costs.

☐ **Streamline product lines**

Entrepreneurs who don't have a lot of available cash should avoid producing too many products in too many styles to sell to too many different types of customers. The more complex a company's product line, the more cash that is required to produce, store, advertise and deliver goods to target customers.

☐ **Hire part-time staff before full-time staff**

Until your company achieves a certain rhythm of predictable revenue generation, minimize your company's operating expenses and payroll taxes by hiring part-time staff and independent consultants.

☐ **Ask for exceptions**

Startup entrepreneurs often assume they have no power to negotiate pricing and payment terms with vendors. Mostly, they don't get price breaks simply because they don't ask for them. Every business in America is hungry for new business, especially from companies like yours that are destined for growth. To the extent that you have a choice in vendor selection, explore opportunities for free goods for sampling, extended payment terms and lower minimum order purchase quantities. Be loyal to vendors who help your company fight its way to positive cash flow.

☐ **Avoid superfluous expenditures**

There is a lot of information out there online and offline to help entrepreneurs manage their new companies—actually too much. Startup entrepreneurs are hit hard by marketers who want to sell them something or trick them into spending extra time at their websites. The advice or products they sell certainly may be good for *their* businesses, but perhaps not so much for yours. During your first few years in business, your time will be better spent soliciting your customers than becoming someone else's customer.

☐ **Reduce tax obligations**

You can preserve your company's cash by taking steps, year-after-year, to minimize tax payments in every legal way possible. At the start of every year, spend some time with your accountant to learn about new tax breaks that might influence when it might be best to hire support staff or buy certain equipment. This is a better approach than meeting with your accountant in April when it's usually too late to take advantage of last year's special tax-saving deals.

Extra Financial Empowerment ··

All is not necessarily lost when a company loses money. Sometimes year-end losses can create cash value to a company in the form of reduced federal and possibly state tax obligations. Most business entities can apply net operating losses or "NOLs" to future income tax obligations for up to 20 years, though the specific rules vary according to the industry of the business. Companies may also use NOLs to recover some taxes paid in prior years by amending their last two tax returns.

···

☐ Celebrate

Achieving positive monthly cash flow calls for a big celebration. Enjoy the moment with family, board members, advisors and staff members. Now set your sights and business strategies to achieving Milestone #3.

$$ Milestone #3: *Year-end Profitability*

"I want to be big!" This is what ambitious startup entrepreneurs often say when they talk to me about the goals of their new companies. Of course, the definition of "big" varies considerably. Most first-time entrepreneurs would be thrilled to manage a company that generates $100,000 in revenue while others define success in the millions.

Still I wonder. Why is it that I've never heard a first-time entrepreneur say, "My goal is to be really profitable"? After all, isn't it more important to earn $1 million after paying all business expenses than to generate $1 million in customer sales? I think so. Bigger profits mean bigger year-end bonuses for business owners too.

The third Milestone of Financial Safety is year-end profitability. When your company reaches this milestone, you will find that more lenders, investors, job seekers, vendors, distributors and collaborators will knock on your door.

The fastest way to achieve business profitability is to stop unprofitable activities. You don't need an MBA to build a "big" and profitable enterprise either. All you need is a willingness to be highly selective in what you do, who you serve, what you buy and how fast you get paid. Precision counts.

There is only one downside to achieving this important milestone—Uncle Sam is now a partner in your business success. Profitable companies usually have to pay federal income taxes and probably state taxes too. Certainly you are legally obligated to pay business taxes, but you are not legally obligated to pay more than the law requires. I know of too many business owners who fret over trimming basic operating costs by 1% or 2% but completely overlook legal ways to save far greater sums through federal and state business tax deductions.

Your next action steps:

☐ **Bill for extra services**

A common mistake of startup entrepreneurs who want to be "liked" by their first customers is to accept special requests which tend to increase the costs associated with delivering a product or service. If a customer asks you for an extra-fast turnaround time that will involve paying overtime to your staff, then charge them a higher rate for the service. If a customer asks you to act as a purchasing agent for their needs, charge them for the use of your working capital. If a customer asks you for a significant "change order" to an agreed service contract, draw up a new service agreement before beginning work to reduce the chance of future payment disputes.

It's your job to manage expectations. If you are too accommodating to special requests during your first months or years in business, then it may be harder to add on extra fees when you get fed up with all the freebies. Your customers will ask in a resentful way, "You never billed for that before, so why now?"

☐ **Shed unprofitable customers**

Every year, review your company's customer list to evaluate your customer relationships in terms of profitability. Sometimes you might have to fire unprofitable customers, that is, customers who complain the most, demand the most, and take a long time to pay the bill. When you free your company from unprofitable customers, you will have more time and resources to pursue profitable ones.

☐ **Lower borrowing and transaction processing costs**

Unfortunately, managing your company's cash costs hard cash. Once a year, compare the costs of deposit, lending and other transaction processing services. If you identify a lower cost provider of comparable quality, give your current provider a chance to match the price. If your current provider is unable to lower pricing, take fast steps to move your account.

☐ **Celebrate some more**

The majority of Americans will never know the feeling of sustained applause, the glory of winning a sporting event, or the thrill of being awarded a trophy. But they can be acknowledged for jobs well done. When your company reaches year-end profitability, take time to acknowledge all the people who contributed to your company's success. Inspirational entrepreneurs know how to stand in awe of remarkable accomplishments. This doesn't mean handing out motivational plaques to employees who are obviously motivated, but creating a moment of appreciation that is heartfelt and real.

$$ Milestone #4: *Earn a Living Wage*

After the financial market meltdown in 2008, there was a popular view that Fortune 500 CEOs were always first in line to get paid, even as thousands of employees lost their jobs. In the small business community, the opposite is usually true. Devoted business founders are last in line to get paid.

I can tell when startup entrepreneurs have not taken any salary for an extended period of time. They slouch and look down a little more than other entrepreneurs. These entrepreneurs are not at all defeated, but they are physically tired from the extra stress associated with not earning a living wage. They work long hours but say they "have nothing tangible to show for it." The situation slowly eats away at their passion, confidence and home life stability.

It's possible to achieve the first three Milestones of Financial Safety and still not have a fully sustainable enterprise because the business founder has to be financially secure too. Most founding entrepreneurs can't survive long without some sort of compensation. The dollar amount can grow over time, but something has to be paid to founders to maintain leadership morale and family support.

Your next action steps:

☐ **Project a salary**

Out of sight; out of mind. If you don't include some personal compensation in your projections, then your product pricing and strategic decisions won't reflect the costs needed to operate a financially-viable business. Be sure to budget salaries for other business partners or staff members who may not now be drawing a salary too.

☐ **Consider commission payments**

Commission checks are my favorite kind of business checks to sign because the expense is tied to incoming cash. If you are uneasy about drawing a salary from your young company, why not pay yourself a small cash commission on new customer account activity? The commission can be a nominal amount or it can match what other industry competitors pay their sales staff for securing new business relationships. You can also develop a bonus payment plan to reward yourself for raising funds from investors, obtaining a grant, or other initiative that brings new cash into your company.

☐ **Accrue unpaid salary**

It's important to have an accurate understanding of just how much you have invested in your business: your hard cash investment as well as uncompensated time. In my experience, knowing this number, motivates entrepreneurs to find customers faster and pay themselves sooner rather than later.

There are two primary accounting methods for recording business revenues and expenses: accrual accounting or cash basis accounting. With accrual accounting, revenues and expenses are "recognized" when they occur, even if cash does not change hands.

If you choose to use accrual accounting, (see Chapter 6 for more information) you can accrue unpaid salary obligations on your company's financial statements. To accrue earned but unpaid salary compensation, simply "book" or record the amount of unpaid salary every month to a liability account that shows up on your balance sheet. You can set the account up as a long-term debt obligation such as "LTD—Officer Salary" or a short-term obligation as "Officer Salary—Payable." The general difference between short-term and long-term obligations is short-term obligations are generally repaid within 12 months.

The amount of unpaid compensation will show up on your company's profit and loss statement too, as an expense. While this may seem to make your company's financial position look worse, it does have managerial value of letting you know what amount of customer revenues it will take for your company to achieve positive cash flow on a monthly basis—when all expenses and employee compensation are really added into the calculation. Of course, once a company achieves a level of consistent cash flow generation and profitability, then the outstanding obligation can be steadily repaid. Talk through salary accruals with your accountant or develop some other way to monitor your total contribution to your company.

Extra Financial Empowerment ···

If you expect to raise funds from independent investors, you may not be able to get investors to pay off outstanding officer or family member loans, accrued salary and other debt obligations. Investors would rather see their cash allocated to initiatives that will increase the overall value of the business, such as developing products and technologies, expanding distribution in new markets, hiring qualified staff, etc. Fortunately, there is a solution to this impasse. Typically, investors will ask entrepreneurs to "roll over" any outstanding debt into equity as a condition of funding. This means that you won't likely get your cash back until your company is sold.

☐ **Celebrate success**
Over the years I've attended a lot of celebration parties for launching a website, securing a round of funding, buying a company, obtaining FDA approval for

a new drug, receiving a big foundation grant, obtaining a patent and so much more. Still, my favorite parties are milestone achievement celebrations because the business is more inclined to stay in business. And that's certainly worth celebrating.

Whenever you feel uneasy or overwhelmed by day-to-day startup business activity, revisit the milestones to help you choose the best way to spend your time and your company's resources. If an initiative is not directly related to helping your company tag up to the next Milestone of Financial Safety, then move on to something that will.

FAQs

Q. **Do the Milestones of Financial Safety apply to non-profits?**

A. Yes. Non-profits close when they run out of cash too.

Q. **Your Milestones seem too regimented. I want to enjoy myself without feeling like I "have to" do what someone else tells me to do—including you. Is there an easier way?**

A. You are certainly not the first entrepreneur I've met who would rather "wing it." Sorry to be tough on you but if your goal is to be an adventurous free spirit, then take up an extreme sport. If you want to be the boss of a thriving business then at some point managing cash has to be a workday priority.

Here's a promise I make to startup entrepreneurs who grumble about managing cash with care. If you focus all your efforts on achieving the 4 Milestones of Financial Safety, then your company will have extra cash flow to pay for your extra fun, extra travel, and "out there" new product development. If the business slips back to an unprofitable position, then tighten your belt and focus your company's staff on achieving the 4 Milestones once again. You'll find out that you will get to do more of the super fun things you want to do, when you have the cash to do it!

Q. **A potential investor asked me about my company's "burn rate." What is it?**

A. A company's burn rate is, quite simply, how much hard cash a company "throws into the fire" every month to pay rent, utilities, wages, website maintenance costs, and all other core costs of operations. For example, if a pre-revenue company has a checking account balance of $20,000 and is burning cash at a rate of $3,500 a month, then the company will be out of cash in less than six months unless investors or lenders step in to help.

Perfect It!

How to Make Your Great Business Idea More Lucrative

The 4 Milestones of Financial Safety provide an easy framework to help you set purposeful goals. If you work as hard as you can to reach these milestones, then your new business will be less likely to go out of business in the first years of operations.

Now, let's up the ante from basic survival to positioning your company for a wealth-building big payday. The purpose of this chapter is to help you create Plan B. To me, Plan B stands for "better." Even though I know you have a great idea for a new business, now is the perfect time for you to make your operating plans more efficient, more effective and of course, more financially rewarding.

By the end of this chapter, you will know…

- What types of customers and customer relationships are most worthwhile in terms of maximizing the financial value of your business
- What types of businesses motivate investors and business buyers to pay top dollar to own all or a piece of your company
- How to position your company so it can grow in value to be worth two, four or ten times what you invested in it
- How to reinvent a "fundamentally flawed" business

This is the money chapter—the "secrets of success" part of *Start On Purpose*. If you enjoy exploring the upside opportunities of business ownership more than the downside risks, then this chapter will be your favorite. It's my favorite too because the information within this chapter can help you achieve your wealth-building goals.

Three Characteristics of Valuable Companies $\boxed{\$\$}$

Why is it that some startup ideas are worth more than other startup ideas? Why is it rational for investors to pay millions to own a piece of a business with no revenues, but pass over a profitable company that has been in business for several generations?

Unfortunately not all revenue-generating businesses have much equity value. It's the seemingly unfair gotcha that catches too many business owners by surprise just at the time they want to sell their company to retire or pursue another career path. They *assumed* their companies were valuable because their companies were valuable to them. But that's not how business buyers, venture capitalists and angel investors size up business value.

"Investment fundamentals" is a common term in the financial community to describe various factors that can increase or decrease the value of a business. The term is used to evaluate publicly-traded stocks as well as privately-held businesses. Fortunately, you don't need to know all of these fundamentals today.

There are, however, three fundamentals of positive business value that I believe every startup entrepreneur should know before investing a penny in a new business. These wealth-building fundamentals relate to your company's future customer base, gross profit margin performance, and brand reputation. Here's what you need to know.

$$ Fundamental #1: *A Brand That Stands for Something*

From a traditional marketing standpoint, a brand is the backbone of a company's public reputation. It is not a tag line or a marketing gimmick, but a highly effective tool to help companies differentiate their products or services from competitors.

Marketing professionals often complain to me that their "brand management" work doesn't get much respect from first-time entrepreneurs because entrepreneurs tend to believe that their company's value comes from its innovative products, not its brand. I understand and agree with this frustration. It is true that most startup entrepreneurs don't give their brands enough thoughtful attention during the first years in business and they pay dearly for this oversight.

Effective brand management is crucial for young companies because customers who are emotionally engaged with a brand are more likely to forgive mistakes in customer service and product performance—and let's face it, fast-growing startups make a lot of honest mistakes and need a lot of customer forgiveness.

Marketers refer to this social phenomenon as a brand's "halo effect." I call it Teflon. Think about Johnson & Johnson. Despite life-threatening medical product recalls and corporate gaffs, the public's emotional affinity for J&J remains mostly unscathed. When consumers "trust" a brand, they continue to buy the brand.

As a finance person, I like to translate business principles into dollars and cents. A brand can become a startup company's most valuable financial asset. Really, an asset? Yes, brands are financial assets when they deliver tangible cash value to growing companies. Here's how.

1. Valuable brands sell themselves

My family is always in the mountains. Like so many other outdoorsy families we've had our share of Subaru Outbacks that seem to go the distance in the worst weather. It's not the most expensive car in our household, but it is the car that delights us most. We are Outback super fans because the brand reflects our let's go spirit. The little car seems to withstand anything—even the large, old growth spruce tree that fell right across the top of our previous Outback. Sure we could have replaced the badly tree-dented car but it was more amusing to keep driving it and retell the story to inquisitive skiers, hikers and campers. When we finally "put down" the beloved car at a little over 225,000 miles, we didn't research other sport utility cars or wait for special dealer incentives. Our next step was automatic—we just bought another Outback. The same color too.

Companies that can book new business without discounts, coupons or other promotional incentives are valuable companies to own. These companies maximize profits by selling to customers who are already "sold" on the brand. Plus, these companies derive added marketing benefits as satisfied customers evangelize their brand preferences to friends and family members who may in turn buy into the brand.

2. Valuable brands can charge higher prices

Companies that motivate their customers to pay a premium price for a product or service get extra business valuation bonus points at the time of business sale. The women's makeup industry illustrates how a brand reputation can influence customer attitudes about product quality and social desirability. Think for a moment about mascara. Women can buy two ounces of Revlon brand mascara for about eight dollars in a drug store or the same amount of Chanel brand mascara in a department store for $30 to $40. The function of both products is essentially the same, yet the overall experience of heightened social status is different for an elite brand like Chanel. Women feel more glamorous, sophisticated and privileged when they use Chanel mascara and are willing to pay more for the extra satisfaction. So it's not the product but the brand that drives the premium price.

The alcohol and soda industry is another product category in which a brand reputation can motivate consumers to pay a premium price. I love Jones Soda's Zilch brand flavored soda—black cherry and vanilla bean are my favorites. I can think of several reasons not to be loyal to Jones Soda. It costs more than other low calorie sodas and I often have to drive out of my way to buy it. Still, Jones Soda is worth it to me because it's got a unique, refreshing kick that is different from other diet sodas. Plus, I like the playful way the manufacturer features photos of its customers on its product labels. Jones Soda's fans embrace the brand's cool nonconformist, colorful attitude and pay more for it.

$$ As you develop your company's brand, remember that customers shop for what they want and love first, and then look at price second. Brands gain financial value when their customers buy into a brand that suits their emotional purpose—be it status, cause alignment, comfort, reliability, nostalgia, exclusivity or whatever else you dream up to motivate your customers to buy over and over again with pride.

3. Valuable brands can be applied to other product or service categories

When customers enjoy a compelling, emotionally-satisfying allegiance to a brand, it's likely that they would favor the same brand in other product or service categories. This aspect of potential future revenue generation is of interest to valuation experts and investors.

Are you a fan of Starbucks Coffee? Even if you are not a caffeine junky, it's easy to admire Starbucks' skillful brand management. Today, you can find the Starbucks logo on ice cream, cold drinks, and candy. Recently the company dropped the word "coffee" from its corporate logo to help Starbucks enter into many more food and consumer product categories, which is good news for Starbucks' shareholders.

Another company that has used brand recognition and loyalty to penetrate multiple highly competitive markets such as mobile phone services, music, airline transportation, vacation travel, consumer money lending, and gaming is British-based Virgin. Virgin's company literature says, "Once a Virgin company is up and running, several factors help to ensure its on-going success." The first item on this list is "The global power of the Virgin brand."

Brands don't have to have a global following in order to drive revenue growth through product line diversification. A small local housecleaning company with a reputation for service excellence, employee honesty and reliability can enter into other in-home-related services with greater ease than a startup competitor whose brand reputation has not yet been established in the local marketplace.

Thinking about brand management in financial terms such as added revenue generation is nothing new. Steve Jobs said that every aspect of what Apple did in terms of product design, retail delivery, product line choices, and marketing influenced customer perceptions of the Apple brand. He characterized these actions as either "brand deposits" that boost a brand's power in the marketplace or "brand withdrawals" that diminish a brand's image and pricing power with customers.

So how can you create a brand with enduring value? Fortunately, you don't have to be an expert in brand management to create your company's brand identity. And you don't have to hire marketing gurus to help you make your first decisions about your brand. What's important as a startup business owner is to take a few purposeful steps in the *right* direction, rather than in no direction or every direction.

Your next action steps:

☐ **Understand the limits of branding**

The moment the Subaru Outback stops being a reliable, rugged little car, that's when our family abandons Subaru as our go-to-the-outdoors fun car. The moment Apple stops making functionally cool, cutting-edge products, that's when the Apple brand starts to lose its cult following. As a startup organization, consistent product or service performance is crucial to developing your company's brand reputation.

☐ **Set your company's lingo**

Brand marketing professionals use many terms to describe their work. The language tends to be ambiguous, imprecise and frustrating for entrepreneurs to grasp. Is it important for you to know the subtle differences between "brand attributes," "brand drivers," "brand values," "brand messages," "brand principles," "brand ethos," "brand conveyors," and "brand focus?" I say, no!

I like simple. If you are new to making brand decisions or can't afford professional brand management assistance, choose just one phrase to guide your first decisions about your company's brand. My choice for startups is "brand promise" because everyone in your company can understand the operating priority and extra commitment associated with the word "promise."

☐ **Brainstorm brand promise options**

Your company's brand promise represents the experience your customers can always count on from your company. When you consistently deliver the same experience to customers then you start to build a reputation for it.

When I first started writing this book and designing complementary online tools for startup entrepreneurs I was not guided by a multi-paragraph mission statement. Of course, I had a strong idea about what I wanted to create and the desired impact of my work, just like you do. And probably like you, I knew the brand name for this work: Start On Purpose.

You would think the name Start On Purpose would not need further brand definition, but it did. "Purpose" implies a lot, but it does not provide enough clarity to guide book content as well as other product and service development decisions. So what did I do? The very same action step that you are about to do. I carefully weighed several factors that would help me differentiate the Start On Purpose brand from other academic and online voices in entrepreneurial education.

To help you define your company's brand promise, organize a brainstorming session with co-workers or a group of business-savvy colleagues. Find a room with a big white board or buy a pad of large-size self-adhesive easel sheets so you can write and post ideas around the meeting room without damaging the walls. The spirit of the session should be open-minded.

Not all of the questions below will be relevant to your specific business interests. As you record your ideas and answers, certain themes will emerge that will help you hone your company's brand promise priorities. Brainstorm the following questions:

- What adjectives best define your competition's brand reputation? Do your competitor's brand reputations look, feel and sound alike? Which competitor enjoys the strongest brand reputation? Why? How can you distinguish your brand from the reputations of other key competitors? How does this compare to what customers value in your industry?

- What adjectives would you like your company or its products and services to be known for in the marketplace? What do you want your customers to say to their friends, family members or business colleagues about what the brand stands for in the marketplace? List at least 10 to 15 adjectives.

- As you make this list, try to stay away from adjectives that describe your company's first products or services. Valuable brands maintain an identity and emotional connection with customers even as their underlying products or services change over time.

- What adjectives imply customer pleasure and satisfaction for your product or service?

- How do you want consumers to *feel* about the company or brand?

- What are some other emotionally-satisfying reasons why a customer would buy your product or service?

- What do you think consumers might think you do? Are there ways in which your target customers might confuse or misinterpret what you do? This consideration is especially important if you are delivering groundbreaking products or services that will be entirely new or unusual in the marketplace.

- What adjectives or phrases might increase confidence in the perceived quality of your product or service? Or, depending on your industry, what adjectives or phrases might help your target customers overcome reservations about buying from a startup organization?

- What adjectives or phrases would *you* not want your company's reputation to represent?

- What adjectives or phrases would turnoff customers or discourage them from buying from your company?

- If your company sells its products or services to a diverse range of customers by age or other demographic factors, would different demographic groups answer any of the questions above differently? If you are uncertain, conduct focus groups, interviews or surveys on the subject.

☐ Pick three priorities

Review the results of the brand promise brainstorming exercise. What adjectives or phrases are listed most often? What themes or words dominated your brainstorm discussions? Narrow down your results to just three adjectives or phrases to represent your company's top brand promise priorities.

For illustration purposes, the three brand promises for Start On Purpose are "easy direction," "gotcha-prevention," and "achievement."

- *Easy direction*: providing easy-to-understand action steps and strategies specifically designed for the startup entrepreneur

- *Gotcha prevention:* providing must-know information to help startup entrepreneurs stay in business by reducing costly beginner's mistakes and needless money loss

- *Achievement:* helping startup entrepreneurs know more, do more, build more, earn more and experience more with confidence

Whenever I write, speak, coach, teach, design online services, participate in conferences, or create videos, on behalf of the Start On Purpose brand, I consider if the content matches these three brand promises. If not, then I have to do more work to achieve the purpose of Start On Purpose.

I'm frequently asked if it's worthwhile to pick just one brand promise to define a startup company's brand. While choosing just one brand promise may seem like the most focused way to proceed, I still favor three promises to give a startup organization more leeway for marketing adjustments as first products and services are tested in the marketplace. Eventually, your customers will help you choose which brand promise will distinguish your company from your toughest competitors.

What's my top brand promise to startup entrepreneurs? I hope that all Start On Purpose books and educational initiatives make it *easier* for entrepreneurs to startup and advance. I always smile a little more when entrepreneurs come up to me and say, "You make things so easy to understand." Ah, such satisfaction!

☐ **Make it genuine**

Valuable brands stand for something. Highly valuable brands stand for something that is authentic. Brands that are fickle and phony run the risk of losing customer trust or being attacked by disappointed consumers or competitors in social media. If you market a product and say it is "all natural," make it all natural. Remember that startups have fewer operating resources to recover from big errors and bad press.

☐ **Make it consistent**

After you have defined what your brand stands for, your next action step is to be consistent in how you message your brand promise online, offline and in everything you do with customers, vendors, employees, and advisors. Consistent brand messaging helps the public remember who you are and what you stand for. And to the extent that your company's brand message penetrates the psyche of your customers, they may repeat that language when talking about your company to friends and co-workers.

$$ ☐ **Put respect into customer service**

Most startup entrepreneurs don't invest a lot of time thinking about customer service needs at the time of a first product or service launch. It's a reasonable oversight since it can be scary to imagine what can go wrong before something actually does go wrong.

In my book, skillful brand management includes developing an effective customer service safety net. When your first customers are unhappy (and some certainly will be as you test out first products or services), only attentive, respectful customer service can turn a bad brand experience into a positive brand experience. How will you protect the long-term interests of your brand's reputation, from common operating glitches and goof-ups?

Notice my emphasis on the word "respect." When your staff members are instructed to treat disgruntled customers with respect, then when problems occur, they know how to take corrective action. Respectful customer service doesn't involve being defensive, stingy or disinterested. Even an offer to fully reimburse an unhappy customer may not be enough to turn a bad customer experience (brand withdrawal) into a good customer experience (brand deposit). When angry customers are lavished with genuine respect, their dissatisfaction and threatened viral gripe can turn into a viral thumbs-up.

☐ **Match distribution channels to brand image**

Where and how products are merchandized can influence customer attitudes about a brand. So your distribution strategies should complement, not conflict with, your brand promise objectives. If, for example, your business objective is to market a line of high end men's golf wear and sportswear, then Nordstrom, Brooks Brothers, Saks Fifth Avenue, and other specialty retailers would be on your solicitation list; not Wal-mart or Sears.

As companies prosper, it can become harder to maintain sales growth without expanding into distribution channels that might not fully match a brand's desired image. But this is a problem for startup organizations too because they are hungry for revenues any way they can get them. Over reaching distribution channels and customer markets can ultimately undermine the loyalty of core customers and the underlying financial value of a brand. This is why many brand marketers develop different brands for different distribution channels. Ralph Lauren, for example, protects its brand image by offering its premium quality merchandize only to prestigious department stores and its lower-priced Chaps brand to discount department stores.

☐ **Test your brand focus**

Here's a great test of brand consistency that you can use throughout your entrepreneurial career. Ask 10 to 20 customers about your brand. What do they say? What adjectives do they use to describe their experience? Your brand messaging needs attention if your customers use too many different words to describe your brand.

Extra Startup Intelligence ··

It is easy to become overwhelmed by online articles and books about product branding, advertising and social media. Yes, read them and learn as much as you can, but keep in mind that most marketing gurus serve well-established Fortune 1000 clients not cash-strapped startup company brands. In a startup company, strategic branding decisions must "establish" public confidence in an unknown brand. In a large corporation, brand strategies seek to "enhance" or "maintain" an existing reputation. When you are ready to hire marketing staff members or professional marketing advisors, use this information to help you hire talent whose experience and expertise most directly matches your company's stage of business development.

···

Fundamental #2: *A Lucrative and Loyal Customer Base*

Here is a business valuation certainty. When the time comes for you to sell your business, not all of your customer relationships will be valued in the same way. This means, that a dollar of revenue earned from one of your customers may not be valued the same as a dollar of revenue earned from other customers. Why?

From a business valuation standpoint, business buyers don't want to buy into a business that may be worth **less** tomorrow than it is today. It's a reasonable concern because no sane business person ever wants to invest in a business at the peak of revenue generation. This is why savvy business buyers and investors (including angel investors and venture capital fund managers) spend a lot of time evaluating the nature of a company's customer relationships for evidence of stability, longevity and future profitability.

The more you can prove that your customers are lucrative and loyal, the more investors and business buyers will want to own an equity stake in your company. Here are the fundamental attributes of valuable customer relationships that I look for when assessing startup business plans and established businesses:

- ### High rates of customer reorder activity

  Nothing says stability to a prospective business buyer than companies that can prove high rates of customer reorder activity. Investors view it as a reliable sign of customer satisfaction and loyalty.

  Notice the emphasis on the word "prove." Business owners must develop reliable customer tracking systems to prove customer reorder rates. A local bakery that can provide detailed reports of families that order birthday cakes year after year will get a valuation bonus point over a bakery that relies solely on random walk-in traffic for revenue generation. Similarly, software companies that motivate satisfied customers to purchase annual upgrades can be valuable companies to own.

- ### Expanding "active" customer base

  During my days of conducting due diligence on acquisition projects, I learned quickly that executives in large companies could produce top-line revenue growth by raising prices or acquiring other businesses. Sometimes these strategies were employed to cover up a company's declining customer base, which is rarely a good thing.

  Savvy business buyers focus on the size of a company's active customer base (customers who buy at least once a year) because it serves as a reliable predictor of future revenue generation. What are the odds of receiving a new order from an existing customer? Some studies report the odds as high as 60% to 70%. What are the odds of generating a new order from a complete stranger? The result can be as low as 5% to 10%.

- ### Diversified customer base

  I would rather own a $100,000 revenue base business that serves 10 different customers than a $100,000 revenue base business that sells to only one customer. Sure, serving just one customer may be administratively easy, but the risk of sudden customer loss is unacceptably high to warrant a high valuation from business buyers.

- **Multi-year contracts**

  The multi-year contract is a highly effective tool to lock down customer loyalty and make it more difficult for your competitors to poach your most profitable customers. Unfortunately, startup entrepreneurs rarely explore ways to integrate multi-year contracts into their business operations.

  From a valuation perspective, multi-year contracts give prospective business buyers comfort that revenues won't drop suddenly after the founder sells out. Further, businesses with a significant percentage of business that is locked down through multi-year contracts are valued more highly than businesses that have to fight for every customer year after year. Multi-year contracts also help entrepreneurs predict working capital and personnel requirements with greater precision.

- **Recurring revenues**

  A close cousin of the multi-year contract is the concept of "recurring revenues." Software service contracts, wholesale club memberships, subscription services, credit monitoring services, cable and cellular phone services, online weight loss programs, and burglar alarm monitoring services, are just a few examples of recurring revenue customer relationships.

  Recurring revenue businesses excite business investors and business buyers because they can project revenues on a monthly, quarterly or annual basis with a high degree of certainty. Further, businesses can generate revenues even if paying customers don't utilize any company services during a billing cycle. For example, athletic clubs typically charge a fixed monthly fee for customer access to gym facilities. Even if a member doesn't visit the club during a month, the business would not be obligated to reimburse the fee to the customer. This kind of customer payment model can help a business maximize revenue generation beyond its actual per-customer operating capacity.

- **Royalty-based revenues**

  I love royalty income that is derived from long-term contracts with resource-rich business partners. Investors do too. Musicians, artists, filmmakers, cartoonists, software programmers, authors, inventors, and owners of mineral resources can earn high profit revenues without all the headaches and risks associated with managing ongoing production, marketing, sales and customer service. In practice, these entrepreneurs license certain rights to their patents, trademarks, copyrights and other property to one or more businesses typically in return for a percentage of their license partner's revenues.

Investors usually value royalty-based revenues higher than "producer" revenues to reflect the lower ongoing costs of future revenue generation. For example, a dollar of revenues earned from the manufacturer of a beauty item may be valued at 1 to 2 times revenues. If the manufacturer's revenue base is $15 million, then the company's worth may be estimated between $15 million and $30 million.

In comparison, a dollar of royalty-based revenues earned from a recognized brand that is applied to that same beauty item may be valued at 4 or 6 times revenues. If the trademarked brand generates $15 million in royalty revenues then that royalty stream may be valued at $60 million to $90 million. That's a big difference all because the owner of a licensed brand doesn't have to spend its cash to produce, market, sell and ship a product to end customers.

Extra Financial Empowerment ···

Here is some good news for authors, musicians, inventors and other self-employed entrepreneurs who receive royalties as a source of revenues. If the entrepreneur reports the royalty income on Schedule E of the entrepreneur's individual tax return, then the royalties are not subject to payroll taxes. As outlined in Chapter 6, the savings can be big. However, if the royalty income is booked as business income and reported on Schedule C then the royalty income is subject to self-employment payroll taxes. Before signing any royalty contract with a business partner, take some time to discuss your options with a qualified accountant. If you sign a contract in a company name, it will be hard to convince the IRS later that you really meant to receive royalty income as an individual rather than through your business, in which case you would be liable for payroll taxes.

···

- **High disconnect pain**

  Some product and service business categories are so fluid that it's easy for customers to change loyalty without notice to the supplier. That's not an ideal situation from a business valuation perspective. Think about this. I can change my shampoo brand in a matter of seconds simply by picking a different bottle from a store shelf. The fast switch is low-risk and pain-free to me. In contrast, changing medical insurance coverage, moving a 401K account, or changing website hosting services always involves more time and administrative hassle.

  Businesses that offer products or services that require customers to learn new protocols, complete lots of paperwork, or change out support gear are in a desirable position from a business valuation standpoint. It's a way for businesses to hang on to revenue-generating customers, even if a customer is not fully satisfied with the experience.

- ### Ancillary revenue generation opportunities

  Ancillary revenues, or "add on" revenues, are favored by companies that like to eeke out extra revenues from their facilities, intellectual property, brand, website, and other company assets. Usually, these revenue opportunities are separate from a company's main product or service operations. For example, most of Amazon.com's revenues come from selling and shipping millions of items from its warehouses each month. However, if you look closely at Amazon.com's web pages you will see that the company allocates precious space for third-party advertisements. From Amazon.com's standpoint, third-party advertising represents an attractive source of revenues because the income stream doesn't take up warehouse space or involve a lot of management oversight. Most importantly, Amazon.com doesn't have to shell out its own cash to create even more cash. Airlines do this too with their branded credit cards. The trick to ancillary revenue generation is finding the right partnerships that won't jeopardize a company's relationships with its core customer or its brand reputation.

- ### B to B relationships

  Would you rather sell your products or services to home consumers or to established businesses and large corporations? The right answer is it doesn't really matter provided that you can build a sustainable business and earn a good living—the mission of the 4 Milestones of Financial Safety. But from a valuation perspective, companies that sell their products or services to other established businesses tend to receive a few extra valuation bonus points than companies that sell only to home consumers. The valuation rationale is that business accounts can order more and possibly pay more for products and services than home consumers.

  Serving a few well-known corporate customers can give relatively new companies fast credibility to capture even more business customers. If, for example, your company designs special engine components for General Electric, then other industrial players such as General Motors, Toyota, Boeing and TATA in India are likely to have confidence in your professional capacity to serve demanding corporate accounts.

  Here's another benefit associated with serving business customers. Bank lenders are far more likely to extend receivable lines of credit on more favorable terms to companies that sell to business customers than home consumers. Again it's a matter of perceived risk. Banks assume that established businesses represent "good quality receivables" because they may have more cash resources than home consumers to pay their bills on time.

Extra Startup Intelligence ··

Government contracts can be a highly desirable revenue source for young companies in terms of increased order size, credit worthiness, and credibility. But not all government work is the same. Businesses that sell products or services to state and local municipalities may have to wait a long time for payment, which is never a good thing from a cash flow perspective. Further, some types of government business impose strict limitations on pricing. Even if your company offers a higher quality product, a government agency may not be able to pay more than the price of a lower performance product.

··

- ▪ **Network potential**

  There are certain types of products or services that become exponentially more valuable as more consumers participate and interact with a business or service. For example, the more people who contribute information to online ancestry sites, the greater likelihood those consumers will have a satisfying experience and find interesting information about their extended family tree. This business phenomenon is known as the "network effect."

  The more people who use a product or service the more inherently valuable, useful and satisfying it becomes for all members or participants. Other types of businesses that benefit from a network effect include online dating sites, product review sites, home swap vacation sites, help wanted sites, auction sites, online gaming, and all kinds of social media hot spots.

  From a business valuation perspective, networks that enjoy high customer engagement are difficult to replicate by competitors. Sure, competitors can try to develop more features at a better price point, but if they can't entice participants to break away from other networks, they become essentially irrelevant in the marketplace. Microsoft's Office products, PayPal's online transaction processing services and Intuit's QuickBooks small business accounting software are examples of business services that have dominated their markets because of the network effect. Because "everyone uses" their services, it becomes harder and more expensive for companies to recruit and train personnel to manage competing services. So even if business customers are not entirely satisfied with Office, PayPal or QuickBooks, they remain engaged because everyone else in their world is.

There are other ways investors evaluate the nature of a company's customer relationships to establish financial value. For advertising-driven Internet businesses, investment analysts look closely at a company's key operating metrics such as "average visitor time on site," "total unique visitors," and "revenue generated per visitor hour."

For illustration purposes, let's compare two masters of the social media universe—LinkedIn and Facebook. In 2012, Facebook's average user spent approximately 6 hours per month at the social networking site. At LinkedIn, users spent less than 20 minutes per month at the site. But this statistic of customer engagement doesn't tell the whole story. LinkedIn generated a robust $1.30 of average revenue per user hour while Facebook fans contributed less than 6 cents per user hour. Which business generated a higher financial return on its customer engagement? Clearly, LinkedIn.

You can use the performance of larger companies such as Facebook and LinkedIn as a reference point to measure your own company's online performance and progress. And if your company's metrics for online user engagement consistently beat Facebook and LinkedIn, consider hiring an investment banker to learn just how much private equity fund managers and big media companies would pay to own all or a part of your emerging business.

Fundamental #3: *Industry-Leading Gross Profit Margins* $$

When I have to read a lot of business plans for business plan competitions or investment purposes, I scan the first few pages of an executive summary and then, by habit, turn my attention to the financial projections. If I don't see a strong gross profit margin story, I start to lose interest in the plan. Why? It's a matter of risk and reward. Low gross profit margin companies are riskier companies to manage and own than high gross profit margin companies.

Companies with high gross profit margins rarely end up in bankruptcy court. They are more able to survive harsh recessions, spikes in commodity costs, or the sudden loss of a big customer. And when unexpected problems arise, entrepreneurs who run high gross profit margin businesses can cut back on less-essential marketing, advertising and administrative expenses without altering core product or service quality. Simply stated, higher gross profit margin businesses have more "margin" for error than lower gross profit margin businesses.

Calculating a company's gross profit and its gross profit margin is really easy. Let's start with the formula for a company's gross profit. It is simply this: The total of all customer sales or revenues received during a period of time (usually over a month, a quarter or a year) minus the direct costs associated with producing or manufacturing the goods or services sold.

For accounting purposes, a company's revenues can include any mix of product sales, royalties, service fees and membership fees. Revenues do not include interest from a company's savings accounts or the proceeds associated with a one-time sale of company assets.

A company's cost of goods sold or "COGS" includes all the direct costs associated with producing its products such as raw materials, assembly labor, production facility costs, and production equipment depreciation.

What types of expenses are not included in a company's COGS? In general, COGS does not include advertising costs, sales commissions, legal costs, accounting costs, donations to charities, and most insurance. These expenses are generally lumped together for financial statement presentation purposes, as a company's sales and general and administrative costs or "SG&A." Expenses associated with researching and developing new technologies are also not included in

Gross Revenues	
- Cost of Goods or Services Sold	
Gross Profit	

a company's cost of goods sold. Here's a fine point. In-bound freight costs associated with raw material purchases are included in COGS; however freight costs associated with selling and shipping finished goods are a cost of sales.

For service-oriented companies, such as an engineering consulting firm, the salaries associated with performing client work are characterized for accounting purposes as the cost of producing service revenue—or "COS." If an engineer travels to solicit a new customer, the hotel, car rental and airfare bills are considered sales costs. If the same engineer travels to perform on-site work for a client, then all travel costs are allocated to COS.

In the example, Venture Bikes sold 15 motorcycles for total first-year revenues of $270,000. The custom bike manufacturer spent $175,500 on various motorcycle parts and labor to assemble and test the bikes. The difference between a company's revenues and COGS is its gross profit. Venture Bikes did quite well in its first year of operations by generating a healthy gross profit of $94,500.

Example 1: Venture Bikes, Inc.

Revenues	$270,000
Cost of goods sold	-$175,500
Gross profit	$ 94,500
Gross profit margin	35%

Example 2: Venture Bikes, Inc.

	Year 1	Year 2
Revenues	$270,000	$384,000
COGS	-$175,500	-$276,000
Gross Profit	$ 94,500	$108,000
Gross Profit Margin	35%	28%

Now let's add a little more financial sophistication to this analysis. A company's gross profit is different than its gross profit margin. One financial metric is expressed as a dollar number ($94,500) and the other financial metric is expressed as a percentage of revenues (35%.) The simple formula to calculate Venture Bike's gross profit margin is: Gross profit/sales or $94,500/$270,000 = 35%.

By itself, a 35% gross profit margin may not seem that impressive, however, when you compare Venture Bikes financial results to manufacturer Harley-Davidson, then the calculation develops some meaning. In good years, Harley-Davidson's gross profit margin averages 36% to 39%. During recessions when consumers don't splurge on new, top-of-the-line motorcycles, Harley-Davidson's gross profit margin can fall as low as 30%.

Notice in the example that even though Venture Bikes' revenues grew by a robust 42% during its second year of operations, the young company's gross profit margin dropped to 28%. Why? Most likely, the company's product costs grew out of proportion to what the company could pass along to its customers. When product costs go up faster than revenues, a company's gross profit margin falls.

Extra Startup Intelligence ···

You can compare a company's gross profit margin performance to other industry competitors on a month-to-month, quarter-to-quarter, or year-to-year basis. For example, let's compare Coca-Cola's gross profit margins to average beverage industry results. Coke's gross profit margin averages about 60%. In comparison, the beverage industry's average gross profit margin is about 42% to 44%.

What's does this tell you? Obviously Coke is a superbly managed business. But there's something more. If you want to start a hip beverage business, you now know what separates good industry performance from bad industry performance. A 10% to 20% gross profit margin for a startup company just won't cut it for very long in the beverage industry. Sure the company might stay in business for some time, but it will struggle because it won't have much extra cash flow to fund ongoing product development, advertising and other business needs. When a startup company's projected gross profit margins are too far below industry competitors, it's time to explore new ways to boost its gross profit margins by increasing product sales prices or lowering product costs.

Here's another example of how you can use your company's projected gross profit margin to fine-tune your company's business plan prior to submission to angel investment clubs and venture capital funds. For example, Microsoft Corporation's gross profit margin ranges between 75% and 82%. This compares favorably to the software industry's average gross profit margin of about 72%. If you are incubating a software business and your business plan projections show gross margins that are well below 40%, guess what? Your business plan will be dead upon arrival at venture capital funds and most angel investment clubs. Why would investors ever want to back entrepreneurs who visualize success at the bottom of industry performance? Simply stated, they don't.

···

Your next action steps:

☐ **Use gross profit margin analysis for R&D decisions**

To the extent that you have a long list of products or services you would like to sell but are short on cash resources, favor higher gross profit margin opportunities first. Provided that there is reasonable customer demand for the item or service, the extra cash flow associated with selling the higher margin product will make it easier for you to fund ongoing operations and customer outreach. As you hire employees to help you develop new products or services, set minimum gross profit margin targets to guide their work too.

☐ **Compare industry margin data**

Set purposeful goals for your company's gross profit margin performance. To get top dollar for your business at the time of company sale, your margin performance should match or exceed top industry competitors.

My two favorite online sources for comparative industry data are MSN Money and Yahoo! Finance. Both resources are free and offer information on publicly-traded companies that will help you develop a sophisticated understanding of the gross profit margin performance of companies in a broad range of industries including consumer products, technology, software, hospitality, food services, advertising, construction, energy production and more.

Start by looking up a company within your industry using its stock ticker symbol. For example, AOL's ticker symbol is "AOL." At Yahoo! Finance you can click on tabs for AOL's business profile, summary of the company's historical financial statements, and comparison of financial results to its competitors within the "Internet information providers" sector. Pay attention to individual company and industry valuation metrics such as price-to-sales and price-to-earnings ratios. Of course, take notes about your industry's average and leading gross profit margins and operating income margins.

☐ **Reinvent product and service mix**

Startup companies that offer commodity-oriented products and services make it too easy for customers to compare costs and favor the lowest price supplier. One way to improve your company's gross profit margins is to explore bundling your company's products or services in innovative ways to disguise separate item pricing. Emphasis should be placed on the exceptional value, extra convenience or other attributes associated with enticing customers to pay more for getting more.

☐ Specialize at something

Every business should offer at least one item or service that can be sold at a premium price to boost a company's overall gross profit margin performance. Ideally, this special item or area of expertise becomes what your business is "known for" in your community. The simple objective is to pick one thing and do it really, really well. Promote the area of specialization and build buzz around the item or service too. Pretty soon, your customers will be touting your area of expertise. A startup diner can market its specialty baked Alaska pie; a graphic designer can become known for corporate logo design; an accountant can become known for forensic accounting in divorce cases; a hair salon can become known for correcting hair color nightmares. When customers know they are getting the best, they are willing to pay extra for it.

You will be well rewarded for taking steps each year to steadily improve your company's gross profit margins. Because investors and business buyers place considerable weight on a company's gross profit margin performance, a 5% reduction in a company's cost of goods sold will probably give your company a greater valuation boost than lowering your company's sales and marketing costs by 5%.

Now you know more about the investment fundamentals that tend to reward entrepreneurs at the time of business sale. If you are thinking about a new initiative that requires a substantial investment in cash, consider if the initiative will directly enhance any fundamental attribute of business value listed above. Will the initiative improve your company's gross profit margins? Will it help lock-in customers into more predictable revenue-generating relationships? Will it lead to a new source of revenues?

When you start to allocate your cash to initiatives that build financial value, then you know you are at last managing your company with purpose. Companies that don't have any meaningful financial value are what I call "fundamentally flawed" businesses. Sure the business idea may be great, but the underlying business itself needs urgent Plan B attention.

FAQs

Q. **I thought business valuations were more complex than what you describe. There's got to be more to it than this!**

A. Yes, you are right, formal business valuations involve many more variables than a company's brand, its gross profit margins, and the nature of its customer base. However, I believe that it is useful to focus attention on the fundamentals that are most applicable to startup entrepreneurs. Knowing these fundamentals can influence the choices entrepreneurs make in business planning. I'd hate to see any entrepreneur spend too much money and time building a business that can't check off any of these three top business fundamentals.

Still, here are some other fundamentals that are worth knowing. Aspire to be the owner of...

- A company with a record of predictable cash flow generation from operations

- A company with annual cash flow that exceeds its reported net income

- A company that can run profitably without the founder's direct involvement

- A company that won't lose its appeal to customers after the founder retires or sells the company, including companies that are named after the founder

- A company that operates in a growing market

- A company that enjoys a strong position in a marketplace in which new competitors cannot enter with ease

- A company that owns a proprietary platform, gateway or distribution network for advertisers or other businesses to reach a targeted customer base

- A company that owns intellectual property that truly blocks competitors from participating in a growing market. [see Chapter 7 for more information]

- A company that can expand in international markets through acquisition or strategic partnerships

- A company that sells products or services that are supported by federal and state regulations—and enforced

- A company that has little to no long-term debt with restrictive covenants that may reduce management's operating flexibility to buy or sell assets, raise funds, etc.

Quit It!

How and When to Leave Your Day Job

A few years ago a woman called me for help with her struggling business. She had a high-powered executive-level resume and corporate contacts throughout North America and Europe. With all this fire power, why was her consulting business in trouble? Simply stated, she "dove into an empty pool."

Let me explain. This very capable executive did what so many other second career entrepreneurs do—she left her salaried job on a whim. She knew why she was leaving her job—it was no longer fulfilling and fun. What she didn't think about was how long it would take to transform her talent and connections into money-making customer relationships. With each passing month, her savings and confidence dropped. Her big regret was not that she started up, but that she started up too soon.

The purpose of this chapter is to help you start your new company from a position of strength. The more administrative and business planning action steps you can do prior to leaving a salaried position, the more you can focus on generating cash once you do start your business.

Expand Your Pre-Startup Intelligence

Think about this. In salaried employment, the costs associated with everyday mistakes are borne by your employer. In your startup, every mistake you make will take time and money to correct—your time and your money. And here's the ultimate cost of too many startup mistakes: your personal savings might not last long enough for you to succeed.

Instead of just getting by in business, your foremost objective as a startup entrepreneur should always be to find a way to get ahead by using your head. Here are some low-cost ways to help you prepare to manage a thriving business.

Your next action steps:

☐ **Explore company-sponsored in-house training classes**

Large Fortune 1000 companies typically offer career enrichment training classes in a broad range of subjects. If your company offers a sales training class, take it. If your company offers a project management or time-management class, take it. If your company offers a financial management class, take it. If your company offers a customer service class, take it. All of these skills will help you become a smarter business leader.

If your company doesn't offer company-sponsored training, research opportunities to attend evening or weekend classes, conferences or seminars with partial or full reimbursement from your employer.

☐ **Take a public speaking class**

Improving public speaking skills ranks very high on my recommended action list for pre-startup entrepreneurs. If you want to succeed in getting what you want, you have to be poised and persuasive in front of customers, bankers, business partners, employees, investors, board members, the media and community leaders.

I'm often asked if a sales training class is a good replacement for a public speaking class. My answer is no. Sales training classes teach students how to solicit customers and negotiate first orders. Public speaking classes improve self-confidence and overall improvisational skills. Of course, not all classes are worth your time and money. Favor classes in which the students talk more than the instructors. Ask to sit in on a class before signing up to make sure the coursework matches your needs.

☐ **Know the numbers that count**

If you are not familiar with how to read an income statement, how asset depreciation can lower business income taxes, or how to calculate a gross profit margin, then sign up for a community college accounting class without delay. Your job is not to become a bookkeeper but to understand the accounting principles that will help you make business decisions with confidence.

Upgrade Personal Finances Too

What do small business lenders and investors say about startup entrepreneurs behind closed doors? Sometimes the real reason why entrepreneurs are turned down for funding may have nothing to do with a company's prospective business operations, but everything to do with the entrepreneur. Investors and lenders are not at all forgiving to entrepreneurs who have a long history of poor money management. Here's what they say, "If someone can't handle their own personal finances, how can they be trusted to manage thousands or even millions of dollars to grow a profitable business?" This is a fair comment.

If you expect that your business will need capital from investors or lenders, now is the time to get your personal finances in order.

Your next action steps:

☐ **Review your credit report**

The Federal Fair Credit Reporting Act requires top credit reporting services such as Equifax, Experian and TransUnion, to provide a free report to consumers each year upon request. The easiest way to obtain a free credit report is through www.annualcreditreport.com. Alternatively, call 877-322-8228.

Check each personal credit report for errors that might lower your credit score or undermine your presentation as a reliable future business partner. Errors are most likely to occur on your address, job status, Social Security number, and marital status. Look closely for credit information that does not belong to you, but belongs to someone with a similar name. For example, credit information for H. Simpson from Springfield, Illinois, may land on the credit report of H. Jay Simpson from Springfield, Massachusetts.

Next, contact the respective credit bureau to report errors, but don't expect fast action. The correction process may take 30 to 45 days. If the bureau fails to make corrections, file a complaint with the U.S. Federal Trade Commission, with a copy to the credit reporting service. This should get some action on your account!

☐ **Improve your personal credit score**

Credit reports are different from credit scores. A credit report provides a history of payments on credit cards, car loans, and other personal obligations. In contrast, a credit score is a numerical assessment of several factors, including details of your credit history, to help lenders make decisions on new loan applications and loan pricing. Most individuals assume that they have just one single credit score. Actually, different credit bureaus calculate their own credit scores; plus large banks can develop their own credit scoring systems too. Two of the most influential credit scoring services are FICO and VantageScore.

These days, if you want to obtain a loan through the SBA's popular 7(a) small business loan program, you will need a personal FICO credit score of over 700 or the equivalent from another credit scoring system to get serious consideration. Angel investment clubs and venture capital funds often obtain credit reports on entrepreneurs to help them identify signs of personal instability or home life distress.

Improving your credit score takes time—it's a process of making incremental improvements to your credit history. In addition to correcting errors to your credit history, here are some factors that will improve your credit score with each passing month:

- Pay your bills on time, especially credit card bills, utility bills, cell phone bills, rent or mortgage.

- Pay down credit card balances that are close to their credit limits. Your credit score will increase to the extent you can lower your percentage of outstanding personal debt against your total available credit lines.

  My strong preference, however, is for you to go one step further. Prior to leaving salaried positions, try to eliminate all outstanding credit card balances. Of course, it's helpful to set aside extra savings for emergency family-related expenses too.

- Don't go "cold turkey" on all debt. While being disciplined about managing money is a very good business-building trait, swearing off all debt can lower your personal credit score. Lenders want to see documented evidence that you pay your bills on time and can manage credit. If you usually pay personal bills with a debit card, checks or cash, consider paying some routine bills with a credit card instead.

- Open a savings account at a bank or credit union. Mutual funds and brokerage accounts rarely report credit information to credit reporting agencies.

- Open a credit card account. For 20-something entrepreneurs who may have limited credit histories, start with a store credit card or a credit card from a community bank. These credit facilities may be the lowest cost way (lowest fees and interest rates) to build a credit history.

Do computer-driven credit-scoring systems hurt or discriminate against business owners? I don't think so. Actually, credit scores may be a way to even out the score for women and minority business owners. Increasingly, business lenders are relying on credit scores to simplify, and sometimes automate, their credit decisions. Automated credit decisions that are based on quantitative metrics can reduce subtle forms of discrimination in credit approval and credit pricing decisions. Plus, individuals with higher credit scores tend to receive lower interest rates on business credit cards, equipment leases, and mortgages.

Family Matters Matter

Here's the real deal about startup entrepreneurship. Not everyone will love your ideas as much as you do. That's Okay. But what if the criticism comes from close friends, siblings, parents and spouses? Shouldn't their support be unconditional? The best way to gain support from friends and family members is to solicit their support; not insist on it.

Your next action steps:

☐ **Consider the consequences of your prospective entrepreneurial career**
It's unrealistic to assume that nothing will change as you move from salaried employment to self-employment. Starting a business is different than starting a new job. Most salaried employees don't invest their whole heart and soul in their salaried jobs, but entrepreneurs do every day. As the boss of your new business, you will work harder and celebrate harder all because it's your company—your baby.

Make a list of the different ways your family members' lives might change (positively and negatively) as a result of your new career pursuit. Think about your new business, from their perspective. Will they see you less? Will you have to travel more? Will the family have to cut back spending? If you work out of your home, will family members confuse your work time with family time? Think through their likely concerns in preparation for upcoming family discussions.

☐ **Explain your career choice to family members**
You don't have to hard-sell your big idea to family members; just explain the personal and professional reasons for changing your career path. To emphasize the seriousness of your career plan, avoid phrases like "It's time I have some fun," "I need to feel fulfilled," or "I'm going for broke." Starting a business is a business. It's not a vacation or a fun way to take time off from the real world.

Extra Startup Intelligence ···

Businesses can be personal assets or personal liabilities. With skillful management, the value of a startup can become a family's largest asset, worth thousands or millions of dollars. If you are planning to marry, consider talking to a lawyer with expertise in family and business law before formally organizing your new business. Your lawyer can advise you of the pros and cons associated with maintaining the business as a "separate personal asset" through a prenuptial agreement rather than as a "joint asset."

Equally, if there is a chance that you might separate or get a divorce from your spouse in the near future, consider holding off starting your business until the divorce is final. This means, no business licenses, corporate filings or business bank accounts. It doesn't matter if you live in a "community property state" or an "equitable distribution state," a family law judge will look at a business started during a marriage as joint property.

Here's a more positive, family-friendly aspect of pre-nuptial and post-nuptial agreements: they can safeguard some family assets from business creditors. It's common for entrepreneurs to personally guarantee bank debt, credit card debt, office space, and equipment leases during the first years of business operations (though I discourage it whenever possible). If the business can't afford to pay these obligations, creditors can turn to the entrepreneur's personal assets (savings accounts, home equity, etc.) for repayment. Families that meticulously keep business assets and liabilities only in one spouse's name can usually avoid losing all family assets in the case of business disaster.

··

☐ Share your plan

Your business plan is your go-to tool for giving friends and family members a detailed understanding of your business objectives. Let them read the document at their pace, not yours. Then schedule "a good time" for your family members to ask questions. Don't dismiss any question since it is likely that you will be asked similar questions by future partners, customers, lenders or investors.

☐ Reassess extracurricular activities

It's naive to think that your new business will have no impact on the time you devote to friends, hobbies, community organizations and leisure time. To minimize future conflicts, guilt and strain, look closely at how you spend your non-working time each month. Take a break from extra commitments for the next 18 months or until your new company reaches positive cash flow.

☐ Determine your survival runway

How many months or years can you survive without a salary? While I appreciate that no startup entrepreneur ever wants to think about this number, knowing the number will help you develop more precise business strategies that will help you beat this looming deadline. If for example, you know you only have nine months of savings to support your entrepreneurial career, then you will be smarter about targeting first customers who are more likely to say "yes" than "let me think about it."

Here's another benefit of knowing your personal survival runway: you can project when you will need to solicit other sources of business funding long before you have exhausted your personal savings. Raising capital from lenders or investors takes time. I guarantee that if you panic and try to force investors and lenders to make fast decisions you will get a fast answer: "No!"

Here's how to calculate your survival runway.

1. Total up all personal savings excluding retirement savings such as IRAs and 401(k)s.

2. Revisit Chapter 1 to determine just how much savings you can safely afford to invest in your startup company.

3. Determine the net savings you have available for personal living expenses by subtracting the amount of savings you will invest in your business from your total savings.

4. Determine your average monthly cost of living. Include an allocation for big annual or semi-annual ticket items like insurance and holiday gifts plus the cost of health insurance, car expenses and any other benefits that may now be paid by your current employer.

5. Divide your total savings allocated to personal living expenses by your total monthly living expenses

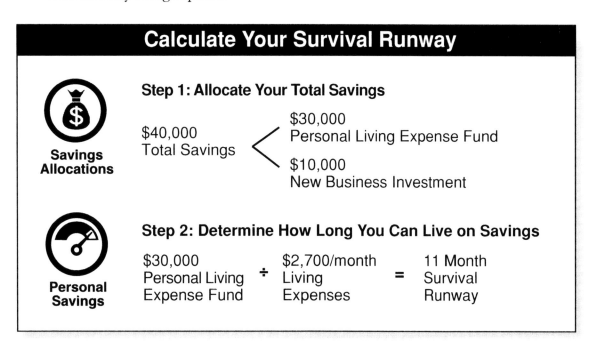

So, how many months can you live on your personal savings without any compensation from your new business? Is it four months or four years? The longer your survival runway, the more time your company has to reach the 4 Milestones of Financial Safety.

Tactical Employment

In eight years of studying why startups fail, I've learned that a primary reason why businesses close is their founders run out of money for personal living expenses before their companies can afford to pay living wage salaries.

One way to extend your survival runway is through tactical employment. Tactical employment is what I call an interim part-time or full-time job that helps entrepreneurs make the transition from salaried employment to self-employment with the least amount of personal financial strain.

Don't think of tactical employment as a dead-end job or a time-wasting career distraction. If you are strategic about your job selection, you will gain a more sophisticated understanding of the day-to-day operating requirements of your proposed new business. Even better, you may get to make some common beginner's mistakes on someone else's "dime and time."

If, for example, you want to start a fast food or retail business that you one day hope to franchise across America, consider working at franchise pioneer McDonald's. In just a few months you can learn the fine points of hiring and training part-time staff, storing inventory and creating franchise store operating protocols.

Another approach to highly productive tactical employment is to work at companies where you ultimately may sell your products. If for example, you want to start your own clothing label or beauty product line, consider working at a retail store that sells those items. With an inquisitive attitude, you can learn what retail buyers and store managers expect in terms of shelf-merchandizing, sales turnover, profit margins, co-op advertising funds, minimum shipment quantities and clearance pricing. It's great to get paid to learn how your target customers will size up your products long before you finalize those products!

Here are some other benefits of short-term tactical employment:

- **Make sure the dream isn't better than reality**
  Imagine how miserable it would be to invest a lot of time and money in a new business and later realize that you hate your new day job. If you love the idea of owning a bakery, spend at least six months getting used to the rhythm and demands of working in someone else's bakery first. If you want to start an art gallery, work in another art gallery first.

- **Keep benefits in place**
  Through tactical employment, startup entrepreneurs can often get health insurance at an affordable cost. Costco Wholesale, REI, Whole Foods, Starbucks and Home Depot are widely recognized for their generous benefit packages for part-time staff.

- **Master customer service**

  All businesses are dependent on happy customers for business survival. By working for companies that excel at customer service such as Amazon.com, Southwest Airlines, Starbucks, USAA Insurance, Wegman's grocery chain, Publix Super Markets, UPS, or Four Seasons hotels, you can improve your understanding on how to serve customers well.

- **Purchase discounts**

  Sometimes entrepreneurs can buy what they need to develop their businesses at a discount through tactical employment. If, for example, you need servers, computers, or office equipment, consider a job at an electronic store or an office supply store that offers generous employee discounts.

Remember, no job is a waste of time. Tactical employment is not about copying another company's intellectual property, but acquiring skills, creating networking relationships and extending your survival runway.

Extra Insurance for a Healthy Start

Before you leave your day job, spend time exploring the market for individual and small business health care insurance. You'll need to know this information to prepare your first financial projections.

Your next action steps:

- ☐ **Visit your doctor**

  Get a clean bill of health before changing employment status. It's emotionally and physically exhausting to recover from a serious illness and start a business at the same time. Further, out-of-pocket treatment costs are almost always less under an employer-sponsored health plan than an individual health plan.

- ☐ **Research COBRA health care coverage**

  Remaining on your former employer's health insurance plan is likely to be the lowest cost health care coverage for startup entrepreneurs and in many cases, their spouses and dependent children too.

  COBRA (Consolidated Omnibus Budget Reconciliation Act) is a federal law that requires companies with 20 or more employees to continue health care coverage for departing employees for up to 18 months, even if the employee quits a job. Here are a few key rules for obtaining COBRA coverage:

- To qualify for COBRA coverage you have to have been covered by an employer's health plan for the previous six months before the last date of employment.

- It's your responsibility to notify your employer in writing of your intent to use COBRA. In general, companies are required to send out enrollment option notices to former employees; however I encourage entrepreneurs not to wait. Ask for enrollment forms and monthly premium costs on or before your last day of work.

- It's your responsibility to pay the monthly premium on time. A former employer is not required to send payment reminder notices. If you drop out of the COBRA plan due to non-payment, your former employer is not required to re-admit you to the program.

Visit the U.S. Department of Labor's Web site (www.dol.gov) and search on "COBRA" for up-to-date regulations related to employer-sponsored health care coverage.

☐ Research alternative healthcare coverage options

If you don't qualify for COBRA or can't piggyback onto a spouse's health care plan, then it's time to do some serious comparison shopping. An insurance broker may be able to help you but don't assume that the broker will always introduce you to the best value option because commission-based brokers make more money when you buy more expensive policies.

Check out the following:

- **SBA.gov.** The Small Business Administration's website offers extensive information about the Affordable Care Act as well as information relevant to self-employed entrepreneurs, business owners with less than 25 employees, business owners with less than 50 employees, and business owners with 50 or more employees.

- **State health care plans.** Many states offer plans to individuals who can't obtain coverage elsewhere. Some state plans have a waiting list for new enrollments so apply early if your state offers a desirable, low-cost plan. Your state's healthcare plan website will have the most up-to-date information, versus other websites, including the SBA's website, which may summarize information about state resources.

- **Association plans.** Many for-profit industry associations, non-profit associations, and wholesale buying clubs offer health insurance as a service to their members. Some plans offer great value to members while other plans offer plans as a way to earn commission income. Again, compare before you enroll. If you do buy a healthcare plan from an association, keep in mind that they are not subject to COBRA regulations. This can be important when there is a change to family status.

- **Independent plans.** Not all medical insurance companies provide coverage to individuals in all states. Self-employed entrepreneurs can lower their monthly premiums (or minimize rapid rate increases) by paying attention to issues that are within your control, especially weight management and smoking. Rates for independent policies also tend to skew higher for individuals with diabetes, depression, and heart conditions.

Keep the *Good* in Good Bye

I get it! I know you can't wait to leave your salaried job to become the boss of your own company. But before you give your final notice, double-check once again for gotchas!

Your next action steps:

☐ **Do it at home**

It's tempting to use a current employer's office equipment and other resources for writing software code, duplicating executive summaries, or communicating with potential customers or investors. A former employer may claim ownership of your new company's intellectual property if it can prove that the work was completed on company property during company time. But there is a more important reason to keep your startup activities away from your employer's offices. It's integrity.

☐ **Avoid borrowing from a 401(k)**

If you intend to leave your employer in the near-term, be aware that most employer-sponsored 401(k) plans require immediate repayment of outstanding 401(k) loans after employees quit or separate from the company. Too often startup entrepreneurs take out 401(k) loans to fund startup costs (not recommended) and then face a shocking repayment bill when they give notice to their employers. It only gets worse. Defaulting on 401(k) loans can trigger costly IRS tax penalties and potentially destroy your good credit rating—something future lenders and investors will review before making business funding decisions.

☐ **Review confidentiality agreements and employment contracts**

Employment contracts can include clauses that may restrict your future activities as a new business owner. Pay special attention to the following:

- **Return of hiring and retention bonuses.** Some corporate employment contracts require departing employees to return a portion of their hiring bonus, moving cost reimbursement, or retention bonuses if employees leave before a specified period of time.

- **Solicitation of customers.** Don't contact any of your current employer's customers and notify them of your intent to startup a competing business prior to your departure date. Also be very careful about taking information about your employer's customers. Certain industries, including the financial and medical industry, have strong rules against employees copying customer information, especially if the information may violate privacy laws.

- **Hiring former co-workers.** Many large U.S. corporations require employees to promise in writing that they will not solicit or start a business with a co-worker. This agreement language is often buried in employment manuals that employees sign at the start of a new corporate job. The chance of threatened litigation increases when a former employee "raids" an office of its top talent.

Extra Startup Intelligence ···

The primary risk of competing against a former employer is the potential legal threat of misuse of an employer's trade secrets and intellectual property. At worst, a judge could issue a temporary or permanent injunction preventing you from actively competing in a certain sector of the marketplace for a period of time. This kind of legal judgment is rare. The best way to avoid nuisance litigation is to keep excellent records of your company's research and development activities to demonstrate that you created your new company's innovations offsite on your own time and dime.

···

☐ **Submit all documented employee expenses for reimbursement**
Every dollar counts in building up your savings prior to starting a new company. Don't quit your job until you have been reimbursed in full.

☐ **Collect unpaid bonuses and sales commissions**
Once employees give notice that they are leaving a job, payment of earned but unpaid bonuses and commissions can become contentious. To the extent that you may be contractually entitled to earn commissions on future customer income, even after leaving your employer, take time to document the obligation. Prepare a written list of customers that qualify for extended commission income. Give the list to your boss as well as your employer's human resource manager at

the time you give notice. Make sure that this list is reviewed and agreed to prior to your last day of work. Also consider proposing an upfront buy-out settlement with your employer to put more cash in your pocket for startup purposes.

☐ **Review the terms of stock-related incentive plans**

Most stock option and stock incentive plan awards terminate immediately or within 90 days after employee departure. Determine the eligibility and tax payment obligations for any stock awards that are vested or may become eligible for exercise within the next six months. Do the math on each award. Not all stock options or stock awards are worth exercising, particularly if the "underlying" stock cannot be liquidated into cash easily.

☐ **Update your network**

Update your contact list to include co-workers and other industry contacts. These relationships should be a part of your ever-expanding eco-system of business advisors and customer leads.

☐ **Give responsible notice**

Two weeks is the minimum amount of notice you should give your employer of your intended last date of employment. Offer to help make the transition as easy as possible for your boss, even if it means staying a few extra weeks. This is not the time to "coast" at work but elevate your productivity to ensure that your last impression is a good one.

Extra Financial Empowerment ···

Entrepreneurs who approach angel investment clubs and VCs for startup funding are often caught off guard when they are asked to produce a list of names and phone numbers of prior bosses. And yes, investors do call every contact, not only to confirm employment dates but to learn more about the character and work caliber of the entrepreneur.

···

☐ **Thank the people who helped you**

I believe in good karma, or at minimum, common courtesy. Take the time to thank the people who helped you succeed in your salaried job. An email is not enough. Pick up the phone, write a personal note, buy lunch or take your work colleagues to their favorite coffee house for an afternoon break. Remember, your former co-workers may one day refer business to your company.

FAQs

Q. **Can't I just quit my job and go on unemployment as a way to support my startup?**

A. Most states don't pay unemployment insurance benefits to workers who quit their jobs without acceptable cause. If you sense your employer is about to downsize the company payroll and is inclined to be generous with severance packages, you might be able to negotiate a friendly, well-timed exit. Here's something else to know: unemployment insurance typically kicks in after a terminated employee exhausts all severance payments.

Q. **My husband and I filed for bankruptcy just last year. How long will this show up on our credit report? How might a bankruptcy affect my ability to go into business for myself?**

A. Bankruptcy laws have changed in recent years. In general, a Chapter 13 bankruptcy filing, which usually involves a repayment plan, can be reported to credit bureaus for up to seven years. A Chapter 7 bankruptcy filing can be reported for up to 10 years. It's important to remember that bankruptcy courts don't directly report bankruptcy information to credit bureaus and won't get involved if information about your bankruptcy is misrepresented on your credit report. It's up to you to update information and correct all errors with credit bureaus.

It's true that most personal credit scores take a big nose dive after a bankruptcy filing but you certainly don't have to wait 10 years to become credit worthy again. One of the best ways startup entrepreneurs can improve their credit rating is through micro-finance organizations. In my experience, they are the most forgiving to entrepreneurs with bad credit histories. You can start with loans as small as $500.

Here's another tip. Because you may be more challenged to obtain credit on reasonable terms from lenders and landlords, choose a startup business that is not cash intensive. For example, it costs more hard cash to start a restaurant than a catering business. Lastly, be conservative in how you manage your new business. Don't commit to spend money before you have it the bank.

Q. **My brother has nothing good to say about my new business idea. Now all I want to do is prove him wrong. The problem is that we are roommates. What should I do?**

A. I suspect that if you asked your brother why he is so negative about your business idea, he would say that he doesn't want to see you "lose money" or "get hurt." You have to admit, these responses come from a thoughtful heart. Still, it's better to start a business in a supportive family environment. Your home has to be a restorative oasis—a place to rest and regroup for the next day of business building. Here are my recommendations:

1. **Show restraint.** If you ever tell a friend or family member that you will "prove them wrong" you position them as an adversary, not an advocate. Don't do it. It will only make your home life more combative and unpleasant.

2. **Ask for help.** The next time your brother is negative about some aspect of your business, invite him to brainstorm potential solutions with you. Sometimes family members just want to feel involved and needed.

3. **Move on and out.** If your home life becomes unbearable, find another place to live. Smart entrepreneurs know when it's time to walk away from a losing battle.

Create It!

How to Name and Structure Your Business with Precision

As the boss of your company, you have a choice. You can do what you want to do, and avoid all the rest…at least for a while. Or you can do things right from the start so you don't have to spend more time later correcting administrative mistakes with the help of lawyers, accountants and other service professionals. The purpose of this chapter is to help you choose the name of your company and set up your company's legal business structure with precision.

Nothing in this chapter is difficult. Actually, the best approach to selecting your company's name and business structure is to keep an open mind. What you initially think might be the best choice for your company may change once you learn more about the tactical implications of these first decisions.

Name Your Company

Entrepreneurs often say their young companies are "their babies." They birth them, nurture them, and experience their heartbreaks and triumphs in deeply personal ways. It's no wonder that entrepreneurs select business names that best reflect their individual spirit and creativity.

For example, did you ever wonder about the origins of Oprah Winfrey's Harpo Productions and Harpo Inc.? It's "Oprah" spelled backwards. Office supply and service store "Kinkos" was named for the red kinky hair the founder sported as a child. Other business owners pick names that have special meaning to them. For example, independent movie producers Harvey and Bob Weinstein named their highly successful independent film production company after their parents, Miriam and Max, to form Miramax Films.

The most common mistake entrepreneurs make when naming their first company is that they make it too complicated. A company name, by itself, can't stand for everything that you represent or want to do as an entrepreneur. Simple can be powerful, memorable and effective. Here are a few creative directions you can take in business name selection:

- **The company is the brand**

  One cost-effective strategy to maximize a new company's marketing dollar is to select one name that will represent both the business organization and its primary product or service brand. Think Bose or T-Mobile.

  The primary risks to this strategy are if the product fails in the marketplace or is tied to some sort of public relations scandal. This is why large corporate entities, especially in the consumer product sector, test one or more brand names for new products that are different than the parent company name. If the product brand turns out to be a dud, the parent company doesn't have to change its corporate identity.

- **The founder's name**

  Michael Dell did it. So did Henry Ford, Martha Stewart, Charles Schwab, Robert Mondavi, and snow board innovator Jake Burton. Their own name became the company name.

  Are there any drawbacks associated with naming a company, its first products or services after its founder? Sure. As detailed in Chapter 7, family name trademarks are usually placed on the "Supplemental Register" instead of the "Principal Register" by the U.S. Patent and Trademark Office at the time of initial federal trademark approval. In general, it is more difficult for business owners to win infringement cases while their marks are listed on the Supplemental Register. Eventually family name trademarks can move from the Supplemental Register to the Principal Register once the public identifies the mark with the commercial product or service rather than the individual. This legal concept is called "secondary meaning." Today most people think about hot dogs or baloney when they hear a reference to "Oscar Mayer," not the man who started the company.

  There is another potential issue associated with using the family name as the new company name. When owners of small service companies put their companies up for sale, they may not receive the highest price possible because the company name may be too closely associated with the company founder. Savvy business buyers will question if the business will continue to prosper when the founder is no longer around. It's a rational concern too. To protect their interests, business buyers may seek to restrict founders and even their extended family members from using the family name again in related commercial pursuits. It happened to the Gucci family, so it can happen to you.

Extra Startup Intelligence ···

Sole proprietors can choose to operate a business under a trade name that is different than a legal business name. This is often referred to as "doing business as" or a company's "DBA." Trade names are allowed to include Baker and Sons, Baker and Daughters, Baker and Company, etc.

Further, trade names are not the same as trademarks. A trade name is used to identify a business, association or organization. Trade names cannot be registered under U.S. trademark law unless the mark also represents a company's goods or services that are actively sold in the marketplace.

···

- **Descriptive names**
  Creating a memorable business name is a daunting challenge for any new business. One way to make the job a little easier is to choose a company name that provides clear clues to your product or service purpose. Office Depot, Inc., Room to Read, DrugStore.com, The Baby Einstein Company, SolarCity Corp., SafetyWeb, Inc., and KitchenAid, USA are good examples of descriptive business names. Sometimes descriptive names can give startup entrepreneurs an advantage in online customer key word search rankings too.

- **The multi-purpose name**
  It's increasingly common for startup entrepreneurs to want to create a business entity that can serve as an "umbrella organization" for several different types of business operations. In these cases, entrepreneurs are best served by selecting a more generic name that is not directly linked to any of their individual "portfolio" company operations. This way, they can buy or sell business entities without any change to their overall parent corporate identity. For example, Warren Buffett's Berkshire Hathaway Inc. serves as the parent company to GEICO, See's Candies, Benjamin Moore & Co., Ben Bridge Jewelers and many other subsidiary business entities.

- **Fanciful and arbitrary names**
  Sometimes new business owners, who operate in crowded product or service markets, have no other choice but to make up a new word for their new company name. The primary benefit of selecting novel, sometimes hip names like Google, Twitter, Smaato or Fandango is that the companies are unlikely to face legal conflicts in trademark registrations.

Choose a business name that can stand out in your specific business category or geographic area without commercial confusion or legal conflicts. If your selected business name also inspires you, that's even better.

Your next action steps:

☐ **Compare three name options**

"Due diligence" is a common term in the venture finance community to describe researching an issue for potential legal, marketplace or financial conflicts. Instead of committing to the first name that appeals to you, conduct some thoughtful due diligence on not just one name but at least three business name candidates.

☐ **Check name availability**

Most states have online tools at their business licensing department to help entrepreneurs check for business name availability. Be careful not to select a business name that is too close to another company's business name within your county or state, especially if the company is a competitor. Another concern associated with similarly named companies is confusion with credit rating services such as the Better Business Bureau. You don't want to be unfairly mistaken for a shady business and have to deal with a lot of phone calls from pesky bill collection agencies.

☐ **Check for domain name conflicts**

Log onto any domain registry service such as GoDaddy.com, Name.com, Yahoo! Small Business, or Network Solutions, to see if your preferred business names are available in one or more top-level domains such as .com, .co, .org, or .net. Resist selecting domain names that involve extra payments to domain squatters because you will need your startup capital for other business building purposes!

There is nothing special about domain name registrars since it is merely an administrative service. It's worthwhile to compare registrar prices. Unfortunately domain and hosting services are high risk areas for international identity theft and small business bank account fraud. Don't provide your credit card or business bank account information to ultra low-cost domain registrars that are not based in the U.S. Be wary if the domain registrar does not have a "Contact Us" page with an active U.S. telephone number or operates with an international domain extension.

☐ **Evaluate search results**

Test your target business names in several search engines such as Bing or Google. Look closely at the paid and organic search listings on the first five pages of search results for each candidate name. Do porn sites appear? Do any major competitors within your industry rise high on the search rankings? How hard will it be for your future customers to find your website?

☐ **Search federal trademarks**

Well-funded trademark owners can make life miserable for entrepreneurs who choose business names that are too similar to their established brand interests. What's the best way to avoid nuisance litigation? Simply choose a business name that doesn't conflict with registered trademarks within your product or service category.

Fortunately, searching for potential federal trademark conflicts has never been easier. Visit the United States Patent and Trademark Office at www.uspto.gov and use the free online trademark search tool called "TESS." Type in your different business name candidates and look closely for conflicts. Also explore your state government's trademark listing service because it is possible for a competitor to file a state trademark application but not a federal application.

☐ **Test ease of use**

Can strangers pronounce and spell your business name candidates without error? Make sure they can. If you choose a business name that is difficult to say or spell, it may be challenging for your future customers to find your company online.

☐ **Research trade name requirements**

Many states require business owners to register trade names, so it is worth checking your state's specific rules if you plan to use a trade name in business. However, notifying your state of your company's trade name will not give your company trademark rights. Visit Chapter 7 for instructions on how to secure trademark rights.

Design Your Company Logo

I know you have been looking forward to designing your company's logo for a long time. It's a creative, fun thing to do. However, let's put your company's logo in proper perspective. A cool company logo, by itself, is not what creates favorable impressions about a business. It's the company's track record with customers that will shape opinions more. Over time, your logo will become a symbol of your company's favorable reputation.

Your next action steps:

☐ **Prioritize spending**

If your product or service brand name is different than your company name save more of your graphic design budget for the logos that will be seen by your customers.

☐ Define message priorities

Create a list of three adjectives to represent what kind of visual impression best represents your company's desired brand identity and promise. For example, one new fashion designer might select "stylish, sleek, and luxurious" to represent her company ethos. Another fashion designer might select "edgy, youthful and fun" to represent his company's creative vision. Different adjectives lead to different logo designs. Your company's target audience can also influence your company's messaging objectives. If your audience is high tech—go there. If your audience is playful—go there. If your audience is patriotic—go there. Review the action steps on brand definition in Chapter 3 before finalizing your company's logo design.

☐ Think about color

If you hire a designer to create your company logo, it's highly likely you will be asked about your personal color preferences. If you hate a color, don't apply it to your company's logo no matter what a designer says works best for business cards, brochures and websites.

Cost is another consideration in choosing logo colors. Do you want a single color logo or a multi-color logo? Multi-color logos will increase the costs of printing business cards, marketing literature, and stationary. Some colors are also more difficult to reproduce online than others. If you want to keep reproduction costs down, instruct your designer to choose standard Pantone colors. Also, explore ways to use logo color to set your new company apart from your competitors.

☐ Consider simplicity

Simple can be powerful, bold and effective. Microsoft is perhaps the most widely recognized example of a company that did not create a separate symbol for its corporate name.

☐ Make it tight

The trend in business logos is to make them small, but distinctive. Even large Fortune 1000 brands are scaling back well-known company and brand logos so they can adapt to Internet and mobile display needs. Federal Express has become FedEx, Kentucky Fried Chicken has morphed into KFC, and Hewlett Packard is now simply HP. Can your logo work within a square icon for easy access on mobile devices?

☐ Test communication equipment

Test your draft logo across all media platforms and business communication equipment. How does your draft logo look when it is sent over a fax machine? Do all design and color elements of your logo remain intact when photocopied or scanned into various electronic devices?

☐ **Postpone tag line development**

Many marketing professionals encourage new business owners to develop a company logo plus a company tag line as part of their work to "brand" a new company. My view is to hold off investing in corporate tag line development until your company's products or services have been in the marketplace for at least a year. Your corporate messaging priorities may change as you gain firsthand experience with customers.

FAQs

Q. **Should I develop a mission statement for my company?**

A. I'm not a fan of mission statements for for-profit startup organizations because they are mostly too vague to provide clear decision-making guidance to employees in a startup setting. As a startup entrepreneur, your mission should be to achieve the 4 Milestones of Financial Safety and align all employees and advisors to this over-riding operating priority.

Well-crafted mission statements are, however, crucial documents for social entrepreneurs who expect to apply for foundation grants and 501(c)3 non-profit tax status from the IRS. A non-profit organization's "mission" will help determine what products or services are exempt from taxation.

Q. **How important is the print quality of a business card?**

A. Here's my general rule of thumb with business cards. If your business card will be given directly to customers, then buy a high quality card stock. Online-only entrepreneurs who rarely meet their customers can afford to spend less. And don't buy business cards from online sources that print their name and website on the back of your business cards! Business cards are intended to connect you to new sources of revenues, not to the business card printer. Here's an extra tip. Select a print font that someone over the age of 45 can read without fumbling for reading glasses.

Choose Your Legal Structure

Once you have selected your company's business name, it's time to determine which type of legal business entity is best for your personal and professional needs. A legal business entity is also commonly referred to as a company's "business organization" or "business structure." Common for-profit business structures include: sole proprietorship, a Limited Liability Company (LLC) or one of several types of partnerships and corporations. Non-profit entrepreneurs typically form corporations, but a few states permit the organization of a non-profit LLC, a low-profit LLC, or a B-corporation (also known as a "benefit corporation") to pursue their social mission.

Why does a company's business structure matter so much? The fast answer to this question is a company's legal structure determines business income tax rates, the "ownership" responsibility of company debts, and the ease in which owners can invite partners and investors into a business.

The following sections highlight some advantages and disadvantages of different business structures with special attention as to how a company's business structure may attract or repel investors. Even if you know what kind of business structure you plan to use for your new business, I encourage you to read through this chapter and learn some of the fine points of different business organizations. Knowing more about these tricky details may influence your decisions about providing credit to corporate, LLC or sole proprietor customers or the best business structure options for your future partnerships with other businesses. A local attorney and business accountant can provide added insight about your state's specific licensing requirements, annual fees and other criteria that may influence your choice of business structure too.

All About Sole Proprietorships

The most popular form of business organization—preferred by over 20 million business owners—is the sole proprietorship. Setting up a sole proprietorship is easy. All you have to do in most states is apply for a business license, pick a company name, open a bank account and print business cards. And voila, a new business is born. Sole proprietors also don't have to create a formal board of directors, hold routine board meetings, and prepare written meeting minutes, which are required for corporate entities.

Sole proprietorships also make it easy for entrepreneurs to start and stop a business on short notice, which is convenient for unemployed Americans who want to earn interim income while they look for full-time salaried employment.

Perhaps the best benefit of a sole proprietor business structure is that entrepreneurs usually pay lower tax rates on business-related income than standard C-corporations. Owners of profitable standard C-corporations can end up paying double taxes—first on business profits and again on any dividend distributions paid to shareholders, which obviously includes the company's founder.

It's commonly assumed that tax reporting is easy for sole proprietors. For the most part, all sole proprietors have to do is add up all relevant business income and expenses and report the results on Schedule C of a personal income tax return. But state and federal tax reporting of any kind involves tricky rules that can take some time to learn. My strong recommendation for all startup entrepreneurs is to meet at least once with a qualified account to understand the tax reporting obligations with a sole proprietorship or any other business structure.

Extra Startup Intelligence ···

Despite all the tax and administrative advantages of a sole proprietorship organization, it is not necessarily the best business structure for every startup entrepreneur. Here are some special considerations:

- **Appealing to investors**

  Startup entrepreneurs who expect to raise money from foreign investors, corporations, venture capital funds, or angel investment clubs should consider incorporating their business. Most professional investors prefer to invest in a standard C-corporation which can issue shares of different classes of stock to an unlimited number of shareholders. Ambitious startup entrepreneurs who are working toward the day they can take their companies public on a U.S. stock exchange or sell to a large corporation should consider organizing as a C-corporation too.

- **Increased personal liability**

  Sole proprietorships are not a separate legal entity from the owner (like a corporation or partnership). As such, when sole proprietors sign business agreements they personally assume the liability for any unpaid business bills. In practical terms, this means that if your business activities can't generate enough cash to repay lenders and other creditors, then a judge may require you to pay the outstanding obligations with personal assets, such as your home, personal savings accounts, and other valuables. In general, IRA and 401(k) retirement accounts are exempt from bankruptcy proceedings, which is the reason why I discourage entrepreneurs from drawing funds from retirement accounts for business investment purposes.

- **Employee incentive plans**

  Cash-poor entrepreneurs often offer first employees and professional service providers the opportunity to earn an equity stake in a business in exchange for reduced cash compensation. The administration of most types of equity grants, particularly stock option plans, is better suited to corporations than sole proprietorship entities.

- **Presumption of business sophistication**

  Unfortunately a sole proprietorship business structure may be perceived as a "small" business to potential business partners, business insurance underwriters,

Internet security rating services, lenders, and other business vendors. This bias may affect what sole proprietors ultimately pay or receive in terms of service value in subtle but meaningful ways.

···

All About Limited Liability Companies

All 50 states now allow the organization of LLCs for business organization and tax reporting purposes. I like to think of the LLC as a gift to time-strapped small-business owners who hate tedious administration and paying top dollar income taxes.

Unlike corporations, LLC organizers are not required to have officers and directors, keep minutes of meetings or even hold regular meetings of its member owners. They also don't necessarily have to prepare formal written resolutions to issue company stock, acquire assets, open bank accounts, or make big changes in the company's business direction.

Like a C-corporation, LLCs can usually issue different types of securities which can help entrepreneurs attract investors. In contrast, S-corporations, which offer tax savings advantages that are similar to LLCs, can only have one class of stock. LLCs also offer an added level of flexibility in structuring agreements with business partners that may not be available to shareholders in corporate entities.

What's often confusing about LLCs is the terminology. Whereas owners of corporate stock are called "stockholders," owners and investors in LLCs are called "members." Corporations are governed by documents called articles of incorporation and bylaws. In contrast, LLCs are governed in most states by articles of organization and an operating agreement. LLCs can also usually be organized as a multi-member LLC or as a single member LLC.

LLCs tend to be more complex than corporations to set up, especially in the development of a LLCs operating agreement. This document is a contract among the member owners of the LLC that often includes guidance regarding what financial contribution each member will make, how profits will be distributed, how members can sell their equity stake and how the business entity can be dissolved. Most states require LLC organizers to declare in the articles of organization whether the LLC will be managed by all members as a group or by a designated manager. A designated manager does not have to be an LLC member.

Provided that LLCs are set up correctly, they generally offer better personal liability protection for business owners than a simple sole proprietorship. For instance, if you obtained a bank loan without signing a personal guarantee, you would generally not be personally liability for missed payments in a LLC business structure— assuming no fraud is involved.

Different states have quirky rules that might be easily overlooked if you are setting up an LLC using online do-it-yourself business organization kits. For example, some states don't allow single-member LLCs, which works against freelance entrepreneurs who want to shield their personal assets from business calamities. Other states tax LLCs with substantial property (such as inventory or automobiles) but not corporations. Good lawyers and accountants know where there are gotchas in your state's laws.

With regard to taxes, LLCs have several filing options. The LLC can be taxed as a corporation, partnership, or sole proprietor, depending on the number of LLC members and its specific "elections" or instructions to the IRS. In general, single member LLCs allow business profits to bypass traditional corporate taxes and pass through to the LLC's member owners, like a sole proprietorship or S-corporation. A multi-member LLC can report as either a partnership or a corporation, including an S-corporation. To be treated as a corporation, a multi-member LLC has to file Form 8832 with the IRS. Otherwise, the multi-member LLC will be treated like a partnership for tax reporting purposes.

LLCs are popular business structures among film producers and real estate developers because LLCs make it easy to segregate investors according to specific project participation. Even better, real estate developers who spend the majority of their time in the real estate profession and are active in the management of the properties can usually write off real estate losses against other forms of income. If you are involved in real estate, your accountant can tell you more about how to structure debt within an LLC to the greatest tax-saving advantage.

If there is a downside to LLC organizations, it usually involves the business structure preferences of angel investment clubs and venture capital funds. Simply stated, experienced investors prefer to invest in entrepreneurial companies that are structured as corporations rather than LLCs.

Why? Let's start with how venture capital funds are organized. Venture capitalists pool together funds from many types of investors including off-shore investors, wealthy private individuals, institutional pension plans, private family foundations, large universities and well-endowed 501(c)(3) non-profit organizations. If a venture capital fund invested in a U.S. pass-through tax entity like an LLC, then the VC's off-shore investors could possibly face unexpected U.S. tax obligations. It's a hassle VCs and their investors would like to avoid.

Another fine point that works against LLC business structures relates to maximizing the big payday for investors and entrepreneurs. The most common way VCs make money is when one of their investments (a "portfolio company") is sold to a larger corporation. If the purchase is structured as a stock-for-stock transaction, then there are opportunities within a corporate structure for a tax-free reorganization. These same tax-saving opportunities are usually not available to most LLC business entities.

If you don't expect to one day raise money from the venture capital community, then don't hesitate to form an LLC if that is your first choice. However, if you want to raise capital from independent investors, then a corporate structure should be your first choice. Sure you can change an LLC to a corporation, but you will need a good lawyer and accountant to help you do it right.

All About Corporations

There are certain pivotal moments in an entrepreneur's journey that are memorable and extremely gratifying. One of these happy occasions is the receipt of a handsome, leather-bound binder that contains dozens of newly printed corporate share certificates. One young entrepreneur told me he felt like a grown-up the day he held the share certificates of his new corporation.

Corporations are a form of business organization that can be set up by one person or a group of people. There are different types of corporations including professional corporations, non-profit corporations, benefit corporations, standard C-corporations and S-corporations.

A corporate business structure is conducive for buying and selling companies, issuing employee stock options, and going public on a U.S. stock exchange. Venture capital funds generally prefer to invest in corporations because of the relative ease in issuing different classes of stock at different times to different groups of investors.

There are two documents that are filed with state agencies at the time of corporate formation: the new corporation's "articles of incorporation" and the corporation's "bylaws." Articles of incorporation usually detail the names and addresses of key officers, the corporation's general business purpose, and guidance on how assets might be distributed upon final corporate entity dissolution. A corporation's bylaws provide operational guidance for the company's board of directors including voting procedures. A corporation's articles of incorporation and bylaws can be amended to reflect changing needs of the corporation with relative ease.

In setting up a C-corporation, startup entrepreneurs are asked to "authorize" a certain number and type of shares of company stock. Authorized shares represent a pool of shares that can be issued at essentially any time to you and your company's potential business partners, board members, advisors, employees, and investors.

Startup entrepreneurs who expect to raise funds from private investors and venture capital funds should authorize two classes of stock—common stock and preferred stock. A good starting inventory of authorized shares could be 30 million shares of common stock and 20 million shares of preferred stock. Some states charge annual licensing fees based on a company's total authorized shares. In such cases, authorize a smaller number of shares to minimize annual administrative costs.

There are other choices entrepreneurs can make at the time of incorporation, including creating certain shareholder's rights provisions in the articles of incorporation that allow existing shareholders—like you—to acquire additional shares in future financing transactions. I find that it is better to negotiate these rights on a per-transaction basis, rather than go through the process and expense of amending a company's organization documents every time you need to raise capital.

Extra Startup Intelligence ···

The primary reason why startup entrepreneurs choose a corporate business structure is to shield their personal assets (homes, cars, antiques, savings accounts, etc.) from creditors in the case they are unable to pay all business debts. This nifty protection, often called the "corporate veil," is especially important to older, second-career entrepreneurs who tend to have more personal assets than younger entrepreneurs.

It's important to note that corporate officers and directors can't always hide behind the corporate veil. Cranky banks, landlords, opportunistic plaintiff attorneys, equipment leasing companies, and suppliers all know that they can tear the "corporate veil" of liability protection by convincing a judge that the corporation's "good standing" was somehow compromised by fraud, gross negligence or reckless bookkeeping. Failure to file state and federal income taxes, renew annual licenses, conduct shareholder meetings, or document corporate meetings are just some of the ways officers and directors put their personal assets at risk for creditor claims.

This is an area where entrepreneurs often say, "I wish I had known better." Here are a few tips for keeping a corporation in good standing:

- **Document loans and advances**
  It's never wise to pay any business invoice directly from a personal checking account. If you have to use personal funds to pay business obligations, write the personal check to the corporation first and then immediately document the sum as a loan advance or new equity investment in the corporation. Equally, don't abuse corporate expense accounts or borrow funds from a corporation without signing a loan document or preparing business expense reports on a timely basis.

- **Keep it separate**
  Set aside one business credit card strictly for business expenses and another card account strictly for personal expenses. Avoid using the business credit card to pay personal expenses.

- **Avoid naked signatures**
  Persistent creditors, who are unsuccessful collecting payments through normal channels, often claim that they thought they were providing a product or service to the business owner rather than a corporate entity. To protect against

this sort of claim, sign all business letters, contracts, leases, loans and purchase orders with a corporate title to signify that you are signing as an employee or officer of the corporation rather than as an individual.

> Mr. Bill MeHere, Chief Executive Officer
> Your Venture, Inc.

- **Correct billing errors**

  If you receive a bill for services from vendors, banks, and landlords that is addressed to you personally rather than to your company name, take the time to ask the creditor to reissue the invoice. Be sure to instruct all staff members to be on the lookout for documentation errors too. Don't leave any ambiguity over the ownership of a debt—if it's a business expense, keep it in the business. Also, do not incur business obligations before a corporate entity is established.

- **Keep administrative promises**

  At the time of incorporation, entrepreneurs outline certain administration obligations in the corporation's organization documents. If, for example, your incorporation documents indicate that the corporation will always have three to five board members, then maintain a board with three to five members. If your corporation's shareholders are required to meet annually during April, then set up a shareholder's meeting every April. If your corporation is required to appoint or re-appoint directors every three years, then do it.

- **Maintain excellent financial records**

  Corporations are required to prepare formal financial statements and keep accounting "books and records" that are separate from personal financial records. Corporations must also keep accurate board of director minutes as well as accurate records of shareholder purchases and sale transactions. This is considerably more work than managing a simple sole proprietorship, but not beyond the capabilities of any entrepreneur who is willing to do it.

  Further, corporations are required to file all tax returns and corporate annual reports on time. Some states are more punitive than others with regard to incomplete documentation and tardy filings. And corporations are required to advise the governing state of incorporation of any changes to the corporation's business address, names of officers or directors, capitalization, articles of incorporation or bylaws.

- **Pay creditors before shareholders**

  Officers and directors of corporations have an ongoing responsibility to manage company assets with integrity. In general, corporate assets should pay off outstanding debts and company obligations before founder's loans or dividend payments to shareholders. A bankruptcy judge can force owners and share-holders to pay back dividends to meet unpaid corporate obligations. Most corporate lawyers also advise corporate officers and directors not to dissolve a corporation while there are debts outstanding, even if the business is no longer in operation, to keep liability protections intact.

- **Separate personal and business assets**

  It's not uncommon for founding business owners to use personal assets such as real estate or equipment for startup business purposes. To clarify ownership, especially if working with one or more business partners, consider developing a simple agreement that acknowledges business use of a personal asset. If you provide personal assets for business purposes, review insurance policies to make sure that the asset is eligible for insurance coverage.

Tax-Saving Solutions for Corporations

C-corporations are required to pay income taxes on net profits. Unlike sole proprietor-ships, partnerships and LLCs, net corporate profits don't flow through to the business owner's personal tax return. Entrepreneurs who have organized their businesses as C-corporations have to report income two ways: first on behalf of the corporate business entity and then second, on the income personally received from wages, bonuses or stock dividends.

It's important to note that while corporate business taxes may seem high in comparison to other business structure options, sometimes organizing a company as a standard C-corporation may not be such a bad deal. The federal income tax rate for the first $50,000 of corporate net income is just 15%, through rates rise quickly as corporate profits increase.

Here are three popular strategies to minimize annual tax obligations:

1. **Zero-out profits.** Privately-held companies can pay out all net income in the form of salaries or bonuses to company owners and managers, so that the business entity has essentially zero taxable profits. The primary down-side of paying out all net profits in the form of year-end bonuses is compa-nies don't have as much loose cash available for rainy day emergencies or to reinvest in the business.

2. **Elect S-corporation status.** With the exception of taxes on certain capital gains and passive income, an S-corporation is exempt from federal income tax. This means that most S-corporation net profits and losses are "passed through" to the individual shareholders on a pro-rata basis. S-corporation shareholders then report their share of business profits or losses on their

personal income tax returns, much like a sole proprietorship or single member LLC.

It's easy to change a C-corporation to an S-corporation for federal corporate tax reporting purposes. All you have to do is obtain approval from all corporate shareholders and file Form 2553 with the IRS at the beginning of the tax year. Check out your state requirements too!

Extra Startup Intelligence ··

There are additional rules and obligations for California and New York City-based S-corporations. In New York City, S-corporations usually have to pay the full corporate income tax rate. Yikes!

··

3. **Draw S-corporation dividend distribution income.** Savvy entrepreneurs can take advantage of a loophole in tax law by drawing compensation in two ways: first by taking a modest but reasonable "market" salary and second by taking extra compensation out of the company in the form of one or more corporate distribution payments.

   The difference is important. Businesses are not obligated to pay payroll taxes on cash distributions, just salary-based compensation. As such, the more S-corporation entrepreneurs can draw distribution-based compensation, the more money they can potentially save in payroll taxes.

   Of course, the IRS is starting to close this tax-saving opportunity. Now the IRS requires shareholder-employees to at least earn a reasonable "market" salary before making cash distributions. A good rule of thumb is to pay at least 65% of total compensation in the form of salary to minimize problems with the IRS.

   Are S-corporations too good to be true? With S-corporations, the devil is hidden in the details. Here's what you need to know. With an S-corporation, the IRS expects that shareholders will receive a cash distribution based on their pro-rata ownership share in the profits of a business. But what if an S-corporation wants to reinvest its net profits back into the company to fund new products and growth rather than pay it out as cash distributions to shareholders? Here's the gotcha. The IRS will still expect to collect taxes on each owner's share of an S-corporation's net profits even if no cash is actually paid to shareholders. This nasty little tax collecting maneuver is called "phantom income tax."

   Are there any other gotchas associated with S-corporations? Unfortunately, yes. Let's start with who can own stock in S-corporations. S-corporation shareholders must be U.S. residents, estates or certain trusts. This means that foreign corporations can't invest in a S-corporation.

There are other limitations to be aware of before selecting an S-corporation as your tax-saving strategy. Whereas standard C-corporations can have an unlimited number of shareholders, S-corporations are limited to 100 shareholders (married couples can count as one), making a public or large private offering to raise funds essentially out of the question. The limits on shareholder count can be an issue to entrepreneurs who want to raise small amounts of equity capital (not donations) from thousands of individuals through crowdfunding sites.

In addition, S-corporations can issue only one class of stock (although differences solely in voting rights can be structured). This requirement doesn't sit well with venture capital funds and knowledgeable private investors who typically insist on receiving preferred stock not common stock for their investment dollar.

Professional Corporations and Professional LLCs

States have different rules regarding what type of professionals can organize a professional corporation ("PC") or a professional LLC. Typically professionals must practice the same profession to qualify for PC or professional LLC organization.

What's the reason for yet another business entity option? For the most part, states reason that professionals (lawyers, accountants, doctors and other medical professionals, engineers, architects, etc.) should not be able to hide behind a standard C-corporation or LLC to avoid liability for malpractice claims.

A PC or a professional LLC helps solve these regulatory concerns. With these business entities, professionals are liable for their share of a firm's business debts plus their own professional negligence. However, professionals are generally protected from the negligent actions or wrongdoings of other professionals within a firm. Some states don't allow professional LLC organizations; only PCs.

There are tricky tax issues associated with the management and tax payment obligations of PCs and professional LLCs. Most PCs pay a flat federal income tax rate of 35% if they are "qualified personal service corporations" and provide certain health, law, engineering, architecture, accounting, actuarial science, or consulting services. However, PCs can file for S-corporation status and pay income taxes at the individual shareholder level rather than corporate level. In comparison, tax treatment for professional LLCs is more straightforward— it's just like other LLCs in terms of allowing pass-through tax treatment, unless its members specifically elect on IRS Form 8832 to be taxed like a corporation.

Partnerships and Limited Liability Partnerships

Just because you might want to go into business with one or more individuals as business partners doesn't mean that you have to choose a partnership as your company's legal business entity.

A general partnership is formed by two or more individuals who manage a business' operations. The partnership can operate under a DBA ("doing business as" name certificate) or the partnership can take on the names of the general partners. Partners are personally liable for the partnership's debts and operations. Since all partners have unlimited personal liability, even so-called "innocent partners" can be held liable when another partner is involved in fraud, negligence or other wrongful actions.

Each partner, unless otherwise agreed in writing, participates in the partnership's operating profits and losses on a pro-rata ownership basis. Partners may split profits equally, or decide that one or more partners deserve a greater share for contributing either more assets or work hours to the business.

A general partnership can also be organized with limited partners who typically invest in the business entity. To enjoy limitations of liability, limited partners must be "passive" which means that they cannot participate in the day-to-day management of partnership operations. Most venture capital funds are organized as general partnerships with many limited partner investors.

The biggest advantage of a general partnership is potential tax savings. Partnership entities do file tax returns but all partnership profits and losses are passed through to the individual partners. Each partner then includes his or her share of the partnership's income or loss on his or her tax return, much like a sole proprietor or LLC member.

General partnerships and limited partnerships involve the development of a detailed partnership agreement that can provide guidance regarding how the partnership will be managed and how profits and losses will be shared. This agreement is structured to comply with state regulations, which, of course, vary.

Limited liability partnerships ("LLP") are yet another kind of business structure option. They are similar to limited partnerships in that they offer limited liability for the partnership's business debts. The primary difference between a limited liability partnership and a limited partnership is the limited liability partnership is not managed by general partners. Further, LLPs protect individual partners from sharing the liability or debts associated with malpractice lawsuits against another partner of the firm.

Special Considerations for Social Entrepreneurs

"Social entrepreneurs" are enterprising individuals who want to make a difference to people or the planet by developing innovative products and services in education, food production, poverty relief, air and water quality, healthcare and more. To them, success is measured in terms of maximizing the impact of their work, not maximizing business profits.

One of the first questions social entrepreneurs ask is if they should form a for-profit or non-profit corporation. It's a good question because the two business structures involve different income tax obligations, funding opportunities and administrative chores. Here are some key considerations:

- **Tax-free revenue generation**

  IRS-approved 501(c)(3) non-profit entities can sell products and services in the marketplace. Even better, they don't have to pay income tax on profits, provided that the earnings are related to the entity's approved social mission. The broader the umbrella of a non-profit's social mission, the greater flexibility the entity has to market a wider range of products and services that are exempt from income taxes. I love it when more cash flow can be re-invested in a social venture's good works, than paid to the IRS! A non-profit organization can also sell "non-program" related products and services, but earnings from these activities are taxable.

- **Administration requirements**

  The accounting associated with maintaining a non-profit 501(c)(3) organization can be tedious and intensive, especially with regard to donor record-keeping and restricted funds (money donated for a particular project). Smaller non-profits with annual income under $200,000 and assets under $500,000 can file a short form 990-EZ annual return.

- **Value of ownership**

  Social entrepreneurs can't own equity in a non-profit organization or sell the entity to the highest bidder. Sure they can earn a salary, but that's it in terms of monetary reward.

- **Funding source availability**

  One factor that can help social entrepreneurs—particularly in healthcare, education and environmental conservation pursuits—choose the right type of business organization, is funding availability. For example, a home healthcare agency that serves rural communities may be able to obtain a larger amount of startup funding through government and foundation grants than through private investors, micro-lenders or commercial banks. Yet, an environmentally-friendly technology company may be able to secure startup funding from venture capital funds, SBIR grants and corporate partners.

To the extent that a non-profit organization is not likely to be self-sustaining from revenues generated from its primary activities, called "program revenues" then the organization must develop other reliable funding sources to fuel startup and ongoing operations. The following is a list of funding sources for non-profit organizations:

- Founder's savings
- Special fundraising events
- Private donors who expect to receive a tax deduction
- Social venture capital funds
- Community investment notes
- Corporate and other non-profit organization strategic partnerships
- Foundation grants
- Government grants

It's dangerous for social entrepreneurs to assume they will be able to raise startup money from corporate sponsorships or foundations without doing any advance homework to learn just how many corporations or foundations are specifically organized to fund their particular kind of social initiative. For example, Social Venture Partners, the Verizon Foundation and the Bill and Melinda Gates Foundation are known for funding U.S. education initiatives, but their areas of funding emphasis differ significantly.

To find a list of grant providers and information about their funding interests, visit Wells Fargo's foundation website for a free foundation grant search tool. A more comprehensive database of grant providers is available through the Foundation Center, which is available for free through most public libraries.

- **B-corporation option**
Social entrepreneurs in Maryland, Vermont, New Jersey, Virginia and Hawaii can form a hybrid organization called a "benefit corporation." Benefit corporations give for-profit social entrepreneurs and their board members the flexibility to maximize their social mission without having to worry that shareholders will sue the company's officers and directors for not maximizing profits and delivering a lucrative financial return to shareholders.

Extra Startup Intelligence ···

The decision to award non-profit status to a new social enterprise rests entirely with the Internal Revenue Service. Even though the review process can take several months, the good news is the approval rate for new tax-exempt organizations is quite high—about 80 percent. Expedited review services may be available to organizations that have grants pending on 501(c)(3) acceptance. Visit www.irs.gov to obtain the most current application forms. Search for Form 1023.

···

Your next action steps:

☐ **Compare business organization fees**

Whether or not you use a local attorney, an online service, or free business organization setup tools offered by most states, your company will be obligated to pay various filing fees and franchise taxes for registering and maintaining a business entity. Oddly, many states, like New York, charge higher fees for the formation of an LLC than a C-corporation. Business entity formation fees also vary substantially from state to state. A basic fee for filing a company's articles of incorporation in Alaska is about $250. In Iowa, the comparable fee is approximately $50.

To compare fees for organizing a new business entity plus ongoing annual business entity maintenance obligations, visit your state's government website. Use the search words "Secretary of State," "Division of Corporations," "Department of Commerce," or "business licensing." Official state government websites have a .gov top level domain name; not .com, .net or .org.

☐ **Select a business structure**

It's time to choose your business entity. If you are unsure of which business structure is right for your business objectives, talk to an attorney or accountant. You can also visit IRS.gov which has helpful information regarding tax and filing obligations of different types of business entities.

As your company's needs change, you can amend most provisions of partnership, corporation or LLC business structures. Further, you can change an LLC to a corporation; a C-corporation to an S-corporation, an S-corporation back to a C-corporation, a sole proprietorship to a C-corporation, etc. There may be some nasty tax ramifications associated with changing business entity and tax payment status, so it is wise to consult qualified tax planning experts *before* committing to a business structure change.

For non-profit social entrepreneurs, a legal entity must be in place prior to applying to the IRS for 501(c)(3) tax-exempt status. You do not have to be a corporation to obtain 501(c)(3) status, however it is the most common way to ensure that your non-profit's officers and directors enjoy some protections against personal liability claims.

☐ **Determine need for legal assistance**

If you intend to form a partnership, corporation or LLC, who will prepare the entity's formal business organization paper work—you or a lawyer? If you hate details or have complex organization requirements, compare the fees of several local attorneys. If you are going into business with a non-family business partner, I strongly recommend that you invest in a customized partnership and buy-sell agreement that is prepared by a knowledgeable business attorney. If you want to set up your business without assistance, visit your state's online tools for new business organization. Most states offer easy "fill in the blank" forms which meet the minimum state requirements for organizing a new business entity.

☐ **Determine need for a trade name or DBA**

Sole proprietors can choose to operate a business under a trade name or a quasi-fictitious business name that is separate from the owner's personal name. This is often referred to as "doing business as" or a company's "DBA."

☐ **Determine need for sales tax permit**

States have different laws regarding what goods and services are exempt from sales taxes. If your business will sell services or products that are subject to sales tax, then you have to obtain a state sales tax permit prior to making a first sale. Visit your state's sales tax department website for permit applications and filing requirements. Most startup businesses are required to pay sales taxes on a quarterly basis. High sales volume businesses may have to pay sales taxes every month.

☐ **Obtain a business license**

Most states and municipalities require new businesses to obtain a business license, including street vendors. Some types of businesses may require additional licensing or may not be able to operate from a home. Business license applications are usually available at state or local government websites. Expect to pay a nominal application fee plus annual business license maintenance fees.

Extra Startup Intelligence ···

Don't advertise freelance services on craigslist without a business license! State tax collectors go to craigslist and other online freelance job sites to find advertisements posted by "underground" businesses that don't have a business license or pay payroll taxes.

···

☐ **Determine need for partnership and stock purchase agreements**

If you are starting a company with one or more partners, skip to Chapter 8 for more insight on how to evaluate a prospective partner's contribution to the new business organization. Once you hand out share certificates to business partners, it's hard to get them back if you don't have the right vesting terms and conditions in place.

☐ **Meet corporate governance requirements**

Corporations are required to organize a board of directors that is elected by the company's shareholders. Since most new corporations are controlled by a founding entrepreneur, the founder usually invites individuals to serve on the company's first board of directors. See Chapter 9 for action steps related to the best ways to identify, solicit, manage and compensate board members.

☐ Assign inventions **$$**

Any design, software code, technology or other intellectual property that was developed by a company founder, partner, friend, family member or hired consultant prior to formal business organization should be assigned to the new business entity in writing. If you don't document it, your new company might not really own it. Venture investors look hard during due diligence document reviews for evidence that all intellectual property is truly owned by the company.

☐ Set up a "master calendar"

Create a single calendar that lists all quarterly and annual tax, licensing, domain renewal and other time-sensitive reporting obligations. Add to this list over time. The IRS website offers a quick list of tax reporting forms and obligations for different types of business organizations which can be downloaded into Outlook or printed out for easy reference. Search for Publication 1518.

It's easy to forget important administrative obligations during the first busy years of business operations. Some administrative lapses are easy to fix; while others are not. For example, the U.S. Patent and Trademark Office does not send out registration renewal notices to trademark owners. If your company doesn't renew a trademark registration on time, the PTO assumes that the mark has been abandoned or no longer actively used in commerce. A master calendar can prevent this kind of oversight.

FAQs

Q. **Should I serve as statutory agent for my new corporation?**

A. A statutory agent accepts legal notices on behalf of a corporation. Startup entrepreneurs can save money if they live in states that allow business owners to serve as their own statutory agent for their corporate entities. Otherwise, they have to hire a firm or a lawyer to serve as their corporation's statutory agent. The gotcha associated with serving as your own statutory agent, if allowed in your state, is your availability to receive legal notices. If you forget to go to your post office for several weeks or are not around to read an important legal communication regarding a threatened or actual lawsuit, you could lose rights even if you are entirely in the right.

Q. **Can I give myself share certificates in my business even though I don't have any money to invest in the business at this time?**

A. Yes, you can receive "founder's shares" in your business even if you don't invest any hard cash in your business at the time of business organization. Presumably, the value of the received shares in a raw startup company with no other assets will be negligible. Still, talk to your accountant to determine the value (or "cost basis") of the received shares for future tax reporting purposes. Ideally, your company's shares will grow in value so that at the time of company sale, you will have to calculate your capital gains tax obligation on a whopping profit. Go for it!

Own It!

How to Take Ownership
of Your Company's Financial Future

What's urgent and must be done today? What can you put off until tomorrow? In addition to achieving the 4 Milestones of Financial Security, I have a few more responsibilities to add to your leadership agenda.

The two themes of this chapter are closely related—capital management and accounting administration. If you avoid these issues or give them half-hearted attention during your first year or two in business, I guarantee that you will have a harder time convincing investors, lenders and other business partners that you are capable of managing a fast-growing company.

Leaders of prospering businesses are accountable for every aspect of their company's operations. Now is the time for you to expand the scope of your leadership by embracing responsibility for accounting, bill collecting or raising capital for your business. You don't have to be an expert in any of these issues or actually do all the work yourself. But you do have to make sure that the work is done by someone on a timely basis.

Think about it. What impression do you think entrepreneurs give to prospective business partners and investors when they say:

- *"We're behind in accounting work and haven't prepared financial statements in a while"*
- *"We're behind in collecting customer payments."*
- *"We're behind in handing out shares of stock to all the people we've promised shares to."*
- *"We're behind on taxes."*

If you want to get ahead, you can't get too far behind on administrative matters!

Fuel for Your Startup

Babson College estimates that it takes an average of $65,000 to start and build a business in America. Startup entrepreneurs typically scrape together about two-thirds of the startup costs from personal savings—or about $43,000. This is a sizable number for most American families. However, don't let this number scare you. There are many prosperous businesses that start with far less capital. Plus, you will need less to fund your business to the extent you avoid the common startup mistakes that are highlighted in this book.

In the venture finance community, the term "capitalization" generally means how a company's operations are funded through an ever-changing mix of short-term debt, long-term debt, equity investments and after-tax business profits. Owners of "well-capitalized" companies anticipate their company's upcoming cash needs and rarely rely on any single funding source to fuel company operations.

Today is an important day in your entrepreneurial career. Today is the day you decide to be a CEO of a well-capitalized business!

Your next action steps:

☐ **Learn about funding source options**

The secret to fundraising is to match your company's stage of business development as well as its geographic location, revenue status, industry and plans for growth to lender's and investor's funding preferences. Here are your options:

Sources of Business Funding

Seed-stage

- Founder's personal savings
- Founder's retirement savings (not recommended)
- Credit card secured by the founder's personal guarantee
- Small loans from micro-finance organizations
- Equipment leases
- Friends and family members' personal savings
- Business partners' personal savings
- Wealthy individuals' personal savings (angels)
- Seed-stage and early-stage venture capital funds
- Corporate investors
- Government-funded Small Business Innovation Research (SBIR) grants
- Commercial loans secured by the founder's personal guarantee and business assets
- Cash flow from business operations

Early-stage

☐ Understand stage of business development

Most readers of this book will be managing either a "seed-stage" or "early-stage" business. Your objective is to learn about funding options that are a good match for your company's current "stage of business development."

The primary difference between a seed-stage and an early-stage business is evidence of business progress. Early-stage companies have generally launched a "beta" version of a website, completed a first-generation prototype, or started to solicit customers. Early-stage businesses may have filed one or more patents, have an active board of directors, and know how they want to build out their management team once more funds are available to the company. Early-stage companies do not have to be profitable but are on a clear "path to profitability." Whereas founders of seed-stage companies talk about what they *think* customers will pay for, founders of early-stage companies talk about what they *know* because they have tested their ideas and product concepts or are actively selling to customers.

Extra Startup Intelligence ···

If you'd like to find the names of regional angel investment clubs, venture capital funds, incubators, micro-finance organizations, SBA offices, and sources of local business plan assistance visit the Start On Purpose website.

···

☐ Plan ahead $$

The time to raise debt or equity funds for your company is not when you are desperate. Different sources of debt and equity funding have different timelines, documentation requirements and application review procedures that won't change just because you say "But I need it now!"

Here's the cruel irony of raising capital for startup companies—entrepreneurs who give investors and lenders plenty of time to get to know their business and leadership objectives, end up raising funds faster than entrepreneurs who push for fast answers.

Plan ahead as follows: For debt, assume that lenders and leasing companies will require 30 to 90 days to make a decision, assuming all required documents are submitted in an orderly way. Micro-finance companies may require borrowers to attend various business management classes or meet with other borrowers on a regular basis. For equity, assume that it will take angel investors and venture capital funds six to 12 months to make a decision *to* invest. These same decision makers can make a decision *not to* invest in less than two minutes based on a fast scan of a poorly conceived executive summary.

\$\$ ☐ **Plan how to invest in your company**

You can invest your personal savings in your new for-profit company in the form of a debt (a loan to your company), equity (an investment) or a combination of the two. Your decision on how you will invest in your new company will affect your company's balance sheet as well as your future personal tax obligations.

Investing in the form of equity is the most common way entrepreneurs capitalize their new companies. The primary disadvantage of investing in a new company in the form of equity is lack of liquidity, meaning you can't convert your stock into cash on short notice.

To the extent that your company is financially able to make interest and principal payments on a personal loan to your business, you can steadily reduce the amount of hard cash you have at risk in your new business. And just because you lend funds to your new company doesn't mean that you won't enjoy the benefits of owning an equity stake in your business too. You will! As long as you don't raise funds from other equity investors, business partners or other individuals, you will still own 100% of your company.

The primary disadvantage of investing in your company in the form of debt is adding some long-term debt to your company's balance sheet. This can be a turn off to commercial lenders as well as angel and venture capital fund investors.

To determine the best choice for your personal financial situation, get some help from a skilled accountant who understands the gnarly tax rules associated with "founder's capital." Different rules apply to debt and equity investments based on your new company's business structure (corporation, LLC, partnership, etc.) If for example, a corporation is "thinly capitalized" and has too much debt and too little equity, then the IRS may decide that the company's debt to a founder is really equity. This kind of tax ruling can have implications on a company's P & L and balance sheet.

Extra Financial Empowerment ···

The best way to win arguments with the IRS regarding the re-classification of business debt as business equity is to have a formal written loan agreement in place which has been approved by the company's board of directors. The business does not necessarily have to make principal payments right away, but the loan should have a maturity date and pay a reasonable rate of interest. If the loan is secured by company assets, consider filing a simple Uniform Commercial Code lien (UCC) with your state—again to help document the formal nature of the loan. Other factors that influence IRS rulings are the company's debt-to-equity ratio and how loan funds are used by company.

☐ Invest in "tranches"

Experienced angel and venture capital fund investors, rarely invest their total available capital in a single company all at the same time. Rather, they prefer to invest in two or more "tranches" based on the company's need for capital and demonstrated progress.

My general recommendation to startup entrepreneurs is to invest approximately a third to a half of their stated investment ceiling (see Chapter 1) during the first year of operations. Over time, most entrepreneurs are "forced" to dig deeper into savings to cover payroll emergencies or pursue opportunities that they just "can't pass up." Further, as businesses expand landlords and lenders ask entrepreneurs to personally guarantee leases and loans, which again increases the amount of personal funds entrepreneurs have at risk in their companies.

☐ Clarify ownership

For entrepreneurs who are married, think through the pros and cons of the ownership of your new company. If you intend to keep your investment in your name only, draw investment funds from your personal savings or checking account; not a joint account. Also, avoid using any personal or joint retirement accounts to fund your new business. Most new business owners don't know that retirement accounts are usually protected from creditors in personal bankruptcy filings. So keep your retirement accounts in tact!

☐ Price your shares

At the time of corporate business formation, founders get to set the "par value" of their company's shares. Often the par value is a low number—a penny a share or less. When entrepreneurs make their first cash investment in a newly formed corporation, they may choose to purchase a first amount of shares at the company's stated par value or some other negligible value. For example, an entrepreneur sets up a new company with a per share par value of $.01. She invests $10,000 in the new company, purchasing shares that she prices at $.05 per share. She receives 200,000 shares of common stock. For personal tax purposes, the entrepreneur's investment "cost basis" on the 200,000 shares is $10,000.

Over time, as your company generates revenues, profits, intellectual property, brand recognition, etc., the per share "market" value of your company's common stock will increase. Future purchases of your company's common stock by you and your friends and family members, your new partners or independent investors at a price above par value is referred to for accounting purposes as "additional paid in capital."

Extra Financial Empowerment ···

A capitalization table (cap table) lists information about a company's shareholders—how much they paid, how much they own, special terms of the securities, and the closing date of the transaction. A well-prepared business plan should include an up-to-date capitalization table. I've posted some information on how to assemble a capitalization table at the Start On Purpose website.

When looking at an investment opportunity, I always check a company's "statement of shareholder's equity" and "capitalization table" as a benchmark for negotiating the price of shares with business owners. Angel investors and venture capital fund managers do too. Expect a battle if your family members pay, for example, just $5 per share for your company's common stock and then you ask independent investors to pay $20 a share just a few weeks later. You'll need a good reason why your company's value has suddenly increased fourfold to satisfy new investors.

···

☐ **Obtain board of directors' approval**

Most corporations require the board of directors to approve all issuances of securities, including common stock awards and stock options. An entrepreneur can negotiate to sell shares of stock to investors or offer shares to new employees, but the deal isn't sealed until the corporation's board says "yes." Board members can approve stock issuances through a written consent resolution that is unanimously approved by all board members or by majority vote at a board of directors' meeting. Board actions should be reflected in written "minutes" of the board of directors' meeting. Auditors and prospective investors often ask to review board meeting minutes to confirm stock issuances. Don't wait months or years to prepare board meeting minutes!

☐ **Issue shares**

When entrepreneurs distribute shares from a corporate entity's authorized share pool then those shares are considered as "issued" or "outstanding." First-time entrepreneurs tend to issue too many of their company's authorized common shares to founders, first employees, and consultants. My recommendation is to demonstrate restraint. Reserve at least two-thirds of your company's authorized common shares for future corporate needs. Yes, you can always take steps to increase your company's pool of authorized shares but you shouldn't need to do it during your first year of company operations!

☐ **Document other administrative details**

The best time to complete paperwork is within a week of any transaction. In addition to documenting board of directors' approval for corporate entities, companies should promptly issue share certificates to new shareholders and record the transaction on the company's financial statements. Paying attention to shareholder details today may affect your ability to attract capital in the future. Investors often "pass" on funding companies that keep poor shareholder records.

Order an Employer Tax Identification Number (EIN)

Once you know the name of your business, your company's primary address and the type of legal business organization, you can apply for a unique 10-digit Employer Identification Number or "EIN." EINs function very much like personal Social Security numbers. You will be asked to provide your EIN when setting up bank and brokerage accounts, filing taxes and bidding on contracts.

Not all business owners have to apply for an EIN. Sole proprietors and single-member owners of LLCs can use their social security number provided they don't have any employees or intend to establish certain kinds of pension, profit-sharing or retirement plans. Sole proprietors who have excise tax obligations, like independent truckers, typically have to apply for an EIN. All organizers of non-profit corporations must apply for an EIN too.

It is my strong recommendation that all new business owners, including sole proprietors, take five minutes to apply for an EIN number. In an era of digital fraud and identity theft, it's good practice to safeguard your Social Security number. An EIN is the safer way to protect your personal credit rating and bank accounts from malicious activity.

Your next action steps:

☐ **Obtain your EIN**

There are two fast ways to obtain an EIN. You can call the IRS at 1-800-829-4933 during business hours Monday through Friday or you can file online at www.IRS.gov. You can also print out IRS Form SS-4 online and fax or mail it to the IRS for processing. If you send your completed SS-4 form by fax to the IRS, you will have to wait about 4 days to receive your EIN number. If you send your completed SS-4 form by regular mail, the processing time may be as long as one month.

Open a Business Bank Account

Once you have a selected a business name, business address and type of legal business structure you can set up a business bank account. Even if you provide part-time services in your own name, establishing a bank account for business purposes will make it easier for you to track business income and expenses.

As companies grow, it is quite common for business owners to set up different bank accounts for different types of financial transactions. For example, business owners can set up a separate account to handle online payments and another account for payroll processing. To the extent that you set up multiple deposit accounts, keep them at the same bank for ease of transferring money between accounts.

Your next action steps:

☐ **Organize documentation**
To open a business bank account you will need your company's EIN number. If your company is organized as a corporation you will need a copy of your new company's articles of incorporation. You may also need to present a copy of your company's board of director's minutes in which you authorize an officer (probably you) to open various bank accounts on the company's behalf. If your business is formed as a LLC, you will be required to present a copy of your company's articles of organization and operating agreement. A partnership is usually required to submit a copy of its general partnership or limited partnership agreement. Sole proprietor businesses typically submit a copy of the company's business license and a DBA certificate, if applicable.

☐ **Confirm that the bank is FDIC insured**
The FDIC (Federal Deposit Insurance Corporation) is a federal government agency that protects consumers against deposit losses if an FDIC-insured bank or savings association fails. Not all banks are covered by FDIC insurance. To find out if your local bank is covered by FDIC insurance, call toll-free 1-877-ASK-FDIC.

☐ **Branch out**
While it may seem convenient to set up a business banking account at the same bank that maintains your personal banking accounts, now is the time to expand your financial network. Sole proprietors have to be extra cautious about bank selection because personal and business accounts of a sole proprietor held at the same bank are covered only up to maximum FDIC coverage, which is currently just $250,000. However, if the business is set up as a corporation or partnership, business accounts and personal accounts held at the same banking institution can qualify for separate FDIC coverage, which is potentially up to $500,000.

☐ **Consider future lending needs**
Another reason to extend your banking relationships beyond a single institution is to set your company up for future lending relationships. If you intend to apply

for a Small Business Association-backed loan in the future, it might be helpful to establish a deposit relationship with a bank that accepts SBA-backed loan applications. You can find a list of SBA partner lenders at your local SBA's website. While local SBA staff members are not supposed to recommend one partner bank over another, they may provide some insight regarding which partner lenders are more active in your community than other lenders.

☐ **Protect your business cash**

The FDIC reports that the most common way that business accounts are compromised is through theft of online banking identities and passwords. Since small businesses tend to have higher checking account balances than individuals, but don't have the support of extensive IT security systems and professionals, they are a prime target of savvy scam artists and hackers. Here are some tips to protect your company's cash:

- **Beware of cyber thieves.** Avoid logging into your business banking account through wireless connections no matter how urgent the situation. Also, be wary of all email communications from your bank or other financial service providers such as PayPal. Many fraudulent "phishing" scam communications are designed with the same "look and feel" as top banks but are typically operated by off-shore thieves. Unless you have specific insurance coverage for phishing scams, once your business cash is gone, it's really gone.

- **Check bank account balances.** Do the reported numbers seem right? Sometimes, small business account theft is organized as a "slow but steady account drain" rather than one massive withdrawal. The thief could be one of your employees, which happened to me and so many other colleagues of mine. (Fortunately, I caught the theft within 30 days because I review company financial statements closely.) Also confirm that the revenues from online advertising networks are directed to your business accounts, not an online marketing service provider's checking accounts.

- **Install security software annually**. Consumer Reports rates anti-virus and security software product options just about every year.

- **Update security information.** Change your bank account log on information and passwords at least every six months and immediately after the termination or resignation of any employee who ever had access to your bank log on information. Ask independent bookkeeping service providers to inform you promptly of any employment changes that might compromise your company's records too.

- **Choose banking partners with care.** Avoid online transactions with financial institutions that don't require "multiple authentications."

☐ **Compare bank fees**

Compare the minimum deposit requirements, monthly fees and other per check charges from at least three banks. Sometimes regional savings and loan companies offer the lowest rates for business checking accounts.

Extra Financial Empowerment ···

It's highly likely that when you submit paperwork to open a business bank account you will be encouraged to apply for a small business credit card at the same time. Don't do it before you compare credit card rates and terms. Most entrepreneurs are not aware that so-called small business "professional" credit cards don't have to follow the same federal credit card regulations that apply to consumer-oriented personal credit cards. With a professional small business credit card, banks can increase interest rates and fees without warning which can make it hard for business owners to budget credit costs on a predictable basis. Professional credit cards still require a personal guarantee of a business owner so there is little benefit to using a professional small business credit card during the first years of company operations, but potentially greater expense and uncertainty.

···

The Home of Your New Business

Starting a business in your home or apartment can be a cost-effective way to reduce the financial risks of new business ownership. At home, you can reduce commuting costs, save on rent, and put your home computers and phone lines to work in new ways. But, starting up at home is not without risk and, of course, a few more taxing details.

Your next action steps:

☐ **Select a mailing address**

Most startup businesses use a home address to complete bank account applications, business license forms and domain name registrations. That's fine from a convenience standpoint, but you might regret exposing your home address to unwanted sales people, irate customers and Internet scams. Consider renting a mail box from your local post office until your company establishes a non-home location.

☐ **Explore general liability insurance**

Most new home-based business owners assume that their homeowner's or renter's insurance will provide coverage for property that is owned by a business but kept in a home. Not so, especially if the equipment is highly specialized or exceeds a minimum homeowner's or renter's insurance coverage limits. Standard homeowner's insurance also rarely provides home-based companies with business interruption insurance or costs associated with employee or customer mishaps in your home.

Extra Warning to Sole Proprietors: Owners of sole proprietorships personally assume the liability for any unpaid business debts. Sole proprietors also assume financial responsibility for problems or accidents with their company's products or services. While a general liability insurance policy won't help sole proprietors pay off unpaid bank loans, it can minimize some of the liabilities associated with product liability complaints or customer trips and falls that can occur in a home. Small business general liability insurance policies for home-based business owners can be purchased for less than $500.

☐ **Keep Uncle Sam happy**

Home-based businesses can deduct a portion of their mortgage interest (not principal) or rent, utilities, house cleaning services, home owner's insurance, real estate taxes and home repairs. The amount of the annual tax deduction is typically based on the percentage of a home's total space that is devoted exclusively to business activities. Home-based business deductions are also allowed for entrepreneurs such as contractors, painters, gardeners, etc. who don't primarily work out of their homes but have no other logical place to conduct marketing and administrative activities.

To calculate your deduction, measure the square footage of your total home and then the square footage of space used for business. Then calculate the percentage of your total home space that is used for business purposes. If 10% of your home is exclusively used for business then you can generally deduct 10% of home-based phone and electric bills and most home maintenance costs on your personal tax return. To the extent that a phone line or cell phone is used exclusively for business purposes, then 100% of the cost is deductible.

Take a picture of your home office to keep with your tax return records in case you ever need evidence of your home-based business for insurance or tax audit purposes. As always, keep important documentation in multiple locations—with at least one copy away from your home office. Fires, floods and bad computer karma can wipe out business records at any time!

Different tax forms are used for different types of business structures. For example, sole proprietors should use Schedule C of a personal tax return to report business income and business expenses. Unfortunately, entrepreneurs can't use the short form Schedule C-EZ to claim home office deductions. Check out Form 8829, Expenses for Business Use of Your Home and IRS Publication 587 and 936 for more information.

No doubt this all sounds complicated, but it's not in practice. Entrepreneurs who form corporations for their new businesses should ask their accountant to explore the potential benefits of "renting" home office space, garage space or barn space to an incorporated business in the form of "arm's length" rental agreement. Then entrepreneurs would report rental income and expense on Schedule E of a personal tax return rather than Schedule C of a personal income tax return. An accountant can determine which approach can maximize your tax deductions within the limits of tax regulations.

There is one more administrative task associated with taking a home office deduction that is rarely written about in the business press. It affects home-owners rather than leased apartment dwellers. At the time a home is sold, the percentage of its sale price that is attributable to the home office isn't eligible for the $250,000 tax exclusion ($500,000 for a joint tax return) on the home sale. It sounds more ominous than it really is. The best course of action is to simply keep track of the amount that has been deducted over the years. Open up a new spreadsheet can call it "annual home office deductions." Update it every year.

FAQs

Q. **Will I become the target of an IRS audit if I take a home office deduction?**

A. In my view, dire warnings about IRS audits are exaggerated. Taking a home office deduction is a matter of comparable risk and reward. According to the IRS' Statistical Oversight Institute data for 2009, only 2% of all personal tax returns were audited. If you can legitimately save $500, $1,000 or $5,000 in annual tax obligations by keeping good records and taking a home-office deduction, then do it. However, the chances of an audit increase if the tax return reports gross income over $100,000. But then again, if you have good records, the IRS can't legally take away the deduction.

Having said this, the IRS is becoming more aggressive about tracking down home-office businesses that are set up for no other reason than to generate losses or disguise hobbies as businesses. At some point, the IRS will expect to see some evidence of business viability to continue accepting home office deductions and losses year after year. You don't necessarily have to generate a profit, but if you are challenged by the IRS you will have to prove your active intent to generate a profit.

Here's a short list of documents that can be used to fight an IRS challenge:

- Prepare a business plan that includes specific strategies that are intended to create profits
- Prepare financial projections that show that the business can one day obtain a profit
- Take photos of the business operation and keep them offsite
- Save communications with targeted customers, even if they don't ultimately become customers

Accounting for the Basics

Consistent, accurate financial record keeping is essential. In my coaching work, it always seems that the companies that are on the brink of financial disaster are run by owners who never bothered to organize their company's accounting for business planning or tax-saving purposes. But that won't be you!

Your next action steps:

☐ **Choose your accounting method**

You will find on various IRS and financial institution application forms a question about the form of accounting that you will use to track financial activity in your new business. There are two options: "cash basis" accounting or "accrual basis" accounting. The difference is really just the timing of when your company will "recognize" or record revenues and expenses.

For example, a novelty lamp manufacturer sells 1,000 lamps to a furniture store chain. Under an accrual accounting system, the company recognizes the sale on the day of shipment. Under cash accounting, the sale is recognized for accounting purposes only when the lamps are paid for by the customer, which could be months later.

Cash accounting is generally regarded as the easiest system to manage, especially for freelance entrepreneurs because it is the way most individuals track income and expenses. Larger businesses favor accrual accounting to help "normalize" financial activity and to avoid monthly swings in profit or loss based on the timing of revenues and expenses. In addition, companies with a lot of equipment and hard assets favor accrual accounting to take advantage of tax deductions for non-cash items such as depreciation. LLCs and corporations can use either method, however if the business has annual gross receipts of $5 million or more, then accrual accounting is required. Other rules can apply too.

☐ Choose a tax year

A company's tax year does not have to start on January 1 and end on December 31. The IRS allows C-corporations, and certain LLCs to choose any 12-month cycle for tax reporting purposes. S-corporations and sole proprietorships have to report taxes on a calendar basis—meaning a tax year ending December 31.

Why would a new business owner want to pick a different time of year to prepare year-end tax filings? Some industries such as consumer retailing choose tax years or "fiscal years" that end on January 31—well after all holiday sales and returns have been processed. Business owners can choose a tax year that suits their personal lives. If you love to ski, you might choose a fiscal year that ends in the summer or fall in order to free up more time in March and April for spring skiing. My strong preference is to choose a tax year that ends in March, June, September or December to coincide with the timing of quarterly payroll tax filing obligations.

☐ Understand key accounting concepts

Investors and lenders don't expect entrepreneurs to be experienced bookkeepers or certified public accountants, but they do expect entrepreneurs to understand certain accounting basics.

For starters, it's worthwhile to understand the difference between "operating expenses" and "capital expenses." While both deplete a company's bank account, they are treated differently for accounting and tax reporting purposes. Here are the basics:

- Operating expenses include salaries, postage, cell phone and Internet costs, travel, entertainment, gifts, office supplies, website maintenance, rent, and advertising. These costs are immediately "expensed" on the company's income statement as they are incurred.

- Capital expenses include the purchase of buildings, office furniture, computers, machinery, trucks, and high-cost office equipment. Unlike operating expenses, capital expenses have a "useful life" of more than one year. A fancy all-in-one photocopier, printer and fax machine is an example of a capital expense. However, printer ink and paper are considered as basic operating expenses.

For accounting and tax reporting purposes, capital expenses are typically "depreciated" or "amortized" over the estimated useful life of the expenditure. Different typcs of assets have different estimated useful lives. For example, the estimated useful life of a computer is three years or less; farm tractors, about 13 years; and milling machinery, about 20 years.

Suppose a business buys a $30,000 machine, with an estimated useful life of five years. The business owner doesn't have to expense the full cost of the equipment when it is purchased because the machine is expected to serve the business for at least five years. To more accurately reflect the ongoing, but certainly declining value of the equipment, on the company's financial statements, the company would expense $6,000 ($30,000 / 5 years) using the "straight line" method in each of the next five years that the equipment is in service.

Extra Financial Empowerment ···

What's the difference between "depreciation" and "amortization"? The two terms are closely related. The general rule-of-thumb is that businesses amortize intangible assets such as patents and depreciate tangible assets such as equipment.

···

☐ **Understand "startup" and "organization" costs**

The IRS allows entrepreneurs to amortize two kinds of costs that are usually associated with the formation of a new company and researching business viability. These costs are called "startup costs" and "organization costs."

Startup costs include most investigative or "due diligence" costs associated with researching a business plan as well as many of the customer survey and testing action steps that are highlighted in Chapter 10. Startup costs can also include rent, payroll, travel, professional fees and other costs that are incurred by a new company before active revenue generation. For accounting purposes, these costs are considered as capital costs (see prior section) rather than operating expenses.

Organization costs include legal and other state filing fees associated with forming a legal business entity and initial employee training and other costs related to securing first production and distribution partnerships. The IRS does not include product research and development costs as business organization costs. Other expenses that don't qualify as organization costs include legal and travel costs associated with selling securities to investors or costs associated with assigning assets to a new business entity, such as patents. Further, eligible organizational costs must be incurred before the end of the first tax year in which the business entity was legally established.

Both startup and organization costs are generally amortized over a 15-year period. However, certain rules apply for different types of business entities and the amounts of allowable expenses during the first year. New business owners are required to "elect" to amortize these expenses by attaching Form 4562 with a company's first tax return. Once a company chooses to amortize these expenses, no changes in the amortization period can be made. See IRS Publication 535 for more information.

☐ Select an accounting package

Intuit's QuickBooks accounting package is the dominant program for independent (non-chain) small business owners. It's easy to use and has features that integrate PayPal and other transaction processing tools into QuickBooks with relative ease. Even better, bookkeepers and tax professionals know the system so well that it is easy for new business owners to find affordable help whenever needed. Most community colleges, SBA offices, and micro-loan centers offer training classes in QuickBooks too.

☐ Hire accounting support

Sometimes it's just faster and easier to hire a part-time bookkeeper to set up your accounting systems and manage first payroll tax payments and related tax filings. If you hire accounting support, make sure that the service provider is well qualified and the nature of the engagement reflects your service expectations. Just because you hire a service provider to manage one general bookkeeping function, doesn't mean that the service provider will automatically perform all other accounting functions for your company, such as prepare your business tax returns. You have to officially hire service professionals to perform specific administrative tasks.

☐ Share financial statements

Get into the habit of preparing company financial statements at least every month. Share and discuss the results with all employees and board members. In startup organizations, it's easy for first employees to become so engaged in product and service development that they forget that success in business is defined by financial success. You can develop a cool website with impressive traffic, but if your company's financial statements don't demonstrate progress, you will have a tough time staying in business or raising capital from lenders or investors.

Extra Financial Empowerment ···

It's amazing to me how many employees of fast-growing privately-held businesses don't know much about their employer's financial status. I ask, "Is your company profitable?" or "Is your company close to cash-flow breakeven?" The usual response from managers and staff members is "They never tell us."

One of the first things I recommend to struggling business owners who want to turnaround their company's operations is to share financial statements with every employee. Trust them. Inform them. Work together. I give the same guidance to startup entrepreneurs too.

....

☐ **Understand payroll tax obligations**

Employers are responsible for filing federal, state and possibly local employment tax returns. Employers are obligated to withhold the following items from employee wages:

Social Security tax ("FICA"): 6.2% tax rate
Medicare tax: 1.45% tax rate
Employee specific income tax withholdings
Other amounts such as wage garnishments, retirement contributions, etc.

Currently, Social Security taxes are withheld on salary income up to $113,700 and all salaried wages are subject to Medicare tax. Employers then, match the tax amount (6.2% + 1.45% = 7.65) plus pay Federal Unemployment Insurance Tax ("FUTA"). Most employers have to pay state and federal unemployment taxes, so rates can vary.

Federal payroll taxes must be paid on a regular basis, usually within a week to ten days of each payroll, depending on the size of the payroll. Penalties are high for late filing. The federal government also requires the filing of quarterly tax returns that summarize all payroll obligations over the previous quarter.

Self-employment taxes are another beast altogether for sole proprietors, unincorporated businesses and independent contractors. Essentially, self-employed entrepreneurs have to pay the entire payroll tax bill—representing both the employee and employer's portion of payroll tax obligations for a total of 15.3%. It's a big tax hit.

Extra Financial Empowerment ....

One requirement that seems to get first-time entrepreneurs in trouble is the obligation to file a federal and possibly state quarterly report and make an estimated payment that should be approximately one-fourth of your total annual income, less business deductions. Self-employed entrepreneurs, who don't file and pay on time, face accumulating interest and penalties. If you are uneasy about preparing your company's first tax filings yourself, seek out local accountants or small business payroll tax firms to do the work for you. Spend your time wisely. Delegate! Check out IRS Publication 505 for more information.

....

☐ Create a technology safety net

One of the most overlooked administrative functions of startup and many small business operations is data backup. If your business is destroyed by a fire, flood or other freak events, your ability to tap SBA Disaster Recovery Loan programs, maximize tax deductions, or prove ownership of assets for insurance coverage will be dependent on your ability to access backup records about your company's past operations.

The following business records should have at least two sources of routine data backup in place:

- Website content
- Customer lists and activity
- Financial information and tax returns
- Corporate contracts, liens, loans, etc.
- Employment records
- Shareholder documents
- Board of director minutes

What are your backup options? Most security experts recommend a mix of backup devices and strategies—both onsite and offsite. These systems can include scanning key documents and placing a hard copy and a digital copy at a safe deposit box or other secure offsite location; changing out back-up hard drives at least weekly; and engaging "cloud" services.

If you pay a hosting service to back up your online data, test the effectiveness of the service at least once a year. If weaknesses emerge, fix them. It is not acceptable to keep all your company's documents and records in a little home office without offsite backup!

Extra Startup Intelligence ···

Laptops can be stolen in airports, hotel rooms or coffee houses. If you have to travel to make a crucial presentation to potential funding sources or a big corporate customer, keep a copy of your presentation materials on a thumb drive that is not kept in a laptop case. And for extra protection, store a copy of the presentation at a free Gmail or Yahoo account. This way, even if you've lost your laptop and your company's servers are down, you have a way to retrieve important documents for presentation purposes.

There is another gotcha associated with data losses that can become a costly administrative nightmare. Some states now charge penalties to companies that lose or compromise sensitive data including credit card numbers and Social Security numbers. Companies may also be required to notify customers of the data breach, which can harm a company's reputation. To minimize the costs associated with malicious or accidental data breaches, add a rider to cover data breach events to your small business liability insurance policy.

∙∙

Plan to Get Paid

If there is a section of this book that will amuse many of my colleagues and closest friends, it is this one. A stylist to Hollywood stars, a painter, a corporate art buyer, an executive headhunter, a software engineer, a valuation consultant, and a consumer product packaging designer all jeopardized the financial health of their businesses because they didn't insist on getting paid.

There are two types of customers you don't want to serve—the chronic slow-payer and the no-payer. It's foolish to think that all customers will pay your bill on time, if at all. The longer you have to wait to collect payments, the more money and time you lose in the chase. While accountants might quibble with me about definitions, sales only count in a startup when you collect a check...that doesn't bounce.

There are many implications of serving slow-payers and non-payers. Slow collections say something about how well you run your business to potential financing partners. Bankers prefer to lend to companies that consistently collect "receivables" within 30 days of invoice rather than 180 days of invoice. Companies with average invoice collections that exceed 90 days are likely to face higher loan origination fees and interest charges—or not qualify for asset-based lines of credit at all.

Especially during a recessionary climate, many of your first customers will purposely test your resolve to collect outstanding invoices. Show them you are serious about the business of running a business!

Your next action steps:

☐ **Know the rules of small claims court**

Before you determine how much credit to give to your customers, visit the website of your local small claims court. In addition to learning what documentation you'll need to file an action, pay attention to your county's monetary ceiling. For example, in Fulton County, Georgia, non-criminal payment disputes can't exceed $15,000. In contrast, civil judges in Richmond, Virginia won't rule on non-payment claims of more than $5,000. Ideally, you never want to offer credit to first-time customers that exceeds your local court's small claims limit. This means that if you bid a job for $7,500 and your local small claims court only takes cases up to $5,000, then make sure you get a $2,500 down payment.

Using your local small claims court as a last resort to collect outstanding invoices is more cost-effective than hiring collection agents. Typically, collection agents will take one-third of any collected amount, provided you have appropriate documentation.

Deadbeats pay attention to court notices. It's a lot easier to ignore a nasty letter from a bill collection service, but much harder to ignore a notice to appear before a judge. Further, no individual or business ever wants to have a court judgment against them that everyone can see online.

There are other fine points of small claims court. Some states require creditors to file in the court where the debtor resides or is located. Other states allow creditors to file in their home town. Again, learn the rules for your state and your specific county. Be sure to visit .gov websites for information on your local small claims court rules; otherwise you can easily end up at a local law firm or collection agency website.

Lastly, keep track of all phone calls and communications to demonstrate to a judge that you took several prudent steps to collect the outstanding bill in a friendly way. Keep your cool in all communications. Don't complain, whine or threaten. Keep conversations entirely focused on the outstanding bill and collection process.

☐ Set short billing cycles

The faster you send out bills, the faster you can receive payment. Service companies should consider sending out new invoices once a week, rather than once a month. Product-oriented companies should bill on the date of product shipment.

☐ Determine billing contact information

When entering into new business relationships with other businesses, obtain key billing information before starting the job, including:

- Name, address, phone number and email address of the new customer's accounts payable department.

- Names and contact information for all individuals or departments who need to sign off on invoices for fast payment processing. If appropriate, send invoices by email to speed payment and reduce mailing costs.

☐ Establish payment due dates

I make a point of buying from U.S.-based small businesses whenever possible. It always amazes me how often I receive invoices from freelance entrepreneurs and other new companies with no detailed payment due date. If you don't list the date a bill is due, how will a small-claims court judge be able to rule in your favor? Service contracts and invoices should stipulate exactly when bills are "due" and "past due," to clarify when late charges can start to accrue.

If you offer a special discount to a customer, consider making the discount conditional on prompt payment. And if you operate a service business such as house painting, don't leave the job site without giving the customer a copy of the invoice. Better yet, try to collect the final payment before you leave the job site.

☐ Get it in writing

For service-oriented businesses of any kind, no work should begin without a signed service agreement. A final service agreement is different than a work proposal. Service agreements should be signed by both parties. They should include a detailed description of the proposed work project, billing rates, payment rules, and how disputes will be resolved. If you have to go to small-claims court, federal court or arbitration to collect payment, assume that the service agreement will be "Exhibit A."

☐ Keep excellent customer records

In general, judges will look for the following documents to rule in your favor: a signed service agreement and proof of work completion (before and after photos, copies of work product, copies of shipping information, etc.). Judges then will look for specific details of billing and payment obligations.

Sometimes slow-payers delay payment by asking for service changes while a job is in progress. These unwritten requests can blur payment obligations. Whenever a customer asks for special changes to a service, amend the written service agreement to reflect change order requests. And, don't forget to charge extra for the additional work.

☐ Penalize non-payment

All service agreements should include a clause that allows you to charge a specified interest rate on overdue invoice balances. You can always waive the interest later, but don't give away this right upfront because it is wonderful leverage in court proceedings. In addition, all service agreements should include language in which the customer agrees to pay all costs associated with bill collection, including reasonable attorneys' fees.

> …Unpaid compensation due Your Company shall accrue interest at the rate of 8% (eight percent) per annum until payment in full. Customer also agrees to reimburse Your Company for all of its costs, including reasonable attorneys' fees, associated with collecting outstanding fees due Your Company. Consulting fees are due within 15 days of the invoice date…

☐ **Establish minimum down-payment policies**

Simply stated, if your customers can't afford a down payment, then they can't afford the entire job. Ask for them. If you offer services to unproven first customers, be sure that the requested down payment amount covers all anticipated initial out-of-pocket costs. In some service businesses, such as painting or construction, you can minimize non-payment risks by asking customers to purchase materials and supplies directly.

Extra Startup Intelligence ···

Certain suppliers may ask your company for partial or full payment in advance of product or service delivery. Before advancing a down-payment, consider the impact to your business if the supplier doesn't deliver your order to your satisfaction. What leverage do you have to get your down-payment back? Put a fair agreement in place that can protect both parties.

···

☐ **Develop an anti-procrastination collection plan**

To minimize indecision and unnecessary angst when dealing with manipulative deadbeat customers, prepare a plan that you and your staff members will automatically implement when invoices become past-due—from any customers. Develop a schedule that lists the exact number of past due days before you place an account on COD status, report the delinquency to credit agencies such as Dun & Bradstreet, or file a claim in small claims court. Here's another collection tip: Consider a friendly "doorstep collection" for local customers. Crafty deadbeats say it's easy to ignore collection letters, but much harder to brush off a friendly but determined business owner.

Extra Financial Empowerment ···

If a customer owes you money that you cannot collect, in whole or in part, you have a bad debt. Bad debts are deductible only if the amount owed has been previously included in your income. As such, companies that use cash basis accounting may not take a bad debt tax deduction because it was never added into business income in the first place. IRS Publications 535 and 550 can provide additional information on what constitutes as a valid bad debt for tax purposes.

···

FAQs

Q. **Does the IRS ever give business owners breaks that are not available to salaried employees?**

A. Depending on how you structure your business for income tax reporting purposes, you can take advantage of laws that allow business owners to sock away more money in tax-deferred retirement savings accounts than salaried employees.

If, for example, you are self-employed and have comfortably achieved the 4 Milestones of Financial Safety, consider setting up a SE-IRA or simplified employee pension-IRA. Here, you can put away up to 25% of compensation after expenses, up to $51,000 a year. In comparison, a salaried employee who is less than 50 years old can contribute only up to $17,500 in pre-tax income to a 401(k) or only $5,500 to an IRA. Even better, high-income business owners can potentially sock away up to $200,000 in pre-tax contributions through a pension program.

Protect It!

How to Protect What Matters Most

A generation ago, most small businesses were valued by the sum of their tangible assets such as inventory, cash, equipment, land and other physical property. Today, the process of valuing startups and other privately-held companies is more complex and highly influenced by the perceived and actual value of a company's intangible assets.

Intangible assets include a company's know-how, patents, trademarks, copyrights, customer lists, trade names, brand names, proprietary processes, and trade dress. Even though you may not be able to physically touch intangible assets, they can have tremendous financial and strategic value to your company as it grows over time.

You don't have to own a high tech business to have intellectual property or IP. Every type of business in America—from restaurants to fertilizer manufacturers—has some element of IP in its operations.

For example, a startup guitar manufacturer may file trademark applications on the novel shape of an electric guitar as well as its brand name. A proprietary curriculum that helps beginners learn how to play the guitar will be covered by copyright. The manufacturer's unique production process may qualify for trade secret protection and, as the company grows, its proprietary customer database may be covered by copyright just like dictionaries. If the manufacture expands online and develops innovative software code to allow customers to design their own custom electric guitar, the software code may be covered by copyright law, patent law and trade secrets. And even a unique fabric design for a guitar strap may be covered by copyright and trademark registrations.

This chapter is not a substitute for professional legal advice. Its purpose is to boost your general working knowledge of the administrative deadlines and documentation needs associated with protecting your company's innovations and most valuable intellectual property.

I hope you read this chapter–little by little–so that you won't ever say "I wish I had known better." The more you know about IP the easier it will be for you to recognize new opportunities to increase the value of your business and collaborate with qualified legal counsel. Enjoy! The world of intellectual property rights is fascinating and fun.

$$ Turning Ideas into Cash

When investors ask entrepreneurs how they intend to "monetize their intellectual property" they are referring to the entrepreneur's strategies to convert a company's intangible assets into tangible business value…preferably cash. Here are some of the most common ways patents, trademarks, copyrights and trade secrets can contribute value to your business:

- Your business can sell a product at a higher price because one or more patents can give your company a temporary monopoly to sell an invention, a new product or a new drug in the U.S. and possibly other countries.

- Your business can sell a commodity product at a higher price than competing brands because of the good will value of your company's brand and trademark protections.

- Your business can license its IP to one or more investors, corporate partners, or brand licensing specialists in exchange for royalties based on sales or other considerations.

- Your business can operate more profitably because of your company's special "know-how" that may be covered by proprietary "trade secrets." Unlike patents, trade secrets don't expire if the secret is closely guarded by its owners.

- Your business can sell its patent for a lump sum to one or more investors, corporate buyers or "patent aggregators." Patent aggregators buy patents not for traditional manufacturing or commercialization purposes. Their business model is to sue infringers to collect large damage awards plus ongoing royalty payments.

- Your business can borrow against future royalty fee income.

As you explore more about the potential strategic opportunities associated with IP, you will see that whenever you combine the fundamentals of business value (Chapter 3) with IP, then your company will be in a stronger position to negotiate more lucrative royalty fees, investment transactions, corporate partnerships and company sale deal terms.

Royalty Rate Primer

A common question entrepreneurs ask as they research and prepare business plan projections is how much do corporations pay to license patents, product-related trademarks, cartoon characters, recipes and other kinds of IP. It's a prudent question to ask before investing in IP development.

The negotiation of licensing fees and royalty rates is not at all arbitrary. In general, royalty rates charged to industry competitors for access to critical technology will be higher than royalty rates charged to companies in other industries. It's a matter of how badly a corporation "needs" a deal to happen. Other factors that can influence royalty rates include the expected license term, the number of years until patent expiration, degree of industry exclusivity, potential for ongoing new product or service development, the potential for a third-party lawsuit, and the comparable costs and time associated with trying to design around the IP.

Higher royalty rates are applied to higher profit margin products and services as well as items that sell at high retail or commercial price points. It makes sense too. Well-recognized characters such as SpongeBob, Dora the Explorer, Angry Birds or Mario might generate a royalty rate of about 5% of net product sales when licensed to a food manufacturer and 8% when applied to children's apparel simply because the profit margins for apparel are higher than most food items.

Ever wonder what celebrities earn for licensing their name to consumer goods manufacturers? Food manufacturers pay big bucks to celebrity food chefs—about 10% of net product sales, which explains why their products are sold at premium prices when compared to other brands. In apparel categories, the rough standard is 12%. In toys, games and entertainment, celebrities receive royalty rates of about 10%. In the uber-high profit margin perfume category, celebrities can earn up to 15%.

Of course, lower royalty rates are paid for less well-known brands. Here are some broad ranges.

Consumer products:	4 to 12%
Food products:	4 to 5%
Apparel:	2 to 15%
Toys and games:	3 to 12%

In the pharmaceutical industry, royalty rates are based on the stage of product development, clinical trial outcomes, patent status, U.S. Food and Drug Administration (FDA) approval status, and the expected consumer and healthcare demand for the medical treatment. Here are some additional guidelines: A patent may get a 1% to 2% royalty; a pharmaceutical product with strong clinical trial support may secure a 3% to 4% royalty; and a proven drug that is ready for commercial sale may secure a 7% to 10% royalty. Pharmaceutical royalties on patented products in blockbuster healthcare categories can top 20% during the first years of product sales.

What will it take for you to license your IP-protected business concept (a recipe, trademark, technology, or product) to a corporate partner who has the resources to market the product successfully? In most cases, it will be up to you to present a persuasive, factual case on why your technology, trademark or product line will be a lucrative business initiative. Then, prospective corporate partners will evaluate the risks and rewards associated with the venture and determine the likelihood that business revenues will recover all the costs associated with packaging, distributing, marketing or integrating a newly licensed product into its operations, pay royalty rates, and make a generous profit. If your projections are reasonable and meet the corporation's minimum "hurdle rate" or profit on invested capital, then negotiations continue. If the proposed business opportunity falls short of the hurdle rate, then the corporation will either decline the opportunity or ask for royalty rate concessions.

All About Trademarks

15 years ago the name "Tory Burch" didn't mean anything in the luxury goods market. Today, the Tory Burch brand and the company's cross-like double "T" logo can be found on shoes, wallets, jewelry, umbrellas, clothing, eyewear, belts, purses, hats, scarves, makeup cases and dog coats covering at least six U.S. federal trademark goods classifications. If thieves broke into a warehouse filled with Tory Burch gear, criminal law would kick in to prosecute the theft. But, if some shady opportunists sold phony Tory Burch-looking jewelry or handbags, then Tory's legal team would rely on intellectual property law to stop the production and marketing of counterfeit goods.

A trademark can be a symbol, word, logo, slogan, design, drawing, advertisement, packaging, publication, name (including personal names of famous people), cartoon character, character used in product packaging or advertisements, radio program, software title, hardware product, websites, decorative item, fabric design and other images that are actively used in the marketplace.

A service mark is a name, word, or symbol that is used by a business to identify its services, such as interior decorating or forensic engineering consulting.

Entrepreneurs can also register trademarks on distinctive sounds such as NBC's famous three note chime or Homer Simpson's "D'OH." Other trademark opportunities can include visual motion marks, colors, product shapes, textures and, to a very limited extent, fragrances.

A trademark is not the same thing as a brand. Brands represent the social reputation and consumer good will associated with a specific product, service or company. In my view, customers are loyal to brand experiences and reputations, not trademarks.

Trademark Protection Options

Despite common perception, entrepreneurs do not have to file a federal registration with the U.S. Patent and Trademark Office (USPTO) to establish trademark or service mark rights. In the United States, entrepreneurs can earn "common law" rights simply by being the first to actively use a mark in commerce, usually within a specific state or community.

Still, filing a federal trademark has its advantages. Federal trademark law helps entrepreneurs expand their business outside of their hometown geographic territory with less chance of trademark conflicts with other businesses. This is especially important for service-oriented businesses who may eventually want to franchise their services or companies that sell products or services online.

Another advantage of filing a federal registration is that it is a low-cost way to announce to the public that your mark is not available for use by other companies in your industry. By registering your mark with the USPTO, businesses that sell similar goods or services will find your mark through routine trademark searches and likely choose another mark rather than risk a fast turndown from the USPTO or a legal dispute.

It's easy and affordable to file a federal trademark directly with the USPTO. The cost varies according to how you file and how many classifications are sought for each trademark. Budget about $275 to $375 per application. If an attorney files on your behalf, expect to pay these same filing fees plus attorneys' fees.

From a legal perspective, not every word, name, symbol or design qualifies as a trademark or a service mark. To gain legal protection, a trademark or service mark has to help consumers and businesses clearly distinguish the "source" or the provider of a product or service.

Here are a few key concepts to know before selecting product or service brand names:

- "Fanciful marks" or "arbitrary marks" are seemingly random names or made up words that have no logical relationship with the type of goods being offered. Both types of marks are considered "strong" candidates for favorable trademark application acceptance. Good examples of fanciful marks include Exxon for automotive gasoline and Zappos for online shoe delivery.

  Arbitrary marks are not quite as strong as fanciful marks. These marks have an existing meaning but convey no information about the product or service. Apple, as a trademark for computers, Ford's Mustang as a trademark for a car and Safari as a trademark for perfume are examples of arbitrary marks.

- "Suggestive" marks provide meaningful clues to the benefits, quality or characteristics of a specific product or service such as Coppertone brand sunscreen. Suggestive marks can qualify for Federal Registration; however they are not as strong as fanciful or arbitrary marks for trademark protection purposes.

- "Descriptive" marks are "weak" marks. They are not good candidates for trademark approval because they describe what a product or service does. For example, blatantly descriptive marks that define a characteristic or quality of an underlying product like "White Socks" or "Prime Beef" would likely be opposed for federal trademark approval by competitors in the apparel and food industries because it can give one competitor an unfair advantage in the marketplace.

After a trademark application is filed, an "examining attorney" at the USPTO will look at existing registrations and pending applications for potential conflicts with a proposed mark. Once a trademark examiner determines that a proposed mark is not on a list of prohibited names and is not similar in sound, appearance, or meaning so as to cause consumer "confusion" within a goods or services product classification, then the examiner will publish the mark in the USPTO's online publication, the Official Gazette.

Assuming no other trademark owner objects to or opposes the potential registration, then the examiner will place the mark on the USPTO's "Principal Register" or the "Supplemental Register." Strong marks are typically published on the Principal Register. Surname marks and other marks that consist of descriptive elements are usually placed on the Supplemental Register.

Marks that are listed on the Supplemental Register can usually block new applicants from trying to register a similar mark. A listing on the Supplemental Register also allows businesses to sue infringers in federal court. However, it is generally more difficult for business owners to win infringement cases while their marks are listed on the Supplemental Register. Also, marks that are listed on the Supplemental Register don't enjoy the same rights to expand commercial use nationwide as marks that are listed on the Principal Register.

Fortunately, the USPTO does acknowledge that through active commercial use and advertising, a "weaker" descriptive mark can, over time, become a "strong" mark. Today, when someone says, "Let's go to McDonald's for lunch" most people assume they have received an invitation to visit the golden arches for a burger and fries. This is because the mark "McDonald's" has developed "secondary meaning" to the general public and is synonymous with a specific burger chain, rather than a person's name. From a trademark protection standpoint, the mark "McDonald's" functions as the identifying "source" of a certain type of food product.

If a descriptive mark remains active in commerce for usually five years, it can move up to the Principal Register under the secondary meaning rule. The move from the Supplemental Register to the Principal Register is not automatic.

Your next action steps:

☐ **Learn about product and service trademark classifications**
There are 34 different product classifications and 11 different service classifications that guide U.S. registrations. A business cannot create a new word, symbol or mark and expect IP coverage in all product and service classifications—just the specific classifications in which the business has an active or upcoming commercial interest.

For example, a multi-media fitness business might explore trademark filings in Class 16 to cover printed materials; Class 9 to cover DVD's and downloadable software; Class 25 to cover t-shirts and clothing merchandize; Class 28 to cover promotional balls and Frisbee-like discs; and service Class 41 to cover gymnasium facilities and training services.

Check out the summary list of U.S. trademark and service mark classifications at the end of this chapter. If you are using an e-reader or pad device and have difficulty reading this chart, visit www.StartOnPurpose.com for an easy view.

Write down the specific classification numbers that cover products or services that you intend to commercialize within the next 18 months. More extensive information about each trademark classification is available at www.USPTO.gov.

Extra Startup Intelligence ··

Sneaky trademark opportunists may try to poach a "famous" trademark for use in an entirely different product or service category. The tactic doesn't always work. Under the principal of "dilution," trademark owners can challenge new trademark filings in different goods and services classes on the grounds that the new filing will disparage the reputation of a famous trademark.

··

☐ **Learn about "intent to use" applications**

The USPTO doesn't allow businesses to warehouse marks in a broad range of goods and service classifications for an extended period of time, but it does recognize the practical need for businesses to secure a mark prior to investing a lot of money in logo design, packaging and promoting a new mark.

If you want to apply for a trademark prior to establishing any common law or usage rights in commerce, consider filing an "intent to use" application (ITU). ITUs are temporary place holders. Companies that file ITU applications should plan on using the mark in commerce within about a year of the filing date. It is relatively easy to obtain an extension of time to file a statement of actual use with the USPTO, so long as you maintain a "bona fide good faith" intention to use the mark in commerce with the goods or services described in the ITU application.

☐ **Search for potential conflicts**

If you choose a name for your new company, product or service that actually infringes on an established mark, you may be ordered to change the name, give up all profits earned on first sales, and pay other damages and attorneys' fees if a court rules in the trademark owner's favor. Certainly no entrepreneur can afford to be on the wrong side of a trademark infringement case.

The more common scenario is that well-funded trademark owners bully entrepreneurs with threatening cease-and-desist letters and legal action until they agree to change their mark. Attorneys representing large corporations don't mind harassing upstart companies and are paid well to do it. You can't blame them because trademark law requires trademark owners to police the use of their marks in commerce.

The best way to avoid the angst and expense of a trademark challenge is to check for availability of your desired mark before launching it in the market. Visit www.USPTO.gov to explore the following online services:

- TESS: a user-friendly searchable database of federally registered trademarks and pending applications

- TEAS: a platform for entering trademark applications

- TSDR: a database for searching the status of trademark applications

Start your research by logging into "TESS." Simply type your desired trademark or service mark name into the TESS system's "New User Form Search." Look closely for similar marks in your selected product or service classifications.

Further, as you search the USPTO's databases, it's highly likely that you will come across marks that are listed as "dead." According to the Lanham Act, a trademark is considered abandoned after three years of non-commercial use. Corporate bankruptcies, product line failures, and administrative error are just a few reasons why marks can be listed as dead for trademark maintenance purposes.

If you come across this kind of notation in the USPTO's databases, do some additional research regarding the timing of cancellation. Ideally you want a mark to be dead for a very long time. Sometimes former trademark owners will seek to reactivate a mark, especially if the reason for a "dead" listing was due to administrative oversight.

Extra Startup Intelligence ···

The basic test for trademark infringement between two allegedly similar marks is whether the mark in question has the potential for causing "confusion" in the minds of the public as to the source of the goods or services. In applying this very subjective "likelihood of confusion" test, the courts and the USPTO will consider a variety of factors, such as if the goods associated with the two marks are sold in the same channels of trade, the degree of similarity of the respective goods, if the relevant customers are sophisticated and discriminating in their purchasing practices, if the marks contain common designs, sounds and meanings, and if there has been any instances of actual confusion between the two marks.

⬜ **Search further**

While TESS is an extensive database, it will not list all potential trademark conflicts because marketers of products and services don't have to have a federal trademark to obtain intellectual property rights. Marks can earn common law rights just by actively using the mark in commerce or they can receive IP coverage through state registrations.

Here are a few more places to search for potential trademark conflicts:

- **State registrations.** Most states offer easy online tools to search existing marks as well as apply for a state trademark or service mark registration. The value of a state search and subsequent registration is to bring out early objections to your proposed mark within your home state as well as from large, well-established industry competitors. Different states have different rules and application requirements.

- **Online search engines.** Type your proposed mark into Google and Bing. Review search results for potential conflicts. If you intend to start a community-based service business, search Angie's List, CitySearch, and Yelp too.

If you hire a law firm to file a trademark application on your behalf, it's likely that the IP attorney will retain an independent firm to help with a more extensive search. Thomson CompuMark is a leader in the field; however there are other online services to explore for service and pricing comparison such as LexisNexis, Dialog and Saegis.

⬜ **Review competing registrations**

You can learn quite a bit about trademark applications from the language used to describe the range of covered goods and services in other approved federal registrations. If, for example, you are developing a business plan for a new restaurant chain, check out the language used in the trademark filings of top franchise and company-owned restaurant chains. Keep track of questions to discuss with your trademark counsel.

⬜ **Acknowledge potential conflicts**

Slow down if you come across obvious commercial conflicts such as a federal registration of a similar mark in your industry classification. As noted previously, marks do not have to be identical to create conflicts under trademark law.

Further, if a conflict exists between your mark and a mark in a pending application that was filed before your application, then the examining attorney will most likely suspend action on your application. Also be aware that it is possible for a new registration to squeak by trademark examiners, but be challenged in the courts later by registered trademark owners.

The presence of a potential trademark conflict doesn't always mean that you have to select a different mark. However, I would not apply a mark with potential conflicts to product packaging or to a website without consulting qualified legal counsel, preferably a specialist in IP law.

☐ Double-check other distinguishing trademark features

A brand identity can be based on more than its letter-based name. Distinguishing features of a mark can include its logo, color scheme, audio components or unique way of packaging goods.

Extra Startup Intelligence ···

A trademark is different than "trade dress." Trade dress protects the overall aesthetic or visual appearance of a product—like the distinctive shape of a Coca-Cola bottle. Trade dress may include "features such as size, shape, color or color combinations, texture, graphics, or even particular sales techniques." Trade dress can become protected if it becomes clearly "distinctive" and consumers associate it with a specific product or service.

···

☐ Determine who will file your trademark application

The online tools for filing trademark applications have become so easy that the majority of new federal trademark filings are made by trademark owners, not their legal representatives. I've found that the USPTO examiners are extremely personable and helpful to first-time filers. If you make an administrative mistake in an application, an examiner will likely contact you by phone or email with recommendations for revision.

If you are unwilling to learn more about the fine points of trademark applications, hate paperwork, or frequently miss deadlines, hire an attorney. If you are determined to own a specific trademark but see potential conflicts from other registrants, hire an attorney. If your company's primary revenue-generating asset will be a licensed trademark, hire an attorney. If you need the help of a skilled advocate to negotiate on your behalf with USPTO examiners, hire an attorney. If your board of directors and investors are uncomfortable with self-trademark filings, hire an attorney.

If you intend to use a lawyer, my strong preference is to hire an attorney who specializes in IP law. The rates charged by IP attorneys are likely to be similar to general practice business attorneys, but the IP specialist will be better versed in recent court decisions that might affect your upcoming filings.

Extra Startup Intelligence ·······································

Copyrights and patents are governed by federal law. Trademarks are governed by both state law and federal law. If you hire legal counsel to manage your trademark filings, consider hiring an IP lawyer who is licensed to practice in your state.

·······································

☐ Establish date of first use

Good record keeping is important when securing and maintaining registration rights. The federal trademark application requires companies to provide a specific date in which a mark was first used in the marketplace. The standard for establishing first use is "clear and convincing" evidence—not undocumented recollection.

Here are some ways to establish the date of first use.

- Save copies of invoices to a first customer as well as proof of customer payment. Make sure the invoice refers to the product or service mark.

- Save copies of invoices to your first out-of-state customer plus proof of payment. This documentation can help demonstrate that commerce was conducted across state lines or between a state and a U.S. territory (such as the Virgin Islands or Puerto Rico) or international country.

- Save copies of bill of lading documents related to a first customer shipment of a product that includes the mark.

- Save copies of work proposals or other proof of soliciting customers which incorporates the product or service mark.

- Save copies of vendor communications about the production or manufacture of packaging or other materials which include the mark.

- Save screen shots of live website pages plus a taped backup drive of the site marked with a date.

- Take photographs of your use of the mark at a trade show or convention.

You do not have to submit your documented proof of first commercial use to the USPTO. However, your use of the mark in commerce has to be something more than token. Keep these documents in a safe place so that you are well-prepared to fight a legal challenge of the timing of first commercial use.

☐ **Organize application information requirements**

Prior to opening a file at the USPTO or interviewing IP counsel, organize the following information:

- **Date of first use of the mark in commerce.** For a more detailed definition of "first use" in commerce, refer to U.S. Trademark Act, 15 U.S. C. §1127 or visit www.uspto.gov.

- **Permanent address and email address.** For startup companies that self-file trademark applications without the assistance of legal counsel, I recommend that entrepreneurs use one email address and possibly a post office box for government communications that are likely to be active for several years. During the first few years of business operations, entrepreneurs often change domain names and office locations, increasing the chance of missed correspondence from important parties like the USPTO.

- **Prepare a "specimen" of the mark.** Read the USPTO's instructions for preparing and submitting examples of the mark to the USPTO. In general, one specimen is required for each class of goods or services specified in the application. Specimens can include digital photographs of labels or packaging. For service marks, the USPTO accepts digital copies of training manuals, brochures, reports, advertisements or other demonstrations of the mark used in commerce.

☐ **Notify the public of your trademark status**

Place a "TM" on your company's products, packaging or literature in the upper right hand corner of your mark. For service marks, place an SM on literature or references to the mark. You don't have to place the TM or SM symbol everywhere on a package or document; just once. Usually, the notice is placed the first time the mark appears.

Trademark registration certificates list the type of product or service in which the trademark may be used, the number and date of registration, the date the application was received at the USPTO and the term of registration. Once you receive a U.S. Trademark registration you can adjust your packaging, marketing literature, and website to include an ® symbol or "Registered in the U.S. Patent & Trademark Office" notice. If you fail to promptly amend your packaging or notify the public of your new federal trademark registration, you may not be able to collect certain types of damages in infringement cases.

The registered trademark symbol is usually placed in the lower or upper right corner of the trademark. When trademarks are used in text, trademark owners are advised to place trademarks in quotes or bold type face the first time the mark is used.

☐ Record marks at the U.S. Bureau of Customs and Border Protection

For a fee, owners of registered trademarks in popular consumer product categories that are listed on the Principal Register (not Supplemental Register) can try to reduce potential infringement by authorizing U.S. customs inspectors to seize imported goods. Visit www.cbp.gov and search for the "Trademark Recordation Application Template." It's important to note, however, that giving information about your trademark to the Bureau of Customs should not give you a false sense of security. Unless you have specific information about an expected shipment of counterfeit goods, the Bureau of Customs will not be helpful in pursuing counterfeit merchandize on your behalf. Let's face it, post 9/11, national security issues take priority over commercial issues.

☐ Maintain consistency

Companies can lose trademark rights if a mark is not consistently used or applied. Develop a "style sheet" to guide employees, ad agencies, PR firms, distribution agents and brand licensing partners on how to apply your mark to product packaging and marketing materials. In general, the overall size and colors of a trademark can change, but the presentation of various trademark elements should remain the same for brand building and trademark protection purposes.

Extra Startup Intelligence ··

Gotcha! Within the first year or two of a trademark registration, entrepreneurs who self-filed their trademark or service mark application are likely to receive several seemingly official invoices and "offers" to manage their trademark registrations plus list the mark in national or international directories. These offers come from companies that grab names off the Federal Register and use fear to sell services you don't need. When you receive these computer-generated solicitations, laugh at them and throw them away! A registration listing at the USPTO is really all you need to provide public notice of your mark in the United States.

··

☐ Consider international options

There are two primary ways to obtain international trademark rights. The first is through the Madrid system, which is managed by the International Bureau of the World Intellectual Property Organization (WIPO). It is important to note that the Bureau does not issue registrations in different countries. Rather, it is a centralized administrative service that simplifies the process of obtaining and maintaining trademark registrations in 89 member countries including China, Russia, Japan, Mexico, and most countries in the European Union.

For American-based businesses, applicants must have filed for a registration in the U.S. before submitting documentation to the Bureau. Fees are based on the number of countries or "contracting parties" sought for trademark or service mark registrations. After the Bureau accepts an application for registration, the Bureau will issue a certificate to the business. This certificate is not a final trademark registration! Each country makes the final decision to accept or deny an application based on local laws or notice of opposition by an existing trademark holder. Of course, applicants can challenge a refusal, ideally with the help of a qualified lawyer. International registrations are generally protected for ten years and can be renewed for additional ten-year terms.

Sometimes it is worthwhile to wait for a U.S. trademark registration before applying to the Bureau to process international registrations because examiners at the USPTO may suggest changes to the description of goods and services that may require subsequent changes to international registrations. Visit www.wipo.int and the www.USPTO.gov for more information.

Another option for international trademark processing is through the European Community Trademark system (ECTM). The European Community Trade Mark system consists of one single registration which applies to all 27 European Union member nations. Visit www.oami.europa.eu for more information.

No matter which route you choose for international trademark registrations, pay attention to the rules and deadlines for establishing date "priority" for your mark. In some cases, you can use the date of your U.S. application with the USPTO to establish priority over other businesses that may want to use the same mark for the same class of goods or services. However, you have to move quickly if you want to take advantage of your U.S. filing date. You will have to file for international protection within six months of a U.S. application.

FAQs

Q. **What are the penalties for infringement?**

A. It's the trademark owner's responsibility to challenge infringement cases, not the U.S. government. Owners of trademarks who are successful in winning court cases can seek treble damages, right to defendant's profits and possible reimbursement of attorneys' fees. Punitive damages may be awarded in cases of willful infringement. From a practical perspective, however, the cost-effective strategy for startup entrepreneurs is to take enough legal action to stop future infringement rather than invest a lot of money on a big court fight.

Q. **Should I file a trademark registration on my domain name?**

A. Domain ownership doesn't by itself automatically entitle domain owners to a federal trademark. Remember that a trademark has to function as an identifier of the "source" of goods or services for coverage under trademark law. If, for example, an entrepreneur owns the domain "gloves.com" it is highly unlikely that the domain would receive trademark acceptance because it would give the domain owner an unfair advantage over all other sellers of gloves in the market-place. Further, it is possible for domain owners to have to relinquish a domain name if it is the same as a registered or common law trademark that is owned by another company.

All About Copyrights

The purpose of copyright law is to protect new creative "works of authorship" from un-authorized reproduction, distribution, display, performance, modification or infringe-ment. Copyright protection can extend to software code, website user interfaces (GUIs), board games, puzzles, newspapers, magazines, books, poetry, articles, films, paintings, plays, scripts, music scores, sound recordings, cartoon characters, book and film charac-ters, photographs, sculpture, stained glass designs, choreography, architectural drawings, and more.

Facts, data, concepts and ideas are not protected under U.S. copyright law, though databases may be. Business tag lines, company names, trade names, product or services names, and marketing slogans are, typically, not covered by the U.S. Copyright Act.

The Value of Federal Copyright Registrations

Copyright protection is automatic. New works are covered by U.S. copyright law from the moment they are "fixed in a tangible medium of expression." This means copyright protections exist from the moment an original work is put on paper, published on a website or committed to a digital format.

Most first-time entrepreneurs assume that their creative works are covered by copy-right law after they affix a © copyright notice on the work and/or when they receive a certificate of copyright registration from the U.S. Copyright Office, in Washington, D.C.

This is true only if you wish to *enforce* your copyright. In the United States—unlike the rest of the world—you must register your copyright with the U.S. Copyright Office in order to bring a claim against an infringer.

The primary value of a U.S. copyright registration is the ability to threaten to sue or actually sue infringers for financial penalties and attorneys fees. You can seek statutory damages (as opposed to actual damages) only if you register within 90 days of the work's publication date or before the infringement began. In cases of "willful" infringement, you can seek actual damages or statutory damages up to $150,000 plus attorneys fees. If you are the plaintiff, the availability of statutory damages may motivate infringers to settle quickly.

Filing a federal copyright registration is really a no-brainer. It's fast, low-cost and usually does not require an attorney's assistance. Registering your work online with the U.S. Copyright Office costs only $45 to register a new work; $500 for expedited processing. Times vary, but my most recent online copyright application took slightly more than three months to receive a federal registration.

For new works owned by a business, copyright registration lasts 95 years from the date of publication or 120 years from the date of creation, whichever is shorter. If the work is owned by an individual, then the copyright lasts for the creator's lifetime plus 70 years. Each new version of a work requires a separate copyright filing.

$$ Ownership Gotchas

Copyright law, especially under U.S. laws, can be complex. Throughout this book there are several warnings about the potential for costly legal conflicts regarding the ownership of IP. Perhaps the trickiest part about preparing a U.S. copyright application is the accurate determination of a work's author and ownership status. If your business hires an independent contractor to take photographs, create cartoon characters, write computer code, or write manuals, etc., then the business doesn't automatically "own" the work, just because you paid for it. There are exceptions to this rule, but for the most part even if your company pays all the costs associated with producing a work, the independent contractor owns the copyright. Yikes!

The best way to shift full ownership and commercial control of a work from an independent contractor to your company is through a written assignment agreement. The copyright assignment can be a standalone document or incorporated into the written terms of a work engagement contract. Obviously, the best time to negotiate the ownership of intellectual property rights with an independent contractor is before hiring, not after.

Who owns the copyright for works created by salaried employees? For copyright purposes, the "author" and owner of a work is the employer if the work was a "work made for hire" by a salaried employee. There are several factors used to determine if an employment relationship exists for copyright ownership purposes, including who has the right to control the nature and production of the work and the nature of the employee's compensation. It is important to highlight that the test for an employment relationship for copyright purposes is different than the test used to determine employment status for benefit and payroll tax purposes. See the next chapter for the IRS definitions of an independent contractor and employee.

Making Money through Copyrights

As the owner of a copyright, you can grant an exclusive or non-exclusive right or license for other individuals, businesses, foundations, educational institutions and non-profit entities to exploit your copyright in the marketplace. One of the biggest mistakes entrepreneurs make in their enthusiasm to partner with larger companies is to grant too many rights or all rights "irrevocably" or "unconditionally" to a first business partner. For example, an extreme oversight might be to license the worldwide rights to artwork, a film or a song lyric to one partner that has commercialization expertise in just one medium or one geographic area. A more prudent approach would be to offer limited rights to different business partners that specialize in a certain type of media, industry or geographic region for a limited period of time—not indefinitely. You can also stipulate in licensing agreements how a work may be used in commerce as well as minimum sales that are required to keep the license agreement in force.

Your next action steps:

☐ **Document your intent**

Many freelance entrepreneurs, writers and artists have two options when preparing copyright applications for their own work. They can file documentation to award ownership rights in a personal name or in their company's name. These tricky decisions may become important in future years to the extent that ownership representations are made to investors, business buyers or other commercial partners. So, if your business plan implies that all IP is owned by your company, then make sure that copyright registrations on software code or cartoon characters do not list you or another author as the owner.

Of course, at any time, you can sell or assign all or portions of your ownership interest to another individual or business entity. However the author's name continues to appear on the copyright notice until 100% ownership transfer. Then, the new owner's name would appear on the copyright notice after the date of transfer.

☐ **Document agreements with partners**

Copyright registrations can be filed with two or more "authors." However, just because two individuals are listed as "authors" on a U.S. Copyright application, does not necessarily mean that the authors will share equally in the income derived from the commercialization of the work. In any commercial relationship, business partners should always develop an agreement or written understanding of how profits and expenses will be shared from the commercialization of a work. If the agreed deal is 50%-50% sharing of profits and expenses, say so in writing. If the agreed deal is 90%-10%, again say so in writing to avoid misunderstandings.

☐ **Develop agreements for employees**

If an employer pays a salaried employee to develop a work, then the employer is generally the "author" of the work for copyright filing purposes and copyright ownership. Still, as recommended in Chapter 8, entrepreneurs can take extra steps to clarify ownership by incorporating language into employment agreements and employee handbooks.

☐ **Document agreements with independent contractors**

If a work project involves the contribution of copyright-protectable works by an independent contractor, develop a written agreement outlining copyright ownership terms—before the work begins. If the independent contractor resists signing the engagement agreement, find another independent contractor who will.

A one-way email or letter notice to an independent contractor stating that the business is the owner of the created "works" is not satisfactory documentation to prove ownership. Get it in writing! Of course, the business has to pay the contractor as agreed to avoid legal challenge to property ownership.

Here is an example of boiler plate language that highlights the ownership intent of a business owner. Assume that capitalized words would be defined in other sections of an assignment agreement.

> …All Work created for Company is the property of the Company and/or Clients and Assigns and Contractor has no current or future claim to copyright or compensation for these materials. Contractor agrees that all Works, to the maximum extent eligible under the U.S. Copyright Act, as amended, shall be considered "works made for hire" so that the Company shall be considered the author of the Works under federal copyright laws; otherwise, Contractor hereby assigns and transfers all right, title and interest in and to such Work to Company and Assigns. At Company's direction and expense, Contractor shall execute all documents and take all actions necessary or convenient

for the Company to give effect to the assignment to, and vesting of owner-ship in, Company of all Works. Contractor has the right to keep copies of his or her work, both print and electronic files of this work. Contractor may use these samples/files in his or her portfolio as representational work...

☐ Understand registration timing

The effective date of a U.S. copyright registration is the date your application is received at the U.S. Copyright Office, not the date that the Copyright Office approves a registration.

Owners of creative works in certain industries such as film and music that are known for copyright pirating can file a pre-registration application on works in process. Works that can be covered by pre-registration filings must be unpublished but intended for commercialization. The pre-registration ap-plication fee is considerably more expensive than a standard copyright regis-tration—over $100 versus just $35. Copyright pre-registrants have to register the final work with the U.S. Copyright office in less than three months after first publication.

☐ Mark all published works

It is not a legal requirement to place a prominent copyright notice on all works. However, a common defense in copyright infringement cases is that the in-fringer had no way to know the work was protected by copyright. This defense is called "innocent infringement."

Copyright owners have flexibility in where to place their copyright notices. Here are some options:

© 2013 Your Venture, Inc. All rights reserved.

Copyright 2013 Your Venture Inc.

Copr. 2013 Your Venture Inc. All rights reserved.

For substantial revisions to a previous work, mark the works as follows:

© 2012, 2013 Your Venture Inc. All rights reserved.

For unpublished works such as book drafts, mark the works as follows:

© Your Venture, Inc. (Work in progress).

☐ Mark website pages with the copyright notice

If your website includes pictures, characters, articles or other works in which the copyright is owned by another individual or entity, you do not have to include the specific copyright notice for these works. Advertisements are an exception and usually include a separate copyright notice.

Each year, you can update the copyright notice for your website as follows:

© 2013 Your Venture, Inc.

© 2008 - 2013 Your Venture, Inc.

Copyright owners often publish a warning statement on their works advising that no part of the work may be reproduced without the express prior written permission of the copyright owner. This statement is not a substitute for the standard © copyright notice.

Under the doctrine of "fair use," purchasers of certain types of material have limited rights to reproduce copyrighted work, for instance making a backup copy of a CD, but not copying a CD for the purposes of resale to others.

☐ **Submit a copy of the work to the U.S. Copyright Office**

You can file a copyright application through www.copyright.gov. In addition to completing a relatively short application, registrants are required to submit a specimen of the work either electronically or by hard copy. There are specific rules for submitting software source code, films, recordings, CD-ROMs, etc. to the U.S. Copyright Office. Legal counsel can provide guidance regarding the circumstances in which a copyright registrant can submit a portion of a work to protect certain trade secrets from public disclosure.

Extra Startup Intelligence ···

With the popularity of YouTube and the technical ease of writing, producing and editing video, new independent production companies are on the rise. Entrepreneurial script writers should consider filing treatments, screenplays and scripts with the Writers Guild of America to complement legal protections offered by copyright registrations.

··

☐ **Record copyright transfers**

Copyright ownership can be licensed, in whole or in part. Copyright transfers can also take place in business contracts, loan collateral, divorce settlements, estate settlements, and through powers of attorney in which copyright owners give other individuals or entities the power to act on their behalf. Legal counsel can advise you of any required changes to public notifications of copyright ownership including providing notice to the U.S. Copyright Office.

☐ **Update corporate records**

Keep a copy of each U.S. Copyright application and certificates of registration in a secure location.

☐ **Set company standards for copyright use and notices**

Teach staff members to be rigorous about affixing copyright notices to company works. Further, because it is a federal crime to infringe on U.S. copyrights, educate staff members on the legal issues associated with lifting works owned by others without proper attribution or permission. As a business owner, you pay all the costs of employee mistakes. If someone wants to reproduce or sell a copyrighted work, they must first get the permission of the copyright holder.

FAQs

Q. **I've been working with a friend on a series of children's books. We haven't yet formed a company. She has drawn all the pictures; I've written the text. Who will own the copyright on the books and the individual characters?**

A. Your question involves issues associated with "joint works." When two or more authors create something with the intent that the separate components will be combined into a single work, then the work is considered a joint work. In your case it would be hard to argue that the pictures and the text were not intended to be commercialized as a single work. Unless you have a signed agreement that specifies otherwise, assume that both you and the illustrator will share ownership in the combined work.

Q. **Do I have to file separate copyright registrations for other countries, especially in Europe?**

A. For the most part, no. There are 164 members of the Berne Convention including Japan, Canada, Mexico, China, Korea, India, Brazil, Australia and most of Europe, South America, Central America and Africa. European Union nations provide copyright protection for the life of the author plus 70 years. Countries that are members of the Berne Convention extend copyright protections for the life of the author plus 50 years, although individual countries may provide a longer period for copyright protection. In general, works by an author who is a national of a country that is a member of the Berne Convention or works first published in a member country can claim copyright protection. As such, you do not have to take administrative action to earn a minimum amount of copyright protection in countries that are members of the Berne Convention, however there may be other opportunities to extend coverage by making additional filings in specific countries. Again, be sure to include the notice of copyright in the work.

All About Patents

In 2011, Congress passed the America Invents Act, the first significant upgrade to U.S. patent law since 1952. The legislation essentially harmonizes the U.S patent system with the patent laws of most other industrialized nations. The passage of this law means most patent-related online articles and "how to" books that were published before 2011 are inaccurate. Be careful. Bad advice always leads to bad decisions.

Under the new regulations, America's patent system moves from a first-to-invent system to a first-inventor-to-file system. It used to be that entrepreneurs didn't have to be the first inventor *to file* a U.S. patent application provided that they could prove that they were the first *to invent* a new technology, product, plant, etc. Now, entrepreneurs who file fast may be rewarded for their efforts. However, entrepreneurs can't file so fast that they fail to "bake" enough key aspects of an innovative concept to qualify for a patent.

It's important to emphasize that only individuals or a group of individuals can apply for a U.S. patent, not businesses. In order for a business to enjoy an ownership stake in a patent, the inventors have to assign their ownership rights in writing to the business.

Other considerations for entrepreneurs is the cost, complexity and length of time associated with preparing patent applications and negotiating issues with the USPTO. Today, most entrepreneurs can file copyright and trademark filings without any or extensive legal assistance. And, assuming that there are no technical conflicts they can receive a favorable action in less than a year. Not so with patents! Today, it takes several years for a patent to issue, which causes considerable uncertainty and angst for entrepreneurs and their investors.

So what exactly does a patent protect? In very simplistic terms, patents can be awarded for new and useful inventions that are not "obvious," meaning that the invention or discovery must not be obvious to anyone who is skilled in the general technology area or "art." The innovation should exhibit some characteristics, features or functions that are "novel" or substantially different from previous inventions and discoveries. This is known as "prior art." Inventors can meet this requirement by creating innovative physical property differences or combining two or more prior inventions together to create a new invention.

Perhaps the most confusing aspect about patents to many entrepreneurs is that you can't patent an idea. But you can patent the innovative, functional aspects of how an idea works in a commercial or industrial application.

The USPTO approves three different types of patents:

- **Utility patent**: The most common form of patent is a utility patent. Utility patents expire 20 years from the date the patent application was filed. The technology or innovation underlying a utility patent must have some "use" or purposeful function.

- **Design patent**: Design patents expire 14 years after the date that the patent is issued, not the patent application date. A design patent cannot have any practical function other than its unique aesthetic or ornamental features. Shapes that serve a function, such as a handle for convenient carrying or car designs that reduce wind friction would not qualify for design patents since they improve the product's overall function or effectiveness.

- **Plant patent**: Agriculture-related plant patents cover new, non-tuber varieties that are primarily produced through plant grafting. Plant patents expire 20 years from the date the patent application was filed. Plant patents are awarded on plants that have at least one unique, distinguishing feature that is not due to varying soil conditions such as acidity. Some plant innovations may qualify for a utility patent.

Inventors don't have to obtain a patent to make, use, sell, offer for sale, or import a product or process in the U.S. However, without a patent, the inventor has no legal ammunition to stop others from copying and commercializing the innovation in the U.S. As such, a key advantage of a U.S. patent is that it gives its owner a statutory monopoly which excludes others from making, using, selling, offering for sale or importing the claimed invention until the date of patent expiration.

Filing Process and Fees

Today, most new patent applications are filed with the USPTO electronically. Filers receive an instant confirmation of the patent filing, which is important for documenting the timing of the filing. While the U.S. Commerce Department has pledged to provide extra resources to the USPTO and open new offices, the USPTO is still woefully understaffed. Today, most utility patent applications take up to two years from the filing date to receive a first "office action" response from the USPTO. Design patents are the exception and typically receive a faster review.

For an added fee, it is possible to speed the review of a utility or plant patent application if the invention may help solve critical health needs. Applications filed with a Request for Prioritized Examination are placed on an examination track to reach final disposition within twelve months. The USPTO will accept just 10,000 requests for Prioritized Examination per fiscal year.

Small businesses pay lower basic application filing, search, examination and patent issuance fees to the USPTO than larger corporations—usually about 50% less. Visit www.uspto.gov for a current fee schedule. And while you are at the USPTO, check out a helpful section of the website called "Inventor Resources."

At the time of application submission, entrepreneurs can also file a non-publication request (NPR) with the USPTO to help maintain confidentiality of the patent filing. Otherwise, every non-provisional patent application is published 18 months after the filing date of the patent application.

In rare cases, more than one inventor may submit a patent application covering substantially the same invention. These cases, which are referred to as an "interference," are largely settled in favor of the inventor who was first to conceive the invention and the first to reduce it to practice. As such, it is very much worthwhile to retain notes, graphs, and documents which can help prove the date of a first invention.

Extra Startup Intelligence ··

For entrepreneurs who are successful in obtaining a U.S. patent, there still are ways that competitors can challenge some or all parts of the achievement. Under the America Invents Act, third parties (meaning your competitors) can seek to invalidate some or all of a patent's claims by petitioning for a re-review of a recently issued patent. Currently, patent challengers have just nine months to file a petition for "post-grant review." A post-grant review will not be approved by the USPTO unless the challenger presents a compelling argument that at least one patent claim will be ruled invalid. In response to the challenge, entrepreneurs can provide information to convince the USPTO to disregard the challenge, cancel the challenged claims or propose substitute claims.

On the surface, the threat of a post-grant review can sound scary to entrepreneurs. However, post-grant review may become a more affordable weapon for entrepreneurs to challenge their competitors' new patent awards too.

It's important to reiterate that the America Invents Act is very new. The USPTO is developing procedures for post-grant review and other new areas of the Act so the patent landscape is changing rapidly. In addition to this regulatory uncertainty, it is expected that the courts will struggle with interpreting these new laws. Will it be easier or more difficult for entrepreneurs to obtain a patent? It's probably too soon to know. What is clear is the decision to file a patent is highly strategic. Hire good legal counsel to help you make the right decisions for your company.

Infringement

Entrepreneurs can develop a false sense of competitive security after being granted a patent. It's safe to assume that the better your company's products or innovations do in the marketplace, the more likely your competitors will try to poach or imitate your best ideas.

Patent owners can file suit in U.S. federal court against companies that make, use or sell, offer for sale, or import an invention without prior approval from the patent owner. This sounds easy enough but from a practical standpoint it is an expensive undertaking. Sometimes it is easier and less expensive for entrepreneurs to hire a highly skilled lawyer to help negotiate a licensing agreement with the infringing company. Licensing income can be based on a myriad of structures including a fixed annual fee, a fixed fee per units sold or a fixed percentage of net revenues.

For entrepreneurs who pursue infringement cases through the courts, judges can issue injunctions against an infringer to prevent continued use or sale of the invention as well as impose monetary damages to infringers. If the judge deems that the infringement was "willfully intentional," then the judge can triple the damage award and order the infringer to pay attorneys fees. Entrepreneurs have to be prepared that infringers may fight back and go to court to try to invalidate a patent in court.

Measuring Potential Patent Value   **$$**

First-time startup entrepreneurs often believe that an issued patent leads to fast financial rewards. Well, maybe. The real deal is a patent can be a lucrative asset if it is part of a well-conceived business plan or an incredible waste of money. Unfortunately, too many innovators learn the hard way that not all intangible assets have tangible value. Said another way, it is possible to spend $100,000 on one or more patent filings that don't have any immediate value to your company in the marketplace.

To potentially maximize the value of a patent, entrepreneurs have to be prepared to present a logical, well-researched business case to investors and prospective licensing partners to prove that the technology advancement can give a company a clear advantage against competitors. Ideally, the patent has strategic versatility and can be applied to several different product applications or industries. Further, entrepreneurs have to persuade prospective business partners that there is an active customer market for the innovation, and that the innovation can be produced and sold in a profitable way. This is the strategic piece that usually trips up most garage inventors who want to sell their invention to another company rather than build their own company around an invention.

Your next action steps:

☐ **Research prior art**
The USPTO will not grant a patent if the underlying innovation has already been covered by other patents or is already in the public domain. Given the relatively high cost associated with patent filings, it makes sense to conduct a

thorough search of prior art to ensure that your big idea has not already been "reduced to practice" or patented by others.

If you uncover potential conflicts in your prior art search, then you can design around the prior art to make sure that you don't infringe on another company's IP. This extra research work is useful because inventors have to distinguish their new innovation from prior art in patent applications anyway.

What counts as prior art to patent examiners? Information that can be accessed by the public without breaking the law or violating confidentiality agreements qualifies as prior art. Prior art can be found in prior patent filings, academic journals, scientific publications, lectures, textbooks, products sold in the marketplace, etc.

Here are some resources to help you search for prior art.

- USPTO: www.uspto.gov plus Patent and Trademark Deposit Libraries located at the USPTO in Virginia and Patent and Trademark Depository Libraries which are located in most states.
- European Patent Office: www.epo.org
- The Software Patent Institute: www.spi.org
- MicroPatent Technology: www.MicroPatent.org
- Google Patent Search: www.google.com/patents
- Lexis Nexis [LexPat]: www.lexisnexis.com
- Questel: www.questel.com

Extra Startup Intelligence ··

Just like trademarks, it's possible to conduct an extensive search and still miss some potential IP conflicts. For example, software can be especially tough to uncover all prior art.

··

☐ **Interview legal counsel**

First-time entrepreneurs, first-time inventors and first-time patent filers all need qualified legal counsel to help evaluate the field of prior art and develop patent claims strategies that are most likely to be accepted by the USPTO. This, I believe, is a non-negotiable.

An experienced IP attorney is going to be well-informed about emerging regulations associated with the Americans Invent Act, the nuances of what constitutes prior art, how international filings can influence U.S. filings, issues related to validity and infringement, and more. Here are some recommendations to help you find competent legal guidance:

- **Find the best.** Visit the Start On Purpose website for a list of top regional and national law firms that practice intellectual property law. Unfortunately, not every community has a highly experienced IP lawyer and the most convenient legal counsel may not be your best counsel. For entrepreneurs who live in rural communities, be cautious about using general business counsel for IP matters. Expand your horizons. Reach out to qualified legal counsel on a regional or national basis.

- **Interview at least three firms.** Interviewing legal counsel takes time. The purpose of an interview is to understand the firm's process, connection base, depth of expertise and fees. Don't expect lawyers to answer many questions about your specific legal case, because they will not want to provide a professional opinion without researching prior art. Expect that larger firms may conduct a "conflicts check" to make sure that they don't already represent an industry competitor or a co-inventor before signing you up as a client.

- **Pay for performance.** Law partners have considerably more experience and expertise than law firm associates. Some associates may have seven years of working experience while other associates are just out of law school. Insist that your money buys experience. Ask who will be doing the work on your account before you settle on legal representation.

- **Buy industry experience.** Consider hiring a law firm that specializes in your specific industry to minimize the cost and time associated with getting a lawyer up-to-speed on key industry issues. Remember, as the U.S. transitions to "first-to-file" patent priority system, it will be important to choose legal counsel who can take fast *and* competent action.

☐ Understand provisional and non-provisional patents

A provisional patent application is a shorter application than a regular patent filing. It does not require written "claims" or drawings. As such, provisional patent applications typically take less time to prepare than a non-provisional application.

From a strategic perspective, filing a provisional patent application may help entrepreneurs lock down a "priority date" for an invention at the USPTO plus allow entrepreneurs to mark innovations as "patent pending" for promotional or fundraising purposes. Provisional patents may be especially helpful to entrepreneurs who have not had the opportunity to develop a claims strategy with legal counsel.

Entrepreneurs have to file a complete non-provisional application within a year of the filing of a provisional application in order to keep the earlier filing date for patent priority purposes.

Are there any gotchas to provisional patent applications? Of course! The biggest problem with provisional applications (especially applications that are prepared without legal counsel) occurs when the inventor fails to fully describe the purpose of an invention and how it is produced. If the written description requirements are not met or are substantially different in the final non-provisional application versus the earlier provisional application, entrepreneurs could lose the early filing date for first to-file priority. This calamity can then lead to even more problems with public disclosure rules and international filings that are detailed in other action steps.

Extra Financial Empowerment ···

Filing a provisional patent doesn't command the same valuation boost within the greater business community as filing a standard patent application because more legal work has to be done to convert a provision application into the all important non-provisional application. It is possible to assign a provisional patent to other companies, though any negotiated royalty rates will probably reflect the preliminary nature of the provisional patent filing.

···

☐ Understand the strategic importance of "claims"

All non-provisional patent applications must include at least one "claim." A claim for patent application purposes essentially defines the scope, novelty, usefulness, industry relevance and non-obvious elements of an invention. Some patent applications are filed with a short list of claims while others can include hundreds of claims with extensive accompanying drawings.

Claims can be either "independent" or "dependent." Independent claims stand on their own and don't relate to any proceeding claim in the patent application. Dependent claims refer to a proceeding or "parent" claim. The subtle differences and relationships between a patent application's claims frequently come into play in infringement cases. The USPTO charges "excess claims fees" on patent applications that include more than a total of 20 claims and more than three independent claims.

The importance of well-drafted patent claims cannot be understated. Skilled patent lawyers try to write claims as broadly as possible to expand potential patent coverage. They also try to use patent claims to effectively block the most likely ways competitors might design around a patent. Technology-oriented investors, especially in large venture capital funds, frequently hire patent counsel to help evaluate the rigorousness of patent claims as part of their due diligence research. Just having a patent is not the source of value to a company; it's the strategic value of the patent claims that can make all the difference to entrepreneurs…and investors.

It is the patent examiner's job to review each claim, accept a claim, dismiss a claim, or re-negotiate the wording of the claim with the inventor's legal representative.

☐ Know key dates

Missed deadlines can represent missed opportunities for entrepreneurs. Here are a few deadlines that matter:

- **First-to-file.** Effective March 16, 2013, the U.S. shifted patent award priority to the inventor who is "first-to-file" rather than the inventor who is "first-to-invent." Entrepreneurs can establish "priority" through the filing of a provisional or non-provisional patent application.

- **Public disclosure.** Entrepreneurs must file a non-provisional or provisional patent application in the U.S. within one year after first disclosing the invention to the public or making the invention available for commercial sale. Disclosure of the invention to third parties that are covered by confidentiality agreements or non-disclosure agreements (NDAs) does not generally start the one-year deadline clock ticking.

  Other European and Asian market countries are not as generous as the U.S. regarding deadlines for filing a patent application after public disclosure. Most countries don't allow inventors to file patent applications on inventions once they have been sold in the marketplace or otherwise "publicly disclosed."

- **Non-provisional application.** Entrepreneurs have one year to convert a provisional patent application into a regular patent application in the U.S.

- **PCT application.** Entrepreneurs can file a blanket country Patent Cooperation Treaty (PCT) application (discussed in the next section) within one year of first filing a U.S. provisional or non-provisional application without losing "date priority" to the U.S. filing. The international priority date for entrepreneurs who fail to meet this deadline is the date of filing the international application. Again, it is crucial to pay attention to the differences in public disclosure regulations between the U.S. and pretty much the rest of the world.

- **Individual international patent filings.** Entrepreneurs have 18 months from the time of filing a PCT application to maintain date priority for subsequent filings in individual international countries called the "national phase" or 30 months from the filing date of the initial patent application in which priority is claimed (such as a filing at the USPTO).

☐ Understand international filings

The commercial power and protections of a U.S. patent do not extend beyond U.S. borders. This means that a visitor to the U.S. can run home to another country and produce and sell a similar innovation to offshore customers. Infringement only begins for U.S. patent holders when opportunists produce the patented technology or product in the U.S. or import the patented technology or product for sale within U.S. territorial borders.

For cash-strapped entrepreneurs, the most economical way to start the process of obtaining a patent in other countries is through the filing of a PCT application, which is prepared in English. The application acts much like the Madrid system for international trademarks in that it does not actually grant intellectual property rights, but simplifies the initial administrative process of securing patent rights in other countries. The final granting of patents remains with the patent offices of individual countries in accordance with their national patent laws. The time involved with examining and granting patents varies from country to country.

After first filing a patent application in the U.S., the primary value of a PCT application is to buy some time to evaluate the costs and likelihood of receiving a patent in other countries. A single PCT filing can help entrepreneurs preserve date priority from the U.S. filing in over 100 countries around the world. Again, entrepreneurs have up to 30 months after the priority date of the U.S. application to file patent applications in member countries—provided the PCT application was filed on a timely basis. See www.wipo.int/pct or www.uspto.gov for more information.

Another way to gain patent rights in international markets is through the European Patent office (EPO) which allows one filing to potentially gain coverage in all European Union (EU) member countries. European patents are good for 20 years from the filing date with payment of ongoing maintenance fees on a timely basis. There are emerging regulations in the EU that will allow entrepreneurs who receive a patent through the EPO to choose to receive "unitary" coverage in all participating member countries. The EPO is also relaxing language translation requirements which will create significant savings for U.S.-based entrepreneurs who already have prepared patent applications in English. Soon the EU will also move to a more harmonized court system which will prevent different EU member countries from interpreting patents in different ways. Visit www. epo.org for more information and, of course, discuss your company's strategy for international coverage with your legal counsel.

☐ **Register to become an e-filer at the USPTO**

If you intend to file a patent application on your own (not recommended), you should create a registered e-filer account with the USPTO long before you rush to file a provisional or non-provisional patent filing. The administrative action steps associated with setting up an account can be time-consuming. And while you are on the USPTO's website, spend some time reading the helpful articles and instructions associated with preparing a patent application.

☐ **Define your invention**

The best way to help your legal counsel understand your innovation and its patent potential is to bullet point the functional aspects and significance of your innovative concept. Your job is not to write the specific claims to your upcoming patent filing but describe your new technology or innovation.

Extra Startup Intelligence ··

Inventors are required to provide a highly detailed description of the innovation as well as information on how to make and use it so that others who are sufficiently skilled in the "art" can practice the invention without undue experimentation. Inventors are also required to describe the "best mode contemplated by the inventor of carrying out his invention."

The longstanding problem with the best mode requirement is that inventors may later identify an even better "best mode" and use this advancement actively in commerce. This real world situation can create a loophole for competitors to try to cancel a patent award or invalidate certain crucial claims within an awarded patent, if the inventor doesn't actively practice the best mode that was described in the patent application. Now under the America Invents Act, the failure of inventors to disclose the best mode can no longer be the basis for patent challenge creating greater protections for inventors. Again, the America Invents Act is new and it will take some time for new regulations to be sorted out in the courts.

··

☐ **Develop drafting strategies**

Before filing a provisional application or a non-provisional application, spend some time with your attorney brainstorming ways to improve the nature and scope of the claims of your patent application. Consider the following questions together: Are there other ways to improve your invention? What happens if you alter it or reshape it? What other elements might be able to expand coverage of your invention to other industry applications? How might future competitors try to design around your claimed invention?

☐ **Restrict disclosure**

Be very careful about what you write in your business plan or post to crowd-funding sites. Disclosure of an invention, including making it available for commercial sale, prior to filing a patent application is a common reason patent applications are denied or challenged by industry competitors. Under U.S patent law, inventors can disclose an invention and maintain intellectual property rights, provided that the inventor files a U.S. patent application within one year of disclosure. It doesn't matter if you disclose the information as the inventor or some other third party discloses it.

☐ **Understand employment and engagement relationships**

The applicant for a patent is the actual inventor or inventors, not the company. As such, at the time of hire, all key employees who may contribute to a company's IP should sign two agreements: (i) a confidentiality agreement to limit disclosure of critical information to non-authorized individuals or businesses; and (ii) a "blanket" assignment agreement in which employees assign ownership rights of all inventions to the company.

It's increasingly common for venture capital funds to require employees to agree in writing that patent filings made up to a year after leaving a company are the property of the former employer. VCs reason that patent filings made soon after an employee leaves a portfolio company are highly likely to have been conceived on "company time."

☐ **Develop NDAs and disclosure policies for employees and consultants**

The rule of thumb in most states is that your company is better off if you have nondisclosure agreements and disclosure policies in writing. Documenting confidentiality and IP ownership and assignment expectations can begin with employment offer letters as follows:

> …Employee will execute the Company's standard At-Will Employment, Confidential Information, Invention Assignment and Arbitration Agreement prior to commencement of employment…

Companies can also include protective language to safeguard innovations in employment manuals and employment contracts. Here is an example:

> …Employee will promptly disclose in writing to the Company all discoveries, designs, ideas, formulas, know-how, processes, techniques, inventions, improvements and data (whether or not patentable or registrationable under copyright or similar statutes) made, conceived, reduced to practice, or learned by Employee (either alone or jointly with others during his or her

employment), that are related to or useful in the business of the Company, or which result from tasks assigned to Employee by the Company, or from the use of premises owned, leased, or otherwise acquired by the Company. For the purposes of this Agreement, all of the foregoing are referred to as "Inventions"...

Companies can include language to safeguard its intellectual property even after an employee no longer works for the company, as follows:

...Employee acknowledges and agrees that all Inventions belong to and shall be the sole property of the Company and shall be Inventions of the Company subject to the provisions of this Agreement. Employee assigns to the Company all right, title, and interest Employee may have or may acquire in and to all Inventions. Employee agrees to sign and deliver to the Company (either during or subsequent to his or her employment) such other documents as the Company considers desirable to evidence the assignment of all rights of Employee, if any, in any Inventions to the Company and the Company's ownership of such Inventions...

Companies can add language confirming the ownership status of developed intellectual property and the employee's agreement to assign intellectual property to the company as follows:

...In the event of termination (voluntary or otherwise) of Employee's employment with the Company, Employee agrees that he or she will protect the value of the Confidential Information and Inventions of the Company and will prevent their misappropriation or disclosure. Employee will not disclose or use to his or her benefit (or the benefit of a third party) or to the detriment of the Company any Confidential Information or Invention...

Companies can also include language that allows it to act on behalf of the employee for legal purposes related to the intellectual property. An example of this type of language follows:

...In the event the Company is unable to secure Employee's signature on any document necessary to apply for, prosecute, obtain, or enforce any patent, copyright or other right to protection relating to any Invention, whether due to mental or physical incapacity or any other cause, Employee hereby irrevocably designates and appoints the Company and each of its duly authorized officers and agents as his or her agent and attorney-in-fact, to act for and in his or her behalf and stead to execute and file any such document and to do all other lawfully permitted acts to further the prosecution, issuance and enforcement of patents, copyrights or other rights or protections with the same force and effect as if executed and delivered by the Employee...

Consulting engagement letters and contracts including hiring of part-time programmers, engineers, designers, etc. may include similar provisions:

> …Consultant agrees that all ideas, inventions, designs, ideas, discoveries, specifications, drawings, schematics, prototypes, models, inventions, and all other information and items made during Consultant's performance of the Services under this Agreement ("Work Product") will belong solely to Company, and Consultant will retain no rights therein. Consultant further agrees to assign to Company all right, title and interest to such Work Product. Upon Company's request, Consultant agrees to assist Company, at Company's expense, to obtain patents for such Work Product, including the disclosure of all pertinent information and data with respect thereto, the execution of all applications, specifications, assignments, and all other instruments and papers which Company shall deem necessary to apply for and to assign or convey to Company, its successors and assigns, the sole and exclusive right, title and interest in such Work…

☐ **Perfect recordkeeping**

Once you have obtained assignments of patent rights from any inventors (if different than you), immediately send the assignments to the USPTO for recording.

☐ **Mark documents and products as "patent pending"**

After a provisional or non-provisional patent application has been received by the USPTO, consider marking related products as "Patent Pending." Patent pending status doesn't provide any protection against infringement because the patent hasn't yet issued, however, the notice may be useful for business and fundraising purposes. Legal experts frequently discourage entrepreneurs from giving any details regarding the timing or contents of a patent filing to prospective business partners or the public. Discretion is best.

☐ **Understand the interests of development partners**

Sometimes patent ownership can be challenged by universities or other development partners if inventions were developed in part with funding, technical assistance or other support from a hospital, medical school, college, or technology incubator. Read the fine print of occupation and technology sharing agreements with any kind of institutional partner for issues related to technology ownership and income sharing.

☐ **Pay attention to ongoing obligations**

Patent owners are obligated to pay ongoing maintenance fees on issued patents. If the patent fees are not paid on a timely basis, then the patent can fall into the public domain.

FAQs

Q. **What do investors think about trade secrets?**

A. Most sophisticated angel investors and venture capital fund managers have a healthy respect for trade secrets. Still, investors know that it is more difficult to sue for theft of a trade secret than sue for patent infringement. Depending on the nature of the innovation, investors may discount the commercial value of the trade secret because of practical disclosure limitations associated with licensing the technology to other businesses, limiting extra revenue generation potential. There are, however, several compelling reasons for entrepreneurs to consider using trade secrets to help fill in the gaps in an IP portfolio that can't be covered by copyrights or patents. Trade secret protection can be applied to processes, formulas, recipes, unpublished computer code, story boards, outlines, technical notes, and even magic tricks.

To qualify as a trade secret, the process or technology must be a new way to make, build or do something and is generally not known to the public. Further, entrepreneurs have to establish that the trade secret has meaningful economic value as a business asset and that it took time and money to develop. Of equal importance, entrepreneurs have to take rigorous steps to limit employee and public access to the technology, recipe or process. Common security procedures to restrict access include keeping trade secret information off a company's computer networks, securing information in off-site bank vaults, handling trash and other documents in a protected way, and restricting employees from discussing or writing about the trade secret. Only a few employees should have access to the information on a strict need-to-know basis.

The most common way trade secrets are leaked to the public is though former employees. If the business took adequate security precautions and made employees aware of the trade secret nature of the information, then a company can likely seek an injunction and monetary damages if a trade secret is disclosed.

The most obvious advantage of developing trade secret protection is entrepreneurs don't have to invest in the preparation of patent applications plus pay filing fees and maintenance fees on registered patents. And whereas a patent may take years to obtain in the U.S., trade secret rights can be obtained immediately. Further, if a trade secret is really kept "secret" then there is no end date of legal protection. In contrast, utility patents expire 20 years from the date of patent application filing and aren't renewable.

Q. **Where can I go for help to determine the value of my patent for licensing purposes?**

A. There are many regional and national resources available to help patent owners who need help evaluating the value of their IP for estate, business valuation, business partner buyouts, business owner divorces and other purposes. Check out Consor Intellectual Property Management, Royalty Source, Royalty Stats, ICAP Patent Brokerage and Big 4 Accounting firms such as Deloitte. Most IP attorneys should be able to direct you to qualified investment bankers or other agents who can help you solicit corporate partners to license your technology in a professional way.

Q. **Why does it cost so much to file a patent with an attorney's help?**

A. Legal fees associated with patent filings tend to be high because of the time and expertise needed to research prior art, prepare patent applications and respond to follow up questions from the USPTO. While I am definitely a fan of bootstrapping and cash preservation, the selection of IP counsel is not a service where cheaper is better.

Q. **I'm preparing projections for my business plan. What's the accounting associated with patents and other intangibles?**

A. In simple terms, the costs your company incurs to file or purchase a patent is considered an asset for balance sheet reporting purposes. Qualifying intangible assets include trademarks, trade names, patents, copyrights, formulas, processes, special know-how, certain licenses, permits and more. The general rule for intangible assets is to amortize them over a 15-year period or the asset's useful or legal life. However, research and development costs that may be associated with a patent application are not included as a "cost" of a patent. Instead, research and development costs are recorded as an operating expense.

Summary of Trademark and Service Mark Classifications

Class 1: Broad range of chemicals

Class 2: Paints, varnishes, lacquers, etc.

Class 3: Cosmetics, perfumes, and a broad range of cleaning preparations

Class 4: Industrial lubricants, fuels, candles

Class 5: Pharmaceuticals, baby food, dietary supplements, fungicides, herbicides,

Class 6: Metal goods, wires, cables, pipes, and ores

Class 7: Machinery, motors, automatic vending machines

Class 8: Hand tools, razors, cutlery

Class 9: Electrical and scientific apparatus, instruments, digital recording media, computers, computer software

Class 10: Medical and surgical apparatus, artificial limbs

Class 11: Gear for lighting, heating, cooking, refrigerating, drying, etc.

Class 12: Vehicles for movement by air, land or water

Class 13: Firearms and ammunition, fireworks

Class 14: Jewelry

Class 15: Musical instruments

Class 16: Paper goods, printed materials, photographs, typewriters, teaching material, etc.

Class 17: Rubber goods, plastics, gum, asbestos, insulation, etc.

Class 18: Leather goods, luggage, saddles, umbrellas, etc.

Class 19: Nonmetallic building materials, asphalt

Class 20: Furniture, picture frames, goods made of wood, cork, shell, etc.

Class 21: Household and kitchen utensils, combs, brushes, glassware, earthenware

Class 22: Tarps, cords, strings, tents, padding, sails, bags, etc.

Class 23: Yarns and threads

Class 24: Fabrics and textiles not included in other classes, bed covers

Class 25: Clothing, footwear, headgear

Class 26: Lace, ribbons, buttons, hooks, needles, artificial flowers

Class 27: Floor coverings and non-textile wall hangings

Class 28: Toys and sporting goods, Christmas tree decorations

Class 29: Meats, vegetables, eggs and processed foods

Class 30: Coffee, tea, cocoa, rice, flour, pastries, condiments, spices, etc.

Class 31: Natural agricultural products, plants, seeds, flowers, pet food, malt, etc.

Class 32: Beer, mineral water, non-alcoholic beverages

Class 33: Wine and spirits, except beer

Class 34: Tobacco, smokers' items, matches

continued on next page...

Service Classes

Class 35: Advertising and business services
Class 36: Insurance, real estate and financial services
Class 37: Building construction, installation and repair services
Class 38: Telecommunications services
Class 39: Transportation, travel, storage, packaging services
Class 40: Treatment of materials services
Class 41: Education, training, sporting, cultural and entertainment services
Class 42: Computer, scientific, research, and design services
Class 43: Hotels and restaurant services
Class 44: Medical, veterinary, forestry, beauty and agricultural services
Class 45: Legal, security, and social services

Team It!

How to Attract Talent—Not Trouble— from Co-founders, Independent Contractors and First Employees

A few years ago I received a letter from a Silicon Valley-based entrepreneur who had just raised a first round of funding from angel investors. He wanted to know all the "sneaky" ways he might lose decision-making control of his company to investors. For the most part, my check list of potential problems and gotchas was similar to his list with one exception—bad first hires.

Get Your Money's Worth

Entrepreneurs who hire unqualified employees or consultants for demanding positions jeopardize their leadership authority and the companies they love. The same is true for going into business with unqualified business partners. Here's why.

Business partners, employees and independent consultants who can't deliver results on time or within budget create extra problems for entrepreneurs. The longer it takes a business to develop a product or launch a website, the more entrepreneurs have to dip into their savings or raise funds from independent investors. If investors are involved, an entrepreneur's ownership position in a startup can drop quickly—from 100% to 50% to 25% and so on. The Silicon Valley technologist got my message. He said with emphasis, "I have to hire *really* phenomenal employees."

Why don't first-time entrepreneurs set high performance standards for their first employees? You would think that ambitious entrepreneurs would hire the best, but they don't. Actually, the opposite is true. Entrepreneurs don't think that they can afford the best or have the time to find the best. They sell their dreams short when they don't have to.

Another factor that contributes to poor hiring and firing practices in startups is the founder's skewed vision of leadership. Entrepreneurs want to be the "good boss"—someone who creates a cool company culture where all employees are appreciated, enthusiastic and collaborative. They dream about hiring happy employees who love coming to work, not firing employees who steal from the company's cash register.

Because entrepreneurs don't want to be the nasty boss, they don't check employee candidate references and don't set up workable systems to review employee performance. They assume everything will work out—until it doesn't. And even then, it takes first-time entrepreneurs a very long time to take corrective action.

Since employee compensation will be one of your company's largest ongoing expenses, it's crucial that you set high standards for work performance. Getting your money's worth means hiring individuals who have the expertise, experience and ethics to help you achieve your goals. By the end of this chapter you'll know how.

$$ Choosing "Worth it" Business Partners

About half of new startups are formed with one or more business partners who are good friends, spouses, siblings or former work colleagues. Unfortunately, in my 20-plus years of venture community experience, I've seen too many of these friendships and family relationships fall apart before the business itself. I think British author William Blake got it right when he said, "It is easier to forgive an enemy than to forgive a friend."

Best friend or family member business partners are expected to be more loyal, more understanding and more hardworking than other employees and investors. They also count on their friends and family members to be unconditionally supportive and defend their actions to co-workers, customers, investors, and vendors. When they don't receive unconditional loyalty, at least one business partner feels betrayed.

I've heard the following statements so many times in my discussions with distressed best friend or family member business partners. They say, "I'm so angry. How could he do this *to me!*" or "He knew how much this company meant *to me!*" When a partner fails to live up to another partner's expectations, it's not just a business problem but a personal problem too.

So is it a bad idea to go into business with a friend or family member? Not at all, but I do encourage prospective partners to take extra steps to minimize potential misunderstandings. It's not enough to assume agreement; you must talk through the nitty-gritty details of running a new business to make a friendship-based business partnership work. If you and your prospective business partner can't agree on operating priorities at the start, save yourself a lot of drama and money loss—don't partner.

Your next action steps:

☐ **Set high standards**
Your standards for admitting new partners should be higher than your standards for hiring first employees. You can fire an unproductive employee at any time but it's not so easy to fire a business partner without involving lawyers.

Before agreeing to go into business, carefully assess what elements of financial value a prospective partner can contribute to your company. Your reasons for going into business should be more purposeful than "it will be fun to work together." Ask the following questions: Does your prospective partner have experience soliciting customers in your industry? Can your prospective partner institute operating efficiencies that will boost company profits? Can your prospective partner develop innovative ideas that have patent potential? Can your prospective partner conceive of new products or services that have salable value in the marketplace? Will your prospective partner's resume make it easier to attract investors?

☐ **Define personal and professional success**

It's easy for two business partners to have a different definition of "success." Is it to generate $250,000 in revenues or $10 million in revenues each year? Is success defined as quickly building up a company to sell at a lucrative price or building a company that can keep both of you employed until retirement? Different dreams involve different levels of effort, risk and funding. Make sure you both want the same things as business owners.

☐ **Agree on a business plan and projections**

During coaching sessions with prospective business partners, I often present the following high-risk scenario. Two eager pilots jump into a small aircraft in search of adventure. Upon take-off and rapid ascent, one co-pilot turns her yoke to bank left; the other pilot turns his yoke to bank right. It's easy to imagine the coming disaster all because the co-pilots didn't take the time to discuss their specific flight plan.

Partners should be aligned on the following business plan issues:

- Service or product development priorities
- Assessment of the company's key competitors
- Target customer list and how customers will be solicited and served
- Pricing and promotion strategy
- Funding strategy
- Specific action steps to achieve the 4 Milestones of Financial Safety
- Priorities for first hires
- Composition of the board of directors, if needed

☐ **Discuss potential problems**

Partners need to be fully aligned on operating and spending priorities. They should also know how their partners might react to terrible business surprises.

Talk through the following short list of "what if" questions:

- What if the company takes longer to develop the business than expected? How long can each partner go without a salary?

- What if one partner needs to take a part-time job to make money to pay family bills? Does that partner's equity stake change in any way?

- What if the company's initial test market fails?

- What if one partner wants to invite another partner into the company?

- What if the company runs out of cash?

- What if a lender insists on personal guarantees from all partners before granting business credit? Will all partners and their spouses agree?

- What if one partner wants to quit?

- What if a prestigious venture capital fund insists on hiring a different CEO as a condition of financing?

☐ Understand your partner's personal financial situation

The typical startup business will take more time and money to reach positive cash flow than initially projected. This isn't necessarily a sign of poor planning, but a reflection of the routine adjustments made in the course of launching new products and services in the marketplace. Prior to securing a domain name or printing business cards, partners should understand the limits of each partner's financial contribution to the new business. Pressuring partners to commit more money than they are able will create undue stress on the working relationship. If one partner can commit more time and money than the other, simply agree to increase the lead partner's ownership stake and decision-making authority.

☐ Exchange credit reports

If a prospective partner has a low personal credit score or has filed for personal or professional bankruptcy during the last seven years, your company may be disqualified from getting bank loans. Typically, all equity partners in a business need a minimum credit score of 700 to participate in Small Business Administration-backed loans, though some more lenient SBA lending partners will allow loan applicants to explain the special circumstances behind a bad credit history.

Venture capital funds usually run extensive credit checks on founding partners and senior management as part of their due diligence procedures. Was your prospective partner ever fired from a job, convicted of a felony, or involved in a Securities Exchange Commission investigation? Better to ask questions now rather than learn the facts in an embarrassing way. If your prospective partner doesn't have great credit, consider holding off on handing out officer titles or company stock. Use stock options instead to minimize scrutiny from outsiders. See Chapter 4 for information on how to order free credit reports.

☐ Maintain "org chart" flexibility

A common mistake among new business partners is to be too generous in awarding executive titles and board seats to prospective partners. Reserve "chief" titles (Chief Marketing Officer, Chief Technology Officer, Chief Financial Officer, Chief Operating Officer, etc.) for the people you may hire after one or more rounds of funding. It's emotionally wrenching to downgrade the titles of partners who may not be able to keep pace with the managerial needs of a fast-growing company.

☐ Agree on job responsibilities

Discuss the specific job priorities of each partner during the first year of operations. Organize priorities into quarterly action plans. Ideally, partner responsibilities should complement each other and help the company achieve the 4 Milestones of Financial Safety.

☐ Discuss work styles

Business partnerships are like marriages. Since you spend a lot of time together you should genuinely like and respect each other's character and work habits. Some partners must work in quiet; while others can work in a noisy coffee house. Talk to your partner about special needs that might affect work performance.

☐ Create some latitude

Resentments build when one partner puts in more time than another partner but still shares equally in all the profits and glory. Talk through your expectations in detail. Are you and your partner committed to work the same number of hours each week? What about vacations and overtime? Agree on times when each partner can leave the office for a day or a weekend without feeling guilty.

☐ Create limits of authority

It's easy for two friends to compromise when there's not much at stake, but as business partners invest more time and savings in a company, different attitudes about spending can emerge. To avoid surprises, talk through how spending decisions will be made and establish a specific limit to spending authority. Can a partner sign the company up for a credit card or book four-star hotels? Can a partner give away free product?

From a practical standpoint, you won't be able to prevent a partner from over-zealous spending or signing a lease for expensive office space, but you may be able to transfer the liability for excess spending to your partner provided you can establish that the partner ignored written company policy. Limits to executive spending authority can be agreed upon by a company's board of directors and increase over time with business progress.

☐ Determine equity split

I'm not a fan of companies that are managed by co-CEOs or 50%-50% partnerships, especially if the partners have not worked together before. It's too easy for casual disputes to lead to unproductive stalemates. What happens when both partners can't agree on strategy, funding deal terms, hiring priorities, or even company work hours? If one partner is really the driving force behind the startup, either technically or financially, then that partner should accept the leadership title and own a little more stock in the company.

☐ Determine the cost basis of shares

There are several ways that business partners can structure their equity ownership in a company. Each business partner can buy shares in the new company at a nominal price per share or at "par value." Business partners can also receive equity in lieu of a salary or as compensation for completion of agreed work assignments. Entrepreneurs can also exchange certain know-how, product designs, patents, customer lists, recipes, software code, etc. for equity in the new business entity.

Extra Financial Empowerment ··

While a company may issue shares to individuals in exchange for work, it is not at all "free." With respect to common stock awards, even though recipients may not receive cash today for services rendered, the IRS still likes to take its share of compensation for the year that the stock was "earned." This nasty tax collection trick is called "phantom income tax."

Fortunately, privately-held companies do have a degree of flexibility in estimating the fair market value of shares of stock. If the shares are granted at the time of business organization and valued at pennies per share, the income tax obligation may be negligible. However, if the individual is granted shares of stock that are valued by the company at say, $50,000, then the individual would be liable to pay income taxes on the estimated value of the shares. Ouch!

To avoid this situation, you can issue stock options, rather than shares of common stock to employees, board members, advisors and other business partners. A stock option gives the recipient the right to purchase a certain amount of common stock at a fixed price for a specific period of time.

For startup companies, most stock option awards have between a five to seven year term before expiration. Typically the price to "exercise" a stock option is set at the company's current per share market value or higher. Also, most stock option agreements require employees and other stock option recipients to work for a company for a specific period of time before some or all stock options can be exercised. If an employee is fired or leaves a company for another career pursuit, any unexercised stock options return to the company's treasury. A securities attorney should be consulted to make sure your company's stock option plan complies with state and federal securities laws.

☐ Determine vesting

$$

If you do give out shares of company stock to new business partners, include vesting provisions that require partners to meet specific performance criteria or work for the company for a period of time. Vesting terms of two or more years are common among startup business partnerships. All issues related to the timing and requirements that affect vesting qualification should be in writing.

The problem with lengthy, multi-year vesting provisions for common stock grants is tax-related. The IRS allows recipients of "restricted stock grants" to delay reporting of the income earning event until vesting restrictions lapse. On the surface this seems like a benefit to stock recipients, but only if the value of the shares doesn't increase during the vesting period. For hot technology or Internet companies, delaying the tax bill can be costly to stock recipients. The higher the value of the company's shares at the time of vesting, the higher the tax bill to the recipient.

Fortunately there is a workaround. Stock recipients have a choice—they can pay taxes on the entire number of restricted shares that are subject to vesting upfront or they can wait to pay the taxes as the annual vesting restrictions lapse. Timing does matter. Stock recipients who bet that the value of the company's shares will go up over time have only 30 days from the date of the stock grant (usually the date of board of director's approval) to notify the IRS of a "83(b) election." This simple tax strategy allows stock recipients (business partners, board members, employees or company advisors) to pay tax obligations at the time of grant when the company's share valuation is low rather than at the time vesting restrictions lapse and the share value is much higher. This election sounds complicated, but the paperwork is relatively easy.

☐ Double-check contributed assets

Sometimes business partners agree to contribute certain assets to a business at the time of formation. If one partner contributes cash and another contributes software code, equipment, other assets or intellectual property, then the IRS will pay attention to the value of non-cash property that is gifted or purchased at the time of business organization. Because the tax and accounting treatment of "contributed assets" can be tricky, I recommend that both partners talk to a qualified accountant *before* entering into business together, not after.

All contributed assets should be documented in writing so there is no potential for costly misunderstandings over the company's ownership of a specific asset. If, for example, your partner purchased a domain name on behalf of the business, then reimburse the partner without delay with a company check and legally transfer ownership of the domain name to your company.

☐ Agree on board representation

Not all founding partners or partner-employees should be on a new company's board of directors. Much depends on each partner's percentage equity stake in the business. A 10% minority shareholder shouldn't have the same voice on board level business issues as a 50% shareholder. Avoid adding spouses, siblings or other family members to your board because outsiders (especially prospective investors) will question their independence in business decision-making.

☐ Develop a partnership agreement

Once you reach agreement on these various issues, it's time to draw up a formal partnership agreement. Ideally, prospective business partners should be represented by different legal counsel. If the prospective partners can't reach an agreement on the nitty-gritty details of how business decisions will be made, what money can be taken out of the business, how new partners can join the company, and what happens if one partner dies or becomes disabled, then the partners will know it's too risky to proceed.

Well-conceived partnership agreements lay out in easy-to-understand terms how profits, assets, debts and other responsibilities will be shared while partners are in business together, as well as how these assets and liabilities will be divvied up when one partner decides to abandon the entrepreneurial cause—for any reason. Partnership agreements can't prevent partner squabbles. But the document can provide a clear cut road map for settling big money conflicts before the business deteriorates to the point where it isn't worth fighting over anymore.

There is no limit to the range of issues that can be addressed in a partnership agreement. Good partnership agreements reflect the needs and spirit of the founding partners' business relationship at the time of formation plus anticipate how the professional interests of the partnership might evolve over time. Here are some questions that attorneys often discuss with partners in the course of drafting partnership agreements:

- Can partners sell their equity stake at any time to any entity—even a competitor—without the consent of other partners?

- What happens if a partner wants out of the business but other partners can't afford to buy out the departing partner for cash?

- What are the instances in which a company or other shareholders may have a right of first refusal to purchase another partner's equity stake?

- Will each partner's equity stake be earned at the time of business formation or at some future date based on vesting schedules or other business contribution?

- What happens if one partner retires, dies, or becomes disabled?

- Will litigation between partners and the company be resolved by arbitration?

- How might the partnership change if one partner is required to split an equity stake with a former spouse as part of divorce proceedings? To the extent that the company or partner is unable to buy out a former spouse, will the spouse (who might be vindictive) enjoy any voting rights or input to board of director functions?

- What are the procedures for selecting one or more independent experts for valuing a business for stock pricing purposes or business sale?

- Are there any restrictions regarding a partner's authority to incur debt on behalf of the company?

- What are the minimum work contributions for partners to retain their managerial position or equity stake?

- What instances can a company buy back a partner's shares and how will the shares will be priced and paid for?

- How will partners share in year-end profits? What happens if one partner wants year-end profits to be reinvested in the business and the other wants to take out excess cash in the form of a stock dividend or performance bonus?

Extra Startup Intelligence ···

Well-conceived partnership agreements often include one or more hypothetical examples, sometimes called "waterfall tables," outlining how income or losses might be allocated to different business partners at year-end or at the time of business sale. Waterfall tables are effective in preventing partner disagreements especially if one partner has any kind of income priority over other partners. It's helpful for entrepreneurs to seek knowledgeable accounting and legal advice to ensure that the structure of the final partnership agreement complies with current tax law and meets the "economic effect test" under Section 704(b) of the Internal Revenue Code. Ask about it!

....

☐ **Document partner share issuances**

Once you have settled the terms of each partner's ownership position, immediately complete all administrative duties associated with a new share issuance including updating your company's financial statements and company records. Don't delay.

FAQs

Q. **I started an online business last year with financial support from a relative. Now the relative wants me to hire his son. The son doesn't know the first thing about my business. What should I do?**

A. No one ever likes to take in the "Fredo" of the family as an employee or business partner. If you are pressured to "include" or "help out" a family member who is not a good professional fit for your new business, consider giving your relative a token amount of non-voting shares of the company's stock that is not subject to buy-back provisions or other standard terms of partnership agreements. This way you may appease some family members by giving your relative a goodwill "piece of the action." But do not hire your relative! Stand firm. Talent should always guide your selection of business partners and staff members, not personal obligation.

Choosing Freelance Workers

There are considerable benefits associated with hiring freelance workers or "independent contractors" rather than salaried staff during the first years of business operations. First and foremost, you don't have to pay payroll taxes on the freelance worker's compensation. If your company hires an independent contractor then the independent contractor's company absorbs all payroll tax obligations plus the administrative nuisance of payroll reporting.

Operating flexibility is another important benefit. If you don't like a consultant's work, you can generally stop work with limited notice (unless you signed a contract that says otherwise). If you don't like an employee's work, you will need more paperwork and time to fire an employee without adverse legal consequences.

When is an independent contractor not an independent contractor? The answer is simple, yet potentially costly. It's when the IRS or your state's labor department says that your independent contractor is really a part-time or full-time employee. If this happens, then the IRS can require a company to pay all "prior period" payroll taxes plus interest and penalties. And penalties can be costly. In California, for example, the civil penalties can run up to $15,000 for each violation or up to $25,000 for engaging in a pattern of "willful misclassifications."

Let's say your new company hires an individual to construct a website. You provide a computer and onsite desk to make it easier for you to collaborate with the designer. Because the designer does a great job, you hire her to create marketing brochures and manage your company's online viral marketing campaign. Pretty soon, the designer doesn't pursue work from other clients because the designer's business has become just your business. This relationship could make your company vulnerable to an employer-employee relationship challenge.

Your next action steps:

☐ **Obtain "independence" documentation**

Once you have interviewed at least three candidates for a work assignment and settled on a top candidate, test the winning candidate's independence for tax purposes by asking for a copy of the consultant's business license and business tax identification number. If the candidate just presents a social security number, beware. My strong preference is to hire individuals who have a local business license and business tax identification number from the IRS. Keep all documentation to establish worker independence in case your company is selected for a payroll tax audit.

☐ **Invoice procedures**

Require all independent contractors to present detailed project-related invoices at least once a month. The independent contractor's invoice should include the company business name and separate work address. Avoid setting up a fixed dollar amount retainer that doesn't fluctuate from month to month.

☐ **File 1099 reports**

At year-end, businesses are required to report to the IRS payments of $600 or more to various independent contractors, service providers and board members on Form 1099-MISC. Business owners are also required to send a duplicate confirmation of total calendar year compensation to all independent service providers, service providers and board members too. You'll need the individual's business name, address and tax identification number to complete Form 1099-MISC.

☐ **Keep documents to support a case of independence**

Keep copies of the consultant's promotional materials to present to tax auditors. During vendor candidate interviews, ask about work provided to other customers within the last year.

☐ **Develop a consulting contract**

All relationships with an independent contractor should be in writing. Contracts can help resolve misunderstandings regarding service expectations as well as establish work independence for IRS purposes. The contract should include the following:

- Provisions that state that the consultant is an "independent contractor" and responsible for all federal and state payroll taxes and benefits, for example:

  > ...Contractor shall not be treated as an employee of Company for any purpose. Contractor understands that Company will not withhold or deliver to the Internal Revenue Service or applicable state and local government taxing authority any FICA, federal, state or local income or other taxes which may be assessed as a result of the performance of the Service. Contractor's fees shall be reported to the Internal Revenue Service on Form 1099. Company will not make or pay federal or state unemployment compensation or worker's compensation contributions or premiums with regard to Contractor. Contractor will be solely responsible for compliance with the payment of all applicable federal, state and local payroll tax and income tax withholding requirements attributable to Contractor as a result of the compensation to be received by Contractor under this Agreement. Contractor agrees to indemnify and hold harmless Company against any liability for premium contributions for workers' compensation coverage, unemployment insurance coverage, Social Security, Medicare or other payroll tax liability attributable to Contractor or his or her employees, if any, providing the Services to Company. Contractor shall not be entitled to and have no claim against Company for any wages, vacation pay, sick leave, Social Security, workers' compensation or employee benefits of any kind...

- Provisions that state that the work is on a non-exclusive basis. A good rule of thumb is your company should not represent more than 50% of a consultant's monthly income; otherwise it may appear as if your contractor is really a de-facto part-time employee.

- Provisions that state the nature of the work assignment and the projected start and end date of the assignment. Update consulting contracts to describe additional work projects as you add them.

- Provisions that confirm the independent nature of work progress. In general, you can monitor progress but not supervise the actual production of work or set the specific hours in a day that the work will be performed, for example:

  > ...In providing the Services, Contractor shall at all times act and perform as an independent contractor to Company, and the relationship between Company and Contractor shall at all times remain that of vendor and client with regard to Contractor's provision of the Services. Each Party to this Agreement shall retain sole control and management of its own business activities, including Contractor's provision of the Services, Contractor's exclusive right to control the manner, method and sequence of the Services performed by Contractor for Company and Contractor's right to retain control and supervise her own employees, subcontractors or agents, if any. Notwithstanding the foregoing, Company may, from time to time, establish schedules or deadlines for the Services to be performed by Contractor. Nothing in this Agreement is intended to create or imply any sort of joint venture, partnership, co-venture or other business relationship between Company and Contractor, nor is it intended to create or imply any sort of employer/employee relationship between the Contractor and Company...

- Provisions that assign intellectual property ownership. There are circumstances in which contributors to certain types of intellectual property may gain ownership rights unless specifically assigned in writing to the business. I recommend you work with an attorney to draft contract language that secures an immediate transfer of all intellectual property rights. If a prospective consultant objects to the language, hire a different collaborator.

  Some sneaky consultant contracts include language that the consultant "agrees to assign" intellectual property to the business, which is different than an immediate transfer of intellectual property. You can assume that the more you need the assignment, the higher the price you will have to pay for the signature! Well-conceived contracts also define which entity (ideally yours) will be responsible to file and maintain any patent or other intellectual property rights.

- Provisions for confidentiality. Many consultants are privy to product and service pricing strategies, customer lists and other important trade secrets. It's your job to state your expectations about how your confidential information may be used as part of a service assignment as well as after a service assignment is complete. Some confidentiality agreements also restrict document production and require consultants to return confidential information to the company after service completion.

> ...Independent Contractor acknowledges that any Company trade secret information imparted to Independent Contractor by the Company regarding the Company ("Proprietary Information") is for the exclusive use of Independent Contractor in connection with the services to be rendered for the Company and may be disclosed in accordance with the terms of this Agreement and Independent Contractor shall not disclose any such Proprietary Information to any third party other than Independent Contractor's own employees, consultants, partners and advisors and other representatives, without the consent of the Company...

For more information about independent contractor status, check out IRS Publications 15. If you want to eliminate any uncertainty about a consultant's independent status, you can file Form SS-8 with the IRS to receive an official ruling. Be aware, however, that the IRS tends to favor employer-employee relationships rather than employer-contractor relationships.

FAQs

Q What if I'm working with an independent contractor who has asked me to "forget" to file a 1099 report?

A. Sometimes independent contractors ask business owners not to report 1099 information to the IRS to help them avoid *their* income tax obligations. Here's my attitude about such requests. There is absolutely no upside advantage for your company, but a lot of downside if you get caught.

Choose High Performance Employees

A senior human resource executive once told me that he believed that 50% of all new hires were unsuccessful matches for employers. That's not much better than a random fair coin toss!

You can avoid the money and time loss associated with bad hiring and subsequent firing by setting high standards for employee honesty, integrity, co-worker collaboration, and job performance. You can't just hope for the best if you want to hire the best. You have to invest enough time to select employees who really know how to develop more products, more partners, more customers, more capital and more revenues for your company.

Unfortunately, your first hire is going to take the most time because you have to create systems to recruit and process employment applications in a way that complies with federal and state employment laws. Further, your must set up productive administrative systems to manage the new employee relationship. Sure, this seems like a lot of nuisance work; however, it is work that will serve your company well if you do it right from the start.

Your next action steps:

☐ **Prioritize hiring**

Startup business owners all reach a breaking point when they just can't do it all. They need help, but they often don't know what items on their daily action list are best handled by a part-time or full-time employee or an independent contractor. My usual recommendation is to hire help for time-consuming administrative jobs first to free up more of the founder's time for cash-generating pursuits.

Unfortunately, this type of thinking is counter-intuitive to bootstrap-minded entrepreneurs. They reason that they can do the easy administrative tasks so they hire top-dollar employees to help solicit or serve customers. Normally, I would favor any initiative that speeds cash generation, but not in this case. Big salaries involve more risk than little salaries during your first year in business. It's less risky maximizing your time first.

☐ **Demand experience and expertise**   **$$**

To help organize your thoughts prior to writing a formal job description, make two lists:

1. **"Been-there done-that" experiences or accomplishments**

Desired work experience should not be defined in terms of years, but specific "been-there done-that" work achievements that demonstrate the candidate is unlikely to make beginner's mistakes. Just because a "marketing manager" has, for example, 10 years of work experience doesn't mean that the manager's experience lines up well with your company's operating priorities.

2. **Work skills that match your company's operating needs**

Work skills or specific areas of expertise can include licenses, professional qualifications, certifications, language skills, and programming capabilities. Expertise can also include less concrete skills related to managing employees and customer relationships, project management, quality control, problem resolution, contract negotiation, market analysis, grant writing, sales proposal preparation, project costing, search engine optimization, etc. You may choose to ask top job candidates to submit samples of work or complete tests to confirm skill levels as a condition of employment.

☐ **Tap your social circle for referrals**

Send the detailed job description to your professional network—what I refer to in the next chapter as your company's "circle of social capital." Get the word out to former co-workers, friends, and service professionals, and through social media such as LinkedIn or BranchOut.

☐ **Develop a standard employment application form**

A resume is not enough. Every new part-time or full-time job applicant should complete an online or written application form. The primary purpose of a job application is to help standardize your company's hiring process to avoid discrimination claims. Service-oriented companies that experience high employee turnover should consider developing web-based tools to streamline human resource (HR) administration. If your company chooses this route, be sure to develop secure systems to protect applicant Social Security numbers and other sensitive personnel information.

☐ **Determine the need for a credit report**

Obtaining credit reports is a sensitive subject, and in my view, probably not necessary for most employment positions in startup companies. Credit reports often contain errors which can lead to wrong conclusions about a job candidate. Further, obtaining credit reports on prospective employees requires employers to comply with the Fair Credit Reporting Act. This federal legislation requires employers who turn down an applicant based on the information in a credit report to furnish the applicant with a copy of the credit report, an action notice and a statement of their rights. That's a lot of extra paperwork.

Still many companies insist on obtaining credit reports for employees, especially if their job responsibilities involve cash. They point to studies that correlate personal financial problems with higher rates of employment-related theft and fraud.

Extra Startup Intelligence ···

Can you ask if a job candidate has ever been arrested, even if the arrest did not lead to a conviction? It depends on your state's regulations. Some states don't require job applicants to reveal arrests or convictions that have been expunged because of successful completion of parole. This means that you may never know if a job applicant has been convicted of theft or other serious criminal charges.

The best way to protect your company is to hire slowly and research job candidates thoroughly. Further, inquire if your company's general liability insurance policy includes "fidelity insurance" which may cover some of the costs associated with employee theft and other misdeeds.

....

☐ **Prepare form releases**

Labor attorneys generally recommend that employers obtain one or more written consents that permit a company to verify a candidate's work history, personal and professional references, credit reports, professional licensing information, and criminal records if required by law for certain types of jobs. Some large universities require release forms to include a Social Security number to confirm identification especially for candidates who have popular names, such as David Smith. A release may be as simple as:

> "I authorize [ ] College to release to [your company name] a copy of my transcript and educational records including the year of graduation.

> Job applicant name:

> Phone number:

> Home address:

> Applicant signature:

> Date:

Keep signed forms for all job candidates in case of a legal challenge from a disgruntled job candidate.

☐ **Review candidate applications and resumes**

Resumes are marketing documents that are designed to highlight a job applicant's best qualities and accomplishments. It's easy to get sidetracked by an applicant's education or professional achievements. If for example, your company seeks a sales manager to develop a network of field sales representatives and distribution partners, hiring a Harvard MBA with no sales experience will probably set your company back.

The most productive way to quickly sort through resumes, online or offline, is to have your job criteria list on hand. If the candidate does not meet your top three criteria for been-there done-that experience *and* expertise, then discard the resume and move on. Don't compromise. If your game is football, don't hire (and pay top dollar for) the trophy-winning polo player.

☐ Set integrity standards

Job candidates who lie on their employment applications and resumes are high-risk employees. Resume fibbers are probably prone to misrepresent the truth to co-workers, customers, vendors and to you whenever it is convenient. You can't afford this kind of employee.

☐ Read "how-to" interview books

There are dozens of books published each year that provide useful employee interview and compensation negotiation strategies. Skim at least two how-to hire books prior to starting a first employee search. Favor books that have been published within the last two years to ensure that descriptions of federal regulations are current.

☐ Prepare for all interviews

Startup entrepreneurs who don't prepare for interviews end up talking too much about the history and goals of the company, rather than asking questions about the career history and goals of the job candidate. These entrepreneurs are likely to hire job candidates who interview well and say they are excited about being a part of a startup organization. I admit that I enjoy talking to candidates who exude an entrepreneurial enthusiasm and willingness to "learn on the job." But I don't hire them. I prefer candidates who have the experience and expertise to move a company forward without making a lot of beginner's mistakes.

To improve your odds of hiring excellence, develop a list of questions that you will ask all job candidates during phone interviews and in-person interviews. This way, you can compare the experience and expertise of different job candidates on an equal footing. Don't ask any questions that relate to a job applicant's religion, age, marital status, or parental status.

☐ Schedule phone interviews

Phone interviews are a great way to focus on a job candidate's skills rather than personality. Plus, phone interviews usually involve less time out of your workday than in-person first interviews.

To get the most mileage out of a phone conversation, focus on how the candidate matches up to your been-there done-that experience and expertise criteria. If a candidate's skills and accomplishments don't line up well to your company's needs, then end the call.

Here are additional recommendations:

- **Lead the discussion.** Tell the job candidate at the start of the interview that the first part of the phone call will be dedicated to learning about the job candidate. Indicate that the candidate can ask questions about your company and the specific job at the end of the call.

- **Listen more than talk.** Ask short questions that don't lead the candidate to obvious answers.

- **Ask questions about every part of the resume.** Some professional interviewers work backwards from the education section to recent employment experience. Others start with work experience and work forwards. Develop a system that you will follow for all interviews.

- **Ask for specifics.** An executive recruiter once advised me to ask job candidates, "Who did you work for at X company?" She said that any hesitation in naming the boss can be revealing. Write down the name. Then ask, "What would X say about your work performance?" Take notes for use in upcoming reference calls.

☐ Give a follow-up assignment

One way to reduce a large applicant pool is to give all candidates a follow-up assignment after a first phone interview. The assignment can be as simple as asking the candidate to call you on a specific day or provide more detailed information on professional capabilities and work accomplishments. If the candidate fails to complete the assignment as specified, drop the candidate from further consideration. In a startup organization you need employees who pay attention to deadlines.

☐ Schedule in-person interviews

If the job candidate is located out of town, schedule a Skype interview as a second or third interview. This is your opportunity to talk about the nature of the position and how a candidate's qualifications can advance your company's operating position.

I'm frequently asked for tips on how to interview candidates for jobs that are outside of the interviewer's domain expertise. Technologists want help interviewing finance people and marketers want help interviewing technologists. Start by asking business colleagues who have experience in these areas to provide interview questions and review resumes. In addition, consider the following backhand question: "I'm a biologist, so I'm not familiar with exactly what a finance manager must do to manage a fast-growing company's financial operations. Tell me what distinguishes a great CFO from a mediocre CFO?" Also ask how job priorities are likely to change over time and what issues might overwhelm an organization if unattended to. Vague answers may be a sign that the candidate doesn't yet have the managerial depth to be a self-starter in a fast-growing startup organization.

There is one question that I encourage entrepreneurs to ask of all job candidates at some time during the interview process. It is, "How might you lose money for my company?" Most savvy job candidates will respond with a smile and say something like, "I will work as hard as I can to make sure I don't lose money for your company." This is your invitation to then ask, "How? Tell me what you will do to prevent avoidable money loss?" If nothing else, this question will tell the job candidate about the culture of your company—to make money, not lose money.

Extra Startup Intelligence ·······································

It's good practice to ask prospective job candidates who are employed by an industry competitor if they have signed any employment-related documents that might potentially restrict their activities at your company, such as a confidentiality agreement or covenant not to compete.

···

☐ Schedule additional interviews

The purpose of a third or fourth interview is to discern the job candidate's emotional aptitude for working in a startup organization. Over time I've learned that not every person is emotionally equipped to handle the pace and stress of working in a startup. If employees are not resilient and don't adapt well to frequent change, they will resist it or complain about it to co-workers, customers or vendors.

In contrast, highly productive employees for startup organizations don't require a lot of hand-holding. They understand that unexpected problems are a part of the startup experience. You want to hire employees who are willing to help clean up problems, not cover them up. Here's some extra interview guidance:

- **Ask about crisis management skills.** "How do you react in a crisis? Give me an example of how you handled an unexpected work problem. Have you ever had to cover for other employees who couldn't get an important job done? What kinds of on-the-job surprises do you hate most?" Pay attention to how the applicant describes the problem in terms of a company's reputation, potential for financial losses, and team work.

- **Ask about past failures.** Great employees learn from their mistakes and can bring keen time-saving, money-saving insights to your organization. If a job candidate doesn't have one or more on-the-job regrets then he or she doesn't have much work experience. Ask all job candidates, "What was the biggest on-the-job mistake you ever made?" Then ask, "What was the second biggest on-the-job-mistake you ever made?" I bet the second question will produce the more revealing answer.

- **Ask about adaptability.** Productive employees for startups are flexible and can work well in imperfect work environments. Ask, "Describe an on-the-job situation in which there was a sudden change in business strategy from upper management. What could management have done better to ease the transition? How did you feel about these changes?"

- **Ask about organizational aptitude.** In every facet of a startup, systems have to be created and improved and improved again. Ask questions about how a candidate may have brought order to prior jobs. Also ask, "What would you do during your first few weeks on the job?" If the job candidate is too vague about job responsibilities by the third interview, slow down the interview process. Spend more time clarifying skills and experience.

- **Ask about competitive drive.** Make no mistake, entrepreneurial companies have to compete aggressively for new business. The only way your company will achieve the 4 Milestones of Financial Safety is to take customers away from your competitors, month after month, year after year.

When several job candidates are well-qualified for a position in a startup or high-growth potential company, I favor candidates who note on their resumes an active interest in competitive hobbies and sports. It doesn't matter if the job candidate competes in chess, bridge or bowling, just as long as the job candidate is wired to win. Competitive-minded employees enjoy team victories and know how to persevere after setbacks. These employees also know from experience the importance of winning the right points at the right time. This subtle but important distinction is highly relevant to startup organizations that rarely have enough operating resources to compete hard for every customer all at the same time.

☐ Call all references

I'm a big believer in new beginnings and career come-backs; however startup entrepreneurs have to pay close attention to prior work performance as a useful predictor of future performance. Call all professional and personal references that have been provided by job candidates. In addition, ask job candidates to provide contact information for their three most recent direct bosses.

Here are some tips for conducting purposeful reference checks:

- **Make the call.** Startup entrepreneurs will always learn more from a phone call discussion than a written job reference. Why? Because reference letters are not likely to address issues related to your job criteria list.

- **Schedule for convenience.** If you ask reference contacts to return your call "this afternoon" chances are that they won't because they can't. Be respectful. Remember that reference contacts are doing you a favor by giving you their time and insights.

- **Raise your expectations.** If your goal is just to confirm employment dates, then you will lose a terrific opportunity to learn about a candidate's strengths and weaknesses. Ask friendly, but detailed questions about a job candidate's character, work commitment, skills and job performance. Even though references are rigged to provide glowing reports they still can reveal information about the prospective candidate if you ask the right questions. For example, you can ask, "Does the job candidate lose her cool under pressure?" or "Can you recall an instance in which the job candidate went above and beyond expectation to get a job done?" Don't forget to ask why the job candidate left the company.

- **Change strategy.** If a former boss is clearly uncomfortable discussing the specifics of a job candidate's work performance, ask the contact to answer questions in terms of a 1 to 10 scale. For example, you can ask, "Compared to your other employees, how would you rate the job candidate's programming skills in C++?" or "How would you rate the job candidate's ability to solve unexpected problems?"

☐ Review online presence

Most job applicants take the time to clean up their Facebook or LinkedIn pages. So, dig deeper. If a resume notes that a job candidate is an active speaker in industry organizations, check out the websites of industry organizations to confirm resume claims. Online searches can also reveal bankruptcies, garnishments, child support payment delinquencies, and arrest records.

☐ Clear equity compensation

A board of directors is usually responsible for approving all new stock-related awards, including stock option and restricted stock award commitments to prospective employees. To the extent that you negotiate equity awards with prospective employees, indicate that all commitments are subject to board of director's approval. The board should also develop vesting guidelines for all employees to ensure that lucrative equity awards are earned over time by employees who perform.

☐ **Craft purposeful offer letters**

Written job offers help clarify your intent and avoid misunderstandings with respect to title, start date, starting pay rate, probation periods and benefit eligibility. Many offer letters include language that employment is subject to final reference and resume confirmations. Employment offer letters can also point to company policy regarding assigning inventions to the company and maintaining confidentiality as a condition of employment.

Best New Employee Administration Practices

New employers waste precious company resources whenever they have to pay penalties or settle disputes with current or former employees because of administrative mistakes. State and federal labor agencies don't accept "I didn't know" as a valid excuse for noncompliance with employment regulations.

Many employment regulations are directed to larger size companies rather than smaller size companies. For example, the state of Connecticut requires employers to pay up to five days of compensated sick leave per year to their employees. But this regulation only applies to "service" employees in certain sized businesses. Similarly, requirements for businesses to offer health care coverage for their employees under the national Patient Protection and Affordable Care Act (aka "Obamacare") apply to businesses with 50 or more employees.

Your next action steps:

☐ **Obtain an EIN**

Not all startup entrepreneurs need to apply for Employer Identification Number (EIN) from the IRS. Sole proprietors, for example, don't have to. However, once a sole proprietor hires an employee, an EIN is required. The fastest way to obtain an EIN number is to call the IRS at 1-800-829-4933 during business hours. You can also file online at www.IRS.gov.

☐ **Understand state and federal labor regulations**

State regulations vary in terms of cost and administrative requirements, especially with regard to worker's compensation and minimum wage requirements. Some states offer free workshops regarding state employment obligations that are worthwhile and allow you to talk to knowledgeable staff members. If you attend any workshops, collect business cards so you can follow up with staff members if you have questions about the following employment issues:

- State unemployment insurance
- Worker's compensation insurance enrollment (may be from a state fund or private insurance carrier)
- Meal time and rest breaks
- Exceptions to minimum wage
- Overtime wage requirements
- OSHA requirements
- Definitions of "exempt" minimum wage employees
- Paid vacations
- "Use it or lose it" vacation policies
- Health care coverage
- Paid sick leave
- Disability insurance (some states require certain employers to carry disability insurance)

\$\$ ☐ **Create a policy manual**

An employee policy manual is a must-have online or offline document for all new employers. Just as a corporate business structure can protect founders from unusual liabilities, an employment policy manual can shield companies from costly administrative and employee management errors. Employment policy manuals also make it easier for employers to fire employees for unacceptable workplace behavior or poor work performance. With an employment manual that clearly outlines acceptable work rules, rogue employees, for example, can't say that they didn't know they weren't allowed to visit porn websites on company time.

A local labor attorney can help you craft an employment manual to meet your needs. You can also ask members of your circle of social capital for ideas on how to prepare your company's employment manual.

Common employment policy components:

- Diversity statement
- Equal employment opportunity statement
- Personal privacy and work area privacy policies
- Sexual and employee harassment policies
- Drug and alcohol abuse policies
- Confidentiality clauses
- Immigration law compliance
- Salary administration, payroll practices, overtime pay and requirements to obtain approval prior to working overtime

- Work hours, holiday schedule
- Policies related to vacation and paid holiday, sick leave, paid time off personal days, leave without pay, military leave, jury duty, notification of absence, and the family and medical leave act policies
- General work place rules and policies regarding conduct including smoking around a premise
- Computer software, email, Internet, telephone and other equipment usage policies including policies for using company property for personal purposes
- Employee records maintenance, including documentation for government contracts and intellectual property filings
- Performance evaluation timing and procedures
- Travel and business expense reimbursement
- Procedures for voluntary resignation
- Discharge
- Severance pay
- Problem resolution
- Conflicts of interest policies

All employees should sign an acknowledgement that they have read the entire policy manual, preferably on the first day of employment. This acknowledgement generally includes a disclaimer that the policy manual itself does not guarantee future employment.

☐ Establish a business expense reimbursement policy

Develop a business expense reimbursement policy to avoid awkward misunderstandings with employees. Can partners and employees fly in business class or first class? Can employees or business partners choose a four-star hotel? Should employees receive approval before purchasing gifts for prospective customers? How often should employees submit expenses for reimbursement? Most employment policy manuals include language stating that submission of unauthorized or non-business related expenses for reimbursement may be grounds for employment termination.

The IRS is another reason to establish a written expense reimbursement policy. IRS Publications 535 and 463 provide clear guidance on the range of expenses that qualify as a business deduction for tax purposes.

☐ Develop an employee confidentiality agreement

Employee confidentiality agreements for employees and business partners are different than confidentiality agreements for prospective vendors, independent contractors, joint venture partners, and investors. For employees, a confidentiality agreement can contain, among other terms, a definition of trade secrets, limitations on how employees can utilize trade secrets, and the types of monetary and injunctive relief that a company can recover if the employee breaches the agreement.

If you don't develop a separate confidentiality agreement document for employees, you can incorporate confidentiality terms into your employee policy manual. It's more likely, however, that a separate confidentiality agreement will carry more legal weight than employment manual clauses regarding codes of conduct.

Extra Startup Intelligence ···

In most states, employers that don't require employees to sign confidentiality agreements lose their legal power to prevent former employees from soliciting their customers.

··

☐ **Understand Homeland Security Regulations**
New employees are required to complete Form I-9, which is issued by the Department of Homeland Security. This document requires employers to confirm that a new employee is legally authorized to work in the U.S. Employers must inspect and evaluate the "reasonableness" of the documentation provided plus retain a copy of Form I-9 and submitted documentation. The following documents can be used to verify employee identity plus establish employment eligibility:

- Unexpired U.S. passport
- Permanent Resident Card or Alien Registration Receipt Card
- U.S. birth certificate copy
- Unexpired foreign passport with a temporary I-551 stamp or I-94 with an unexpired arrival-departure record which includes an endorsement of the alien's non-immigrant status if that status authorizes the alien to work
- State driver's license
- U.S. military card
- Voter registration card or other identification card provided the document contains a photo and other information such as name, date of birth, gender, height, eye color and address
- Native American tribal document

☐ **Create systems to process new employees**
A new employee's first work day should begin with the employee completing all payroll and "company-protecting" paperwork. Employers lose leverage to obtain

signed confidentiality agreements and blanket assignments of future intellectual property developments from new employees after the first day of work. Just make it a company policy that no work begins until all required documentation is complete. Advise new employees to bring the documents to satisfy I-9 requirements on their first day of work too.

Here is a sample documents list to use to process new employees. Other documents may be required based on your company's industry or state requirements.

- Form confirming receipt, review and acknowledgement of terms set forth in the employment manual
- Form 1-9: Employment Eligibility Verification Form
- Form W-4: Employees withholding and allowance certificate
- New hire reporting form. Some states require notice of new hires
- Employee confidentiality agreement to protect your company's trade secrets and other confidential information
- Employee non-compete agreements to prevent employees from working for competitors. Note: Some states don't enforce or recognize non-compete agreements though many companies still require new employees to sign them.
- Non-solicitation agreements to prevent former employees from contacting your customers or staff members after leaving
- Emergency contact form: Every employment file should contain some guidance on the employee's preferences regarding contacts in case of a medical emergency
- Health care policy enrollment forms

☐ Share big picture objectives

Startup companies that enjoy high rates of employee productivity share strategic information with staff members. Schedule time with new staff members to allow them to ask questions about your company's business plan, projections and operating objectives. No staff member should ever be considered as "too low in the organization" to make a difference. In addition, explain the 4 Milestones of Financial Safety to new staff members so they appreciate how and why you make strategic decisions for your company. When everyone is working toward the same objectives, milestones are achieved faster.

☐ Set quarterly work objectives $$

Of course, no one likes performance reviews. Poorly planned and executed, they can be uncomfortable, confrontational and counter-productive. If planned well, they can be motivating and fun for the entire organization.

It's amazing to me how few small businesses conduct regular employee reviews. Owners of struggling businesses frequently tell me that they don't "have time" to conduct employee reviews in a formal way. This means they lose the opportunity to improve employee performance and employee morale, which are essential to turning around any money-losing company.

Over the years I've tested, refined and tweaked various initiatives to boost staff member communication and productivity in startups and fast-growing companies. I have found that quarterly staff reviews are more effective and less stressful than annual reviews. Annual reviews are not compatible with a fast-changing organization. It's too easy for employees to drift off course, especially if top managers travel extensively.

My recommended format for conducting quarterly reviews is what I call the "3-2-1 Precision Employee Review" program. It works well for startups because it is not administratively intensive or punitive. It's a simple, efficient and effective vehicle which ensures that your priorities are known throughout your growing organization. And, of equal importance, critical information about the real status of your company's operations—the good and the bad—is communicated to you in a healthy no-blame way.

Here's how the program works. Start by scheduling a private meeting with every staff member to discuss and establish top priorities for the upcoming quarter. Employee performance goals are organized around the following components:

1. **Three "Do or Die" Deliverables**
   The most important component of the quarterly performance review is the 3 Do or Die Deliverables. These three "deliverables" are specific actions to be achieved within the upcoming quarter. Emphasis is placed not on what employees *want*

3-2-1 Precision Employee Review Program	
3·2·1	3 - "Do or Die" Deliverables 2 - Stretch Goals 1 - Point of Pain

   to accomplish but what they *will* accomplish—do or die. After all, startups die when first employees can't complete their work on time or on budget.

   The phrase "3 Do or Die Deliverables" eliminates any ambiguity about an employee's top priorities. In startup organizations, there never is a shortage of work to do. However, with Do or Die Deliverables, employees are less likely to get distracted by less important work assignments. This helps other inter-dependent team players in technology or product development companies, complete their work on time too.

2. Two Stretch Achievements

As part of each employee quarterly review, the employee is asked *to suggest* at least two additional goals or purposeful initiatives that can stretch the employee's skills and creativity for the company's benefit. The goals should be ambitious and not so easy that employees are robbed of the joy of working extra hard to do something special. When employees are given a little bit of latitude to excel in something that interests them, they can accomplish great things for your company. If the stretch goals are not achieved, it's not a big deal, provided of course that the employee completes the Do or Die Deliverables first.

3. One Point of Pain

The last component of the 3-2-1 Precision Employee Review Program is the most innovative in terms of startup staff management. Because startup organizations have fewer operating resources to address surprise problems, they have to be more attuned to identifying little problems before they morph into big, costly problems. In advance of the quarterly review meeting, all employees are asked to think about one looming gotcha that may have the power to damage the company's reputation, customer relationships or competitive position. When employees know they won't be scolded for honesty, they can be constructive and forthcoming with information that can sometimes save a company from disaster.

For example, I once asked an executive sales manager of a company that was about to go on a fundraising "road show" if there was any event he could think of that would cause him to lose a big chunk of business to a competitor. It turned out that the sales manager's international revenue base, which represented 60% of the company's profits, was tied to just one sales rep. If the sales rep quit suddenly, the company would have no backup in place or understanding of the service issues that the company's international customers might require.

Within 48 hours of this discussion the company organized a thank you package for the sales rep that included a raise, a larger travel expense budget, stock options that steadily vested over a 4-year period, and an extra bonus that would be paid upon completion of the financing. The sales rep was also asked to teach a sales and customer service workshop to the company's sales and marketing staff, which the rep was thrilled and honored to do. The company also committed to hiring additional sales reps who would report to the super star performer to create a more stable base for the company's growing international sales activities. When companies take the time to think about the unthinkable they have the opportunity to solve problems before they happen.

The 3-2-1 Precision Employee Review Program works well in startups because it doesn't involve a lot of paper work. Just one page says it all—three agreed deliverables, two agreed stretch goals and the employee's commitment to be on watch for one point of potential pain that may be lurking in their immediate area. After you have finished the review discussion, give a copy of the 3-2-1 goals to the employee and place another copy in the employee's HR file.

Here are some other fine points of the 3-2-1 Precision Employee Review Program:

- Everyone participates. The 3-2-1 Program only works if it involves all part-time and full-time employees, unpaid and paid interns, company founders and business partners. And yes, the 3-2-1 Program can be adopted by self-employed freelance entrepreneurs who want extra motivation to set quarterly goals.

- Schedule meetings in advance. Conduct quarterly review meetings within a short window of time. Ideally, try to complete all meetings within one or two days preferably shortly after the close of a calendar quarter.

- Create a two-way conversation. The program is designed to encourage collaborative discussions between bosses and employees. If Do or Die Deliverables and Stretch Achievements are simply "assigned" to employees, then the program will turn into an unproductive corporate employee review that everyone will hate.

- End non-performance. If an employee fails to achieve the 3 Do or Die deliverables for two quarters, put the employee on notice for potential termination. Employees who miss three quarterly objectives should be dismissed. Your company's cash has to buy talent and performance to succeed. Success in the Stretch Achievements should not be a substitute for completing the 3 Do or Die Deliverables.

- Pain point follow-up. It's unlikely that any startup organization will ever be able to address every point of potential pain that is identified by its staff members. Still, it's your job to acknowledge each employee's observations and develop a way to address the most pressing problems. It's vital that you and your top managers don't ever reward spiteful finger pointers. The point of identifying points of potential pain is to motivate an entire organization to uncover potential problems and improve performance, not disparage employees.

- **Celebrate.** Create a tradition of celebrating individual achievements rather than employee birthdays! After every quarterly review period bring your company's staff members together to acknowledge notable achievements and get psyched up for the next quarter ahead.

FAQs

Q. **What is the minimum documentation I need to fire an employee?**

A. Before taking any action, find out if your state is an "at will" employment state. Most states are. Unless a company has signed an employment agreement with an employee, at-will employment allows employers and employees to terminate an employment relationship at any time, with or without cause, and with or without notice. Of course, at-will employment does not allow employers to discriminate against employees or arbitrarily fire employees without providing prior warnings of unsatisfactory work performance and allowing employees a "good faith" opportunity to correct unsatisfactory work performance.

There are two documents that give employers what I call the "fire power to fire." The first set of documents is the written quarterly performance reviews. Conducting quarterly reviews allows startup entrepreneurs to hone in on problems quickly and resolve problems in less than 180 days. Companies that rely on annual reviews may have to pay for unacceptable employee performance problems for a year or more.

A company's employment manual is the second document that helps employers to manage employee problems in a straight-forward way. Well-conceived employee policy manuals lay out exactly what types of behavior are unacceptable, such as disparaging co-workers, sharing confidential information about the company on social networking sites, theft of company property, etc. Ideally, all employees should have signed a form notice on the first day of employment stating that they read the policy manual and agreed to its terms. Because the employee agreed in writing to abide by the company's work rules, employees can't claim, "I didn't know." Case closed.

Q. **Will conducting quarterly review meetings with employees just encourage employees to ask for quarterly raises?**

A. No, quarterly review meetings are designed to boost employee satisfaction with their job and minimize the frustrations associated with feeling "in the dark" or "out of the loop." If you want to keep your best employees motivated and in love with your company, give them the opportunity to collaborate with the top boss in a purposeful way. When adjustments need to be made, it's easier to thoroughly explain new initiatives in private quarterly meetings rather than through a series of fast chats in a lunch room or hallway. When employees feel they are respected by the top boss, they don't look for other jobs—even higher paying jobs.

Q. **What employee records should I keep and for how long?**

A. Ever-changing privacy regulations have increased the complexity of employment regulations. Employment professionals recommend that employers keep separate employee files as follows:

1. Solicitation and hiring document file. This file can include candidate solicitation cover letters, a resume, signed employment application and authorizations to obtain references and credit checks, results of any job-related tests, reference confirmation results, offer letter, job description, emergency contact information, employment contract, signed confidentiality agreement, signed assignment agreements, or signed non-compete agreement.

2. Payroll file. Signed W4 tax withholding form and ongoing payroll information.

3. I-9 file. The Department of Homeland Security can request to inspect employer I-9 files at any time. 1-9 documentation must be kept for three years after the hire date or one year after the employment ends, whichever is later.

4. Benefit information file. Healthcare, retirement and incentive-based stock program enrollment and participation records.

5. Performance review file. Quarterly and annual performance records plus other notes, awards, citations, or job-related event or written warnings.

Network It!

How to Select Qualified Advisors and Board Members

By the ninth chapter of this book you know my operating priorities for startup businesses. You must maximize your time and limited resources to bring in cash from customers, investors or lenders. And you need to avoid beginner's mistakes so your company can achieve the 4 Milestones of Financial Safety as quickly as possible.

But while you focus on developing your company's capital resources, it's easy to overlook another form of capital that can speed startup progress. It's social capital.

Starting out on your own should never mean going it alone. Even sole proprietors and part-time entrepreneurs who prefer to work alone can benefit from a thriving ecosystem of advisors, board members, mentors, service professionals and other entrepreneurs. It's all about surrounding yourself with insightful individuals who can help you accomplish more, especially in the months before your company is able to hire permanent staff.

When is the right time to reach out to a circle of social capital for strategic guidance? How about today? Just about every highly accomplished entrepreneur I know can trace their success to a handful of advisors who stepped up to provide contacts, reassurance and shrewd negotiating guidance. They recall how their special advisors "believed in me when no one else did." This chapter will help you find and collaborate with individuals who can help get your company to the "next level" of operating achievement.

Your next action steps:

☐ **Prioritize social capital needs**

The notion of effective networking has morphed during recent years. You can spend a lot of time attracting "friends" and "followers" and never generate cash from your social networking efforts. As a startup entrepreneur, all your social and professional networking affiliations should be purposeful. Favor strategic quality over quantity.

Where do you need the most help? Is it pricing your products or services, fundraising, preparing government grant proposals, or soliciting first customers? How confident are you in creating budgets or projections? What makes you uneasy?

Unless you are facing an immediate cash crisis, invest your time in developing a circle of advisors who can provide direct assistance for the next 18 to 24 months of operations. Start by picking two managerial areas or business disciplines for help; plus try to identify at least one successful entrepreneur who has been in business for over five years to serve as a mentor.

Here's a shortlist of organizations where you can meet business owners for networking purposes: Young President's Organization, Women President's Organization, Rotary Club, MIT Enterprise Forum, TiE, SCORE, and Entrepreneurs Organization. Check out your alma mater for referrals too.

☐ Qualify advisors

Failed business owners often tell me that bad advice accelerated their financial troubles. I hear the following phrases quite often: "I assumed they knew better" or "I trusted him to know more."

Not everyone who offers advice is qualified to do so. It's your job to size up the value, relevance and accuracy of the recommendations given to you by paid and unpaid advisors. Here's a framework that has served me well in the venture finance community.

1. "Been-there done-that" advisors

The best advisors have direct experience in what you want to know or do. Pay attention to them because their advice is likely to be highly valuable to your organization.

If, for example, your goal is to identify a business partner in Europe to distribute your product, ask members of your circle to refer you to another business owner who has already researched, negotiated, planned, funded and successfully commercialized products for the vast European market. Ask the business owner about mistakes, gotchas, unexpected costs and cultural challenges to help you avoid making similar mistakes.

2. "Wired and wise" advisors

Look for advisors who don't have big egos and freely acknowledge when others have far more relevant experience or expertise. Wired and wise advisors listen closely to your needs, ask clarifying questions and then make time-saving referrals to others who are "more active in the space." It's worthwhile to ask these advisors for guidance on the best way to follow up on their referrals too. Be gracious, thankful and thoughtful in how you keep wired and wise advisors in your circle of social capital.

3. **Self-interested advisors**

Whenever I write about the integrity lapses of professional service providers, franchise brokers, self-directed IRA agents, insurance brokers, and commercial real estate agents I get a lot of angry flame mail with lots of exclamation points. It's true that not all service providers misrepresent information to business owners, but certainly enough bend the rules for entrepreneurs to be cautious.

No one will ever watch out for your business or your company's cash as well as you. As you listen to advice from any source, always consider if the advisor has any financial interest that might influence their recommendations. And of course, if someone says "you can't lose," always assume you can.

4. **"Wannabe" advisors**

Entrepreneurs will encounter service professionals and other advisors who genuinely want to help a young company prosper, but lack the expertise to be reliable sources of information. Here's a perfect example of how damaging wannabe advisors can be to unsuspecting entrepreneurs.

A couple of years ago, I received a phone call from a former Wall Street stock broker who convinced a rookie entrepreneur that he could raise millions in funding for his startup clean-tech business. He reached out to me through my column thinking that I could give him some advice on how to raise money for the clean-tech entrepreneur. After a grandiose presentation that made little sense, the stock broker finally admitted to me that he didn't know the first thing about valuing startup companies, angel investors, venture capital funds, term sheet negotiations, Department of Energy grants, etc. But his lack of expertise didn't stop him from charging the clean-tech entrepreneur a $4,000 monthly retainer. What a waste of money!

The company's founder probably assumed that anyone who ever worked on Wall Street knew how to raise money for a technology-oriented startup. Not so. Certainly the entrepreneur was duped, but whose fault was it really? The ex-stock broker who misrepresented his expertise or the entrepreneur who didn't ask the right questions?

The best way to qualify potential advisors—both paid and non-paid—is to ask clarifying questions about their expertise and experience. Ask, "What work have you done recently in X?" "What was the outcome?" "What can I expect in pursuing X with you?" "Tell me about your process and expected timing of your work?" "Can I have a list of references for clients you have served in the last few years?" Listen closely to the answers. Always interview at least three candidates for any professional service assignment.

☐ Set social capital assistance thresholds

Most startup entrepreneurs don't tap their circle of social capital enough to help them clarify strategy or negotiate important agreements. They say they "just had to make a decision on the spot." Really? I can't think of many startup situations that don't allow time to make a few phone calls.

Here's a way to bring some thoughtful discipline to your decision-making. Seek guidance from at least one been-there done-that advisor whenever a decision involves a certain amount of money you can't afford to lose in a new initiative—it could be $1,000 or $10,000. As your business progresses, increase your social capital assistance threshold by thousands or millions of dollars.

☐ Respect advisors' time and position

I can tell a lot about the mindset of an entrepreneur by how he or she asks for help from advisors. Self-involved entrepreneurs who don't yet understand the nuance of productive relationship building measure the value of mentors, board members and other advisors by how fast they turn over contacts—especially funding contacts—for the entrepreneur's direct follow-up.

The real deal is advisors worth knowing won't hand over all their best contacts during a first phone call or meeting. It's up to you to earn their trust. If you plan to raise money from investors in the future, you will hear the expression "get comfortable" quite a lot. If investors can't "get comfortable" with a business plan or the character and capabilities of a company's management team, a deal just won't happen.

☐ Learn how to ask for referrals

To develop a circle of social capital you must learn how to ask for help without awkward hesitation or apology. The request may be as simple as "I'm looking to hire a part-time bookkeeper who can set up and manage QuickBooks. Do you have any ideas or know of someone I can talk to who can provide recommendations?" The more specific you are about your needs, the easier it is for people to help you.

☐ **Communicate achievements**

Your circle of treasured business advisors and mentors is a special asset of your business. In an era of instant communications, it's easy for truly important news to get lost in random tweets and text messages. When your company has achieved an important milestone or sales achievement, share the information with your circle of advisors—both paid and non-paid. This communication is not a press release, but a personal message about your company's advancement. As appropriate, consider informing your circle of your company's next big goals too. When your circle knows what you want to accomplish, they can think creatively and productively about how they can help you succeed.

FAQs

Q. How many times should I call or email a referral without becoming a pest?

A. My general recommendation is to contact a referral no more than three times with at least five days between each attempt. This is the same recommendation I give to entrepreneurs who are pursuing angels and venture capital investors. Be patient. If possible, ask executive assistants and other administrative gatekeepers for guidance on how and when to communicate with a target advisor. Further, don't flag any communication to a target advisor as "top priority" or leave crazed pleas for help on a voice mail message. Your first impression should be professional.

As you develop your business, you won't be treated warmly by every person you solicit for help. Shake off the rejection and don't spend any time second guessing your request. In most cases, the individual's life is just too busy at the moment to help an ambitious entrepreneur. Move forward.

Your First Board of Directors

It amazes me how often I'm asked to be on the board of a startup or early stage company. I'm flattered of course, but most invitations come from startup entrepreneurs who haven't yet asked if I have the time to serve the company or if I have any financial interest in a competitor.

Your first board of directors can be a tremendous asset or a time-consuming liability. High-functioning board members work in a collaborative way. They don't panic when problems surface but provide steady, thoughtful guidance to solve problems quickly and with a minimum of cash loss. Productive board members don't grandstand, manipulate, offend or dominate debate. They listen, observe and speak up only when their questions or comments add to the conversation. And on a good board, the personalities and skills of the various board members mix or "jell" in a productive way.

In contrast, dysfunctional boards don't agree on a company's strategic direction, its funding requirements or when the company might be a good candidate for sale. A dysfunctional board can become a time-consuming liability rather than a productive resource, especially when a company is losing money at a rapid rate.

Experienced board members—especially members of the National Association of Corporate Directors, understand their fiduciary obligations of board service. Board members work for companies, not for entrepreneurs. Further, it is their collective job to represent the interests of all company shareholders and try to "maximize shareholder value." This means that board members may be required to vote in favor of a generous buyout offer even if the founding entrepreneur would rather continue to run the business as an independent entity.

Here are some key duties of corporate board members:

- Approve the issuance of securities including common stock, warrants, preferred stock and stock option grants to employees
- Approve a company's annual business plan and operating budget
- Approve "material" contracts that can have a significant impact on the company's financial status or operating position
- Examine the reasonableness of the company's overall strategic plan of operations
- Mentor key members of the company's management team
- Set limits of executive authority and ensure that the company has reasonable controls in place to protect company assets
- Hire and fire the company's CEO (particularly if the CEO does not own a majority of the company's outstanding voting shares)
- Ensure that the company meets its primary fiscal, legal and regulatory obligations
- Evaluate risks that can cause the company to fail, often called "enterprise risk"

Entrepreneurs should have a practical understanding of what falls outside of a board member's job description. It's not the board's job to solve all business problems. They are not miracle workers. If, for example, you tell board members in the eleventh hour that your company is almost out of cash, don't expect them to be able or willing to connect you to a fast fix of cash. You can, however, expect them to be really annoyed that you didn't do a better job projecting and disclosing your company's cash requirements.

Board member selection is an important decision that involves strategic planning and good judgment. You want to identify board members who have the time and inclination to deliver meaningful value to your company, so that your company does indeed grow in value. You can do this!

Your next action steps:

☐ **Complete a draft business plan**

Before asking business professionals to serve on your new company's board of directors, you should already have a good idea of what you want to accomplish in quantitative terms, what markets you want to enter, and your company's general business model for revenue generation. If an entrepreneur is too vague about the company's strategic objectives and requirements to achieve profitability, prospective board members might decline participation until the entrepreneur has more concrete goals in place.

Extra Startup Intelligence ···

Board members can assume certain financial liabilities for management screwups. For example, if a company fails to pay payroll taxes, board members can become personally liable for the shortfall including interest and penalties. For this reason, many experienced business people turn down board seats until the company has reliable financial systems in place or has raised a certain amount of money to pay company obligations.

···

☐ **Set board composition criteria**

The minimum and maximum size of a corporation's board of directors is usually set at the time of legal formation. Startup boards should not be so big that board functions become unwieldy. Start with a board with no more than one to three independent directors and keep some seats open for potential representatives of investor groups or individuals whose experience and expertise match what you want to do next in business.

☐ **Keep friends and family members at home**

The best board members have independent professional relationships, not personal relationships with founding entrepreneurs. Asking friends and family members to join your company's board of directors will definitely make it harder for you to convince other board members and investors that you are serious about the business of running a business.

☐ **Skip rookie directors**

First-time board members may not know what constitutes good board behavior; experienced board members generally do.

☐ **Seek complementary skills**

A well-balanced board is made up of independent directors, the founding entrepreneur and possibly representatives of the financial community to the extent you raise funds from equity investors. It's not wise to select directors from one field of expertise—for example all successful technologists or all marketing executives.

Independent members of your board of directors should change over time, especially as the scope of your business changes. The same board that will serve your company during its lean pre-revenue period may not be best-suited to oversee a multimillion dollar company pursuing international sales, corporate partnerships, acquisitions and product line extensions.

I'm frequently asked if startup entrepreneurs should ask their accountant or legal counsel to join a first board of directors. My standard response to this question is, "Expand your horizons." Entrepreneurs can already count on their lawyers and accountants for guidance on professional issues. Yes, keep them in your circle of social capital, but focus on attracting board members with the skills and experiences that your company needs to reach the 4 Milestones of Financial Safety with special attention to revenue generation.

☐ **Ask for referrals**

Work your circle of social capital for board candidate recommendations. Talk to other successful business people who have developed independent boards for ideas on how to expand your network. Recently retired executives may look forward to an entrepreneurial opportunity to remain engaged in an industry. Lastly, check out regional executive search firms. Occasionally, search firms may accept stock options in exchange for making first introductions to capable board members.

Extra Startup Intelligence ··

Just because someone you respect recommends a board candidate, doesn't mean that you have to invite the candidate to your board. If a candidate is an intimidating know-it-all, move on to other candidates. You know your own managerial limits—good board members should be able to help you reach beyond those limits without intimidation or needless anxiety. It helps if your board members have a good sense of humor too.

··

☐ **Estimate time commitments**

Startup entrepreneurs should be prepared to advise prospective board members of the approximate number of in-person meetings that will be held each year. Of course, experienced board members understand that there will be times when a company will need additional phone or in-person meetings, especially on time-sensitive issues related to securities transactions.

☐ **Determine compensation package**

Cash-starved companies usually offer prospective board members an annual award of common stock or stock options to compensate them for the time dedicated to board service. All stock-related compensation should vest in one year or less. Highly experienced directors who are willing to roll up their sleeves to help a startup company might expect an equity award of 1% to 4% of a company's outstanding shares plus subsequent annual stock option awards. Once a company reaches a comfortable level of cash flow and profitability, board members may receive a cash fee for board meeting attendance. If a board member is asked to travel on the company's behalf, then the company should provide prompt reimbursement of agreed upon travel-related costs.

☐ **Research board candidates**

Every board member of your company should have an impeccable reputation. Entrepreneurs who expect to raise funds from independent investors should make sure all board members can stand up to professional scrutiny from prospective auditors, investors, government contractors, and grant providers. Research online for any events or issues that might be potentially embarrassing to your company.

Collaborate with board members

Extra Startup Intelligence ···

How can you get the most mileage out of board members? Outside of scheduled board meetings, invite individual board members to brainstorm with you on specific issues. Ask "What if…?" "How would you approach…?" "Are there any partners who can…?" "What's the best way to…?" It is up to you, not board members to initiate these important discussions. When in doubt or in trouble, communicate more, not less with board members.

···

FAQs

Q. **I raised a small amount of money from a local business owner who sits on my board. Now that I am in advanced discussions with a venture capital fund for additional funding, he says that he will invest more money too. Should he be involved in negotiating with the VCs?**

A. It's a positive sign that your first investor has expressed a willingness to invest "along side" the VC fund in the upcoming round. However, his involvement in negotiations is a conflict of interest. As the CEO of your company, it's your job to negotiate deal terms with investors with your company's legal counsel at your side. Your goal is to negotiate the highest possible valuation to minimize dilution to all existing shareholders. Once you have a "term sheet" of agreed deal terms in hand, give it to the first investor for review. As a board member, the investor has a fiduciary obligation to vote what's best for the company, not what's best for any single investor.

Q. **I'm worried that VCs will fire me from my own company. How can this happen?**

A. Concerns about maintaining executive "control" typically come up after an entrepreneur raises one or more rounds of funding from angel investors or venture capital funds. Because angels and VCs typically receive one or more board seats as part of a major funding, the founding entrepreneur can steadily lose voting control of the board of directors and the power to influence a company's strategic direction and management.

Still, the last thing board members and investors ever want to do is sack a company founder. It's emotionally wrenching for company employees, board members and investors. Trust me; investors are much happier scouting for new investments than managing companies through chaotic management transitions.

In many ways, a company's founding CEO is very much like a football quarterback. Investors don't bench top-performing CEOs who "make their numbers."

Questions regarding leadership competence arise when board members face too many money-losing surprises, hear too many excuses, or watch the CEO finger point to everyone else except the person in charge.

Here are a few more recommendations:

- **Choose independent directors before investors do.** Independent directors, who are networked closely to investors, in subtle but meaningful ways, will favor the interests of investors over executive management. My preference is for entrepreneurs to identify and establish good working relationships with one or two highly qualified board members before a first round of capital is raised from angel investors or VCs. Maintaining control of a company is directly related to maintaining the confidence of a majority of board members.

- **Get an employment contract.** From a corporate governance perspective, most CEOs report to the company's board of directors. Employment contracts that are negotiated with a pre-funding board of directors tend to be more lenient to founding entrepreneurs than employment contracts negotiated after funding. However, if a pre-negotiated contract is considered "abusive" in terms of compensation or performance measures, new investors will either renegotiate the terms of the employment agreement as a condition of financing or simply walk away from a funding transaction.

- **Communicate with candor.** Startup and early-stage board members who have built companies of their own or served on other for-profit company boards fully expect there will be unforeseen problems and delays associated with reaching company milestones. What they don't accept is any delay in learning about brewing company problems from management. Entrepreneurs who promise to deliver the bad news just as fast as the good news maintain board member trust.

- **Report all news.** I recommend startup entrepreneurs give board members a biweekly or monthly summary of good news and bad news. It's easy to do and gives board members a higher level of confidence that they know what's going on. This simple report helps prevent board members from overreacting to any single communication of bad news.

- **Watch the numbers.** Experienced board members and certainly investors pay attention to the numbers. They have to in order to meet their fiduciary obligations. Board members will expect to see quarterly and annual budgets, projections and estimates of cash requirements to sustain operations.

Choosing Paid Advisors

There will be times when even the most cash-strapped entrepreneurs should engage attorneys, accountants and other professionals. My preference is to hire specialists rather than generalists. Why? Because specialists understand nuances and can reach conclusions faster with less research. This translates into better service and typically a lower service bill.

You don't need a top attorney to incorporate a business, but you do need one at your side to review big-dollar deals involving intellectual property, joint ventures, real estate, brand licensing, and securities transactions. If you live in a rural area with limited service expertise, search out domain experts in regional metropolitan areas.

When researching service professionals, pay attention to how many years they have been in practice. Some "associates" in professional practices can have 10 years of experience whereas others might be right out of school. Experience and expertise, which are two different things, always rank highest in my service professional hiring decisions. Tenured service professionals are also more likely to have a broader social capital network for you to tap as well.

Your next action steps:

☐ **Interview three candidates**

For all paid service relationships, including marketing, website design, legal, and accounting, interview at least three service candidates. In most cases a first meeting with a service professional will be free of charge, provided that you make clear that the meeting is exploratory in nature. During this meeting you will have the opportunity to learn more about the service attitude of the professional, their special areas of expertise and pricing policy. You will find that when service providers know they are competing for an assignment, they work harder to demonstrate their expertise so you have a better appreciation of their skills before you make a decision. I'm never disappointed.

☐ **Match scale to operating needs**

The size of a service provider's firm should be a factor in your hiring decisions. Large professional service firms that are set up to serve big corporate accounts are just not staffed or priced to serve most startup and early-stage companies. And if you do hire a big firm, you may end up in the hands of the firm's least experienced professionals.

For example, if you intend to launch a promotion campaign to support a sales test in a regional grocery chain, hiring Weiden & Kennedy would be overkill. Weiden & Kennedy specializes in creating cutting-edge advertising for Fortune

500 brands such as Nike, Target, and Electronic Arts. Similarly, you probably don't need to hire a "Big Four" accounting firm such as Deloitte or KPMG to prepare your company's first tax returns.

☐ Avoid fast decisions

It's unwise to hire any service provider, independent contractor or vendor during a first meeting. Ask for a written proposal and take the time to review it. With a written proposal in hand, you are in a strong position to clarify assignment expectations, negotiate better pricing terms and ask questions about instances in which additional fees might be charged.

☐ Just say "no"

Too many startup entrepreneurs over the years have told me that they signed contracts with vendors they didn't like or trust. They ignored their good instincts and allowed high pressure sales representatives to intimidate them into buying products or services that their companies couldn't afford or really need. The best way to manage manipulative sales representatives is to end conversations and email communications as soon as possible. No means no. And certainly, don't waver if someone who is trying to sell you something says, "I think you are making a mistake."

☐ Make the call

If you interview three or more candidates for a project, at least two candidates will not get your business. I always call (not email or text) any professional who I met for a first interview but decided not to hire. This courtesy call is not to negotiate a better price but to establish a positive, professional image for your company in your local business community. It often works out that the candidates that didn't get a first assignment might prove to be the perfect fit for a future project.

☐ Communicate payment timing

Service providers to startup businesses take on high risks of non-payment. They understand that new companies cannot predict cash flow with the same degree of accuracy as larger, more established companies. You can enhance your social capital by being honest with service providers about payment. When you build a reputation for prompt payment, then service providers will work harder for you. And if you can't pay in a timely way, pick up the phone to explain the situation and payment status—long before they call you asking for payment. If you duck payment in an irresponsible way, assume that your best advisors will opt out of your circle of social capital.

FAQs

Q. **Do I need to organize an advisory board? I hear that this is now the preferred way to build credibility. What do you think?**

A. During the first year of a company's operations, change is the only constant day-to-day reality. Concepts that you thought would be the winners when you first formed your company, may be off your priority list after first customer testing. This means that social capital advisors with different levels of expertise and experience will be needed as your plans evolve.

For time management purposes, my preference is to avoid setting up a formal advisory board during the first year of operations. It takes your time and your money to organize meetings to the extent you have to reimburse advisory board members for travel costs. You can derive the same advisory benefits by reaching out to advisors on a less formal basis as you need them.

Another problem with startup advisory boards is accountability. In haste, entrepreneurs sign up big names and hand out generous stock awards before really working through exactly how advisory board members will contribute to a company's growth. Unlike employees and corporate board members, advisory board members really don't have to be accountable to a startup organization. My preference is for entrepreneurs to hand out stock awards for work well done, rather than work that might never happen.

It is true that high growth potential startup entrepreneurs who approach angel investment clubs and VCs assume that an advisory board is a requirement for funding. Here's the real deal. Investors will not base their funding decisions on the caliber of advisory board members. They will, however, be impressed if well-known individuals reached into their pockets to invest in your business. That's a far better demonstration of confidence in your company's growth prospects than simply joining an advisory board.

Of course there are exceptions to every rule. Advisory boards make sense if they help speed revenue generation. They can be useful if the members are genuine representatives of a target customer audience and can help test and fine-tune products and services before market launch. For example, advisory boards can advance medical technology startups to the extent that healthcare professionals have tested and "approved" a new product or service concept.

Q. **I don't have much extra cash to pay an attorney to incorporate my new business. Can I use stock?**

A. Sure you can pay for services with your company's common stock, provided your attorney agrees to this form of payment prior to starting work on your account.

But here's the gotcha—not to you but your attorney. As highlighted in the last chapter, if your company issues stock in exchange for assets or as payment for services rendered, a value must be assigned to the stock for 1099 tax reporting purposes.

Test It!

How to Stress Test Your Business Model and Customer Appeal

Mount Rainier in Washington State is regarded as one of the most treacherous mountains to climb in the United States. At 14,400 feet, it has its own weather patterns and 25 major glaciers—more than any mountain in the lower 48 states. Mount Rainier is so challenging that only about half of the 10,000 or so climbers who try to summit each year are successful. And every year, some climbers die trying.

Entrepreneurship has a lot in common with mountain climbing. It's thrilling and fun. I find that first-time climbers are different from first-time entrepreneurs in how they approach the climb to the top. Novice climbers want to know the "easy" way; entrepreneurs want to know the "fast" way. Unfortunately, the fastest route for entrepreneurs can also be the steepest, hardest, and most dangerous. Any unexpected obstacle can lead to a tragic fall, especially if you are all alone in your endeavor.

Choose the Easiest Way to the Top

I like easy; actually I preach easy. I bet that you've been warned that starting a business is "hard." Well, it is hard and frustrating whenever you have to stop, retrace your steps and start all over again. The journey becomes even harder if you don't have the cash to make a second attempt to "summit."

What route are you laying out for your entrepreneurial journey? The hard way that can overwhelm your personal savings or the easier path of least resistance? If you like easy, you'll love the trauma-saving purpose of this chapter. When you identify glitches and gotchas early in the business incubation process, you can solve them before they lead your company to the entrance of the dead business graveyard.

This chapter will help you:

- Find resource-rich partners to share the expense of starting up your business
- Double-check that your idea can become a viable business

- Pinpoint competitor weaknesses to make it easier for you to target and secure first customers, even take away a competitor's customers

- Avoid big "disconnects" between what you offer and what your customers want

Now let's explore the easiest routes to the top!

$$ Partner to Conserve and Create Cash

First-time climbers gain stability and confidence when they are roped to several more experienced climbers. Similarly, startup companies can advance with less operating risk when they hitch up to one or more established business partners. In the venture finance community, partnership relationships are often referred to as "joint ventures," "strategic alliances," or "strategic partners."

The most desirable kind of business partnerships are what I call "piggyback" relationships. Entrepreneurs benefit most when they partner with established companies that already know the market terrain and can carry more than their share of the load.

Notice that this section received a **$$** because the financial rewards of piggyback partnership relationships are significant. Piggyback relationships can help conserve your company's cash by reducing operating and overhead costs. Or they can accelerate revenue generation by getting your company in front of your partner's distributors and end-customers—saving your company some of the pain associated with hit-or-miss sales solicitations.

Angel investors and VCs think highly of entrepreneurs who pursue partnerships because it is a sign of effective leadership. If you secure a partnership relationship that has meaningful strategic or cost-saving value to your company, mention the achievement on the first page of your business plan.

Where can you find piggyback relationships? Probably right in your home town! It's a matter of being creative and opportunistic. Brainstorm the following questions with mentors, board members, best friends, spouses and other professional colleagues to identify candidates for potential partnerships.

- Can you think of a company, church, warehouse, school or other location that may have some extra space where you can incubate your idea at a low monthly cost or rent free? In my experience, entrepreneurs are more likely to get free space if they make a specific request for a specific period of time—not forever.

- Can you postpone signing a lease for office space or a retail store by incorporating your business operations into another company's existing operations? Can you test your retail concept in a mall kiosk rather than investing in a full scale retail store? Can you provide an established retailer a commission on your product revenues in exchange for counter space?

- Is there a company that already owns certain equipment that you need to develop your products that might not be utilized on a full-time basis?

- Is there a way to speed product research and development by sharing technology, people, or facilities with another company?

- Are there one or more partners who can help you shrink the costs associated with building a "supply chain" for producing your product?

- Can you piggyback onto another company's proprietary distribution network to reach more customers?

- Is there a company that already does business with one of your target customers? Can your product or service be incorporated into their business relationship to speed revenue generation without having to go through the process of introducing your company to decision makers by yourself?

- Can you speed access to larger customers by serving as a sub-contractor on a large government contract? Visit SBA.gov for information on how to become a small business contractor. Read about special opportunities for minority, women and veteran-owned businesses too.

- Can you get your grocery, home improvement, health, or beauty aid product into chain stores through a private label relationship?

- Can you cross-license technology between your company and another company to speed access to your target markets without costly IP challenges? Can you partner with a larger company to tap a larger war chest to fight off IP property litigation or infringement cases?

- Can you partner with one or more complementary websites to reach a wider audience?

- If you are a social entrepreneur, can you flow program revenues and grants through an established non-profit to minimize accounting and administration in exchange for a fixed percentage management fee?

Most startup entrepreneurs assume that joint ventures and strategic partnerships are just for bigger, well-established companies. Actually, corporate executives know that there are many strategic benefits associated with partnering with smaller, more entrepreneurial companies. At the top of the list is innovation. The culture of smaller companies inspires creativity, productivity and problem solving. Smaller companies meet deadlines with less hierarchical interference so that new products can be developed and rolled out faster than most large corporations. Plus, small businesses generate approximately 13 times the number of patent awards per employee as large corporations.

As you consider different partnership opportunities, prioritize what types of relationships will help you obtain more cash-paying customers or spend less cash during the first two years of operations. Pursue several initiatives all at once. Don't get discouraged if a partnership doesn't emerge on your time schedule. Keep at it. Remember this: you can't get what you want if you don't ask for it.

Listen to Your Target Customer

What's the cost of guessing what customers are willing to pay for? It may be more than your initial investment in packaging, inventory, promotions, trademark registrations and more. If you make too many mistakes during the first two years in business, you may have a hard time convincing investors that you are a good steward of their money. Investors do understand that entrepreneurs will face unexpected problems in any product or service rollout. These issues are mostly forgivable. However investors won't write checks to overly confident entrepreneurs who don't bother to test their ideas in some way before a commercial launch.

Your next action steps:

☐ **Understand target market motivations**

Do your target customers really want to buy your type of product or service? Notice my emphasis on the word "want"—it's a more powerful purchasing motivation than "need."

Most Americans don't *need* to buy donuts but they do. Dunkin Donuts, Krispy Kreme and thousands of independent donut shops across the country prosper because Americans want to buy something that is sweeter and more satisfying than a low fat, 100% whole-grain bagel. Investors reason that it takes a lot of cash and advertising to convert "should buy" customers into "want to buy" customers.

As such it's crucial to select your target market with precision. For example, a startup organic snack baker can make an impressive, highly quantitative case that the majority of American adults need to eat lower calorie, chemical-free snacks. But is the baker's target market all overweight Americans or is it health food lovers who already are passionate about eating organic foods? It's the latter. While the demographic numbers are far smaller, the easiest way to prove there is active, ready-to-buy demand for organic snack food is to reference existing organic food buyers.

☐ Understand market size dynamics

Is the general market demand for your type of product or service growing? Ideally, you want to compete in markets that are growing. You've probably heard the expression that "a rising tide lifts all boats." In a marketplace that is growing there is an ever rising tide of active customers who can generate enough business for large industry competitors as well as new entrants. Conversely, shrinking markets make it tough for startups to succeed. Inevitably, cash-rich competitors will lower prices to maintain market share. And as we know from Chapter 3, gross profit margins suffer whenever entrepreneurs have to engage in a price war with competitors.

Extra Financial Empowerment ·····································

Markets that are growing more than 10% to 20% per annum make it easier for entrepreneurs to raise capital from investors. A market growth rate of 40% or higher is the kind of market climate that excites angel club members and VCs. More mature markets that may be nearing the end of a market life-cycle with less than 1% growth rates are not fertile ground for investment capital, at least from "sophisticated" investors.

·····································

☐ Test end-customer appeal

Is your beloved hobby a good candidate to become a viable business? Is your cool website concept a service that can capture customer loyalty in a profitable way? Sometimes what you want to do most in business may not be what customers want to pay for. Who's right? The customer of course! When entrepreneurs don't listen attentively to customer preferences, they end up wasting a lot of time, money and opportunity. This is when stubborn determination can be an entrepreneur's most destructive managerial trait.

During the concept testing phase of business development I tend to favor one-on-one conversations with target customers rather than focus group meetings. It's too easy for one group member to act like the alpha dog and influence or silence other participant feedback.

The key to purposeful research is determining what you want to learn in advance. What are your priorities? For example, is your purpose to test product price sensitivity, product performance or how your concept matches up to top competitors? To get the most information from test candidates, avoid long written surveys because they rarely provide the kind of detailed insights that are most helpful. Also, consider asking test candidates to weight their responses using a 1 to 10 point scale. This way, you won't give a response more or less consideration than the test candidate meant. Lastly, try not to educate testers about the purpose of your product or service before asking questions.

Here are some questions to ask during customer feedback sessions:

- How did you use or test this product? For how long? Did it work on the first try?
- Did it work differently than you expected? What were you hoping for?
- What worked right? What didn't work right?
- How would you improve the product or service?
- How can we make what we do more convenient for you?
- Who do you think would be most inclined to buy this product or service?
- What is the best attribute/characteristic/feature of the product or service?
- Would you like to place an order today?

Extra Startup Intelligence ···

Seek feedback from prospective customers who are not friends or family members. Friends and family members will be influenced by their desire to support your dream. They also probably know too much about your startup to give you an unbiased view of what should be improved prior to commercial launch.

···

☐ **Test for service glitches**

Evaluate every possible way a customer may interact with your business. Ideally, enlist one or two other people to do this important evaluation of your business operations. Select testers who represent different age groups, levels of technology proficiency or gender. Ask the testers to give you a report of what is good, bad, didn't work, or needs improvement about your company's operations, customer service, website, and more. Pay attention to these reviews because most product, service, website and customer service functions tend to be overly influenced by company convenience rather than customer convenience. Study the results and try not to dismiss recommendations too quickly by saying, "We can't do that because…"

☐ **Adapt to customer feedback**

I've never worked with a company, nor built a company of my own, in which the original startup vision was not substantially improved after customer focus groups, product trials or "beta" testing. As you continue to test and refine your first products and services with prospective customers, consider the following questions:

- What can we eliminate from a product or service product line to reduce the ongoing costs of production, inventory warehousing and management?

- Do we offer customers too many choices that may detract from the easy, satisfying experience of buying from our company? Is the product or service that we highlight as "our best" the same thing that our target customers view as "our best?"

- What words did target customers use most to describe what they wanted most from a product or service company like ours? Do these words match our brand promise? Do these words match highlighted words and headers on our website and other customer-oriented literature?

- What can we do to make it easier for a customer to (i) make a decision to buy our product; and (ii) use our product successfully? What can we do to improve our instructions, packaging, website or service features to match customer questions?

- Do our target customers understand how we are different and better than our primary competitors?

- How can we improve our online ease of access? What metrics can we use to monitor the ongoing effectiveness of our website for prospective customer engagement, customer service, and brand building? Do we deliver online what customers want most? Is our online presence optimized for mobile devices? Do we utilize different landing pages to help get online traffic to desired information faster?

Extra Startup Intelligence

What's the primary purpose of your company's website? Is it to educate visitors? Is it to boost traffic to maximize ad revenue potential? Is it to solve customer service problems? Is it to prompt visitors to buy on impulse? Is it to direct traffic to other websites to maximize referral fees? Is it to answer potential customers' most common questions—like hours of operation or driving instructions? Whatever it is, try to do it on your site home page without annoying Flash graphics!

☐ Test two key financial assumptions $$

Perhaps the most costly mistake startup entrepreneurs make is scraping together just enough funds to "start" a business, but not raising enough funds to keep the new company's doors open for months and years to come. It's like starting out on a month-long mountain hike with only three days of food and supplies.

Conduct some "what if" spreadsheet analysis to expose weaknesses in your business model assumptions. Start by determining what amount of cash will be required to:

- Complete and test a product or service prototype
- Secure a first paying customer
- Achieve monthly positive cash flow
- Achieve year-end profitability

When you know exactly how much money you need to achieve certain milestones, you will make smarter spending decisions. You also will be able to answer questions from prospective lenders and investors with less guesswork.

Next, test the amount of quarterly sales that you project during your first two years in business. How many new customers does this represent each quarter? Compare your company's projected rate of new customer generation to your resources. Is it a practical result? Who will secure these customers? How much time will it take? If you underestimate the amount of time it takes to secure new customers, the amount of cash you will need to support your company's actual operations will be considerably higher! I prefer the opposite scenario—it's better to overestimate the amount of time it takes to secure first customers and enjoy the use of some extra cash.

Business Model Basics

A "business model" is a popular term that is used in business schools and in the venture finance community to help students and entrepreneurs describe the flow of payments from customers to product or service suppliers. Business models should be logical and easy to understand. Your job is to test your company's business model to make sure your company will have the operating capacity to attract and serve an ever increasing number of customers...and get paid for it.

If you are planning to raise capital from angel investment clubs or venture capital funds, be prepared to describe your business model with precision. You should be able to describe how cash will flow to your company, preferably with industry-leading gross profit margins (Chapter 3). This is not the time to talk about the cool features of your company's primary products and services.

Here's another fine point related to business models. Investors care about making money. They will ask you questions about how *your company* will make money and how *investors* will make money from owning an equity stake in your business. Know the difference. Revisit Chapter 1 for a brushup on the profit motivations of investors.

Your next action steps:

☐ **Explore different business model options**

Some business models are straightforward and rely on a traditional exchange of products or services between one seller and one buyer, like a lawn care service or a restaurant. Other business models, like Groupon or PayPal are more complex and require considerable cooperation and systems integration among various partners and vendors plus a high level of brand trust to succeed.

Over time, businesses may change their business model to adapt to market trends. Last century, traditional magazines and print newspapers generated revenues from advertising, subscriptions and the occasional sale of mailing lists. This century, publishers have to be more creative in order to maintain revenues in an era of free online content.

Here are some common business models:

- **Refill business model**

  The economic value of a refill business model, sometimes called "razor-razor blade" business model, is easy. Companies develop a long-term revenue-generating relationship with an individual or business by pricing a primary gadget or device at a relatively low entry cost. Then, in order to continue using the primary product, customers have to purchase higher profit margin refill items.

  This business model is used in a broad range of consumer product categories including printers, coffee makers, water filters, game consoles, and more. This business model is risky if first customers don't use the product enough to require frequent purchase of replacement components. The upside to this business model is the opportunity to create strong brand loyalty and minimize customer interest in competing options. Customers rationalize that since they have already make a considerable investment in the primary item, they don't want to waste money buying into another razor-razor blade system.

  From a business valuation standpoint, refill business models get high valuation marks because they can lead to predictable future revenue generation. These businesses can also earn valuation bonus points to the extent that they know exactly who their customers are, where they live, and how long they have been loyal to the brand.

- **Transaction fee model**

  Companies that employ a transaction fee business model charge a fee or commission for each use of a company's proprietary technologies, platforms, or other assets. Some transaction fee businesses bring together buyers and sellers such as financial services companies, sales representatives, real estate brokers, crowdfunding sites, auction sites, product distributors, transaction processing services or vacation rental services.

The biggest challenge to entrepreneurs is to raise enough capital to build a "best in breed" service infrastructure that can support a high volume business. And, of course once the systems are built, the business has to incur substantial marketing costs or partner with established businesses in order to attract enough customers to support ongoing business operations. For personalized, service-oriented transaction fee businesses such as real estate sales, the challenge to entrepreneurs is to be a highly disciplined manager of a business with "feast or famine" cash flow.

- **Subscription or membership model**
Subscription model businesses typically charge customers a flat fee to use a product or service on a monthly, quarterly or annual basis. I like subscription business models for startup companies because customers typically pay upfront in full before utilizing a company's services. Ideally, customers are so satisfied with the service that they will automatically renew at the end of the subscription term without promotional incentives.

The problem with subscription services for startup companies is once a customer pays upfront, it can be challenging for entrepreneurs to measure customer satisfaction with a service. Unless entrepreneurs expressly ask subscribers for feedback, they won't know if customers are satisfied until they are prompted to renew the service at the end of a specific term. As such, the percentage rate of service renewal becomes a more important indicator of long-term business viability than the rate of new member growth. Entrepreneurs who intend to raise capital from investors will need to present compelling service renewal statistics to gain investor support.

- **"Per-seat" model**
A close cousin of the subscription business model is what is called a "per-seat" business model. Companies in the enterprise software industry often charge their business clients a monthly, quarterly or annual fee based on the number of end-users, not the number of corporate entities served. LinkedIn, for example, charges corporations and executive recruiters an annual license fee of over $8,000 per end user for its

LinkedIn Recruiter service. The more users within a corporation, the more revenue for LinkedIn. The primary advantage of a per-seat fee structure is revenuc predictability. Even if certain individual users don't actively use the software or service, the company still gets paid based on the availability of the service for use.

- **"Freemium" model**

Companies that employ a freemium business model provide a certain amount of free products or services to customers to entice them to buy into a higher level of paid products or services. This type of business model can help reduce initial customer resistance to buying products or services from a company that is not yet recognized or respected in an industry or community.

There are risks to freemium business models. The first is that customers are so satisfied with the free service that they have no motivation to upgrade their account to paid services. This situation places freemium companies on the fast track to business failure. The second risk is that a company's active customers end up paying a super premium for products or services in order to subsidize all other freemium account activity. This situation could make a company more vulnerable to customer loss to lower priced competitors. To minimize these risks, entrepreneurs have to limit free trials or set specific end dates for free service.

- **Advertisement/sponsor-supported model**

Magazines, newsletters, online content providers, arts groups, documentary film producers, television networks, local community groups, and trade conference operators support business operations through paid advertising or sponsorship fees. In most cases, the amount of revenues generated from advertisers is based on the size and demographic profile of the audience who may see the advertisement. Other factors that influence advertising and sponsorship rates includes the nature of the specific advertising vehicle and how well the advertisement shows off the brand—known as the quality of the "branding experience." A right column text ad is considered a lower quality branding vehicle than a "pre-roll" video advertisement.

The advantage of an advertisement model is it can be a relatively easy way to generate business revenues, particularly for online content providers who sign up for an ad network service such as ValueClick Networks, 24/7 Real Media, Yahoo Network, Specific Media, Google Ad Network, Microsoft Media Networks or others. These companies manage all aspects of soliciting advertisers and processing payments to online entrepreneurs. However, with growing competition among ad networks, the rates paid to content publishers continue to fall—even as low as $2 per thousand. Ad rates for video content and other premium quality branding experiences typically generate higher rates per thousand.

Another risk to entrepreneurs who rely on an advertisement-only business model is the challenge to create enough audience traffic in the first months in business to sustain growing operations. It's tempting for entrepreneurs to add gimmicks that boost traffic but dilute or muddy the website's brand promise. Seeking advance payments through advertising sponsorships may help mitigate these problems, but the time it takes to meet and persuade key decisions makers in media buying firms, advertising agencies and corporate headquarters may be excruciatingly long for most startup companies. It's easier for them to allocate sponsorship dollars to established companies with a built-in audience.

- **Brand, trademark or IP licensing model**
  Sometimes entrepreneurs can make more money by licensing their intellectual property to established companies that already have all the systems to produce, market, and collect payments from end customers than doing it all themselves. With most licensing partnerships, entrepreneurs don't have to raise a lot of startup capital, obtain office space, manage staff or solve nuisance problems that are a part of every company's day-to-day existence. Cash flow comes back to the entrepreneur in the form of a fixed-fee royalty on each product sold.

  The primary risk of licensing to entrepreneurs is that the licensee doesn't adequately promote the product or technology within a geographic territory or industry, maintain the quality and image of a licensed brand trademark, or pay royalties on time.

☐ Test business model participant motivations

Some businesses are really easy to understand—like a hair salon. Other business models are more complex and dependent on other companies to serve customers and generate revenues.

The most reliable way to test a business model is to list or graph every type of individual or entity or "business model participant" that will play a role in the process of producing, distributing, serving or collecting end-customer payments for your company. It's not good enough to just *assume* various business model participants will want to work with your company, you have to test it.

Consider the following questions as you develop and test your company's business model and business plan. These are the kinds of questions I ask entrepreneurs when reviewing business plans for investment due diligence purposes:

- Why is each business model participant financially motivated to work with or buy from your company? What is the nature of their financial motivation—is it to make more money or reduce operating costs? Exactly, how much money can each participant make or save by working with your company? Is it enough for the participant to really care about?

- Does the participant have minimum financial requirements for doing business with your organization? For example, most buyers in national chain retail stores have minimum gross profit margin hurdles to qualify new products for shelf placement consideration. Similarly, companies that distribute products to hospitals, grocery chains, drug store chains and other kinds of business networks have minimum unit sales expectations they use to justify allocating warehouse space and other company resources to a new product.

- What other strategic benefits will each participant gain from doing business with your company as compared to other business options?

- Will the participant have to incur out-of-pocket costs (equipment investments, employee training, etc.) in order to work with your company as a partner, producer, or distributor? How can you reduce these upfront costs?

- Will the participant have to replace a long-standing business relationship in order to work with your company? If so, how might the competitor defend its turf?

- Does the target participant require special packing, shipping, unique product coding, anti-theft devices, or other non-standard operating requirements? Does the participant have additional corporate safeguards or warranties for international production?

- Does the participant require additional insurance, a minimum company net worth, a personal guarantee from the company's owners or other criteria to start a new business relationship?

- What other obstacles may exist to securing participant buy-in?

- A common challenge to startup entrepreneurs is predicting just how fast they can set up relationships with key business model participants in order to start serving customers. If your business model requires prospective partners or key participants to change their operations or incur considerable cash startup costs, try to prove the value of your proposed business relationship by starting with a small test initiative.

☐ **Test business model payment risks**

Testing the flow of customer payments will help you uncover any gotcha issues that might affect the speed and certainty of revenue collection. Here are some questions to consider:

- When will a customer be billed for services?

- Who will pay the bill? What are some product quality and customer service issues that may cause customers to stop payment for legitimate reasons? What are some reasons why customers may try to avoid payment?

- Who will physically or virtually collect the bill? What is the cost for payment processing? If you are using a payment processing company, what is their motivation to be accurate and timely in payment processing? How can your company confirm the accuracy of reported transaction activity?

- Do any elements of the projected flow of payments to your company rely on other parties investing in new accounting systems or payment systems? Have these systems been adequately tested?

- How are international customer payments processed? Is there a risk of currency devaluation?

- Can you contractually penalize customers or payment processing intermediaries for non-payment or slow payment?

- What are some other opportunities for fraud or theft in payment processing?

- What are the cash flow implications if a partner/customer holds back invoice payments for any period longer than 30 days?

Size Up Your Weakest Competitors

The title of this section is not a typo. From a tactical perspective, charting the strengths and weaknesses of the market loser is just as important as charting the strengths and weaknesses of the market leader. Here's why.

The 1st Milestone of Financial Safety is revenue generation. Given this strategic emphasis on fast revenue generation for business survival, doesn't it make sense to pursue the "low hanging fruit" in your target market first? I think so. It is likely to be far easier and less expensive to lure a disgruntled customer from a mediocre competitor than a happy customer from a well-managed competitor.

My approach to competitive "landscape" research for business concept testing is multi-dimensional. Very rarely does a startup have a truly superior technical or concept advantage that will give an entrepreneur enough time to win a market before well-funded competitors catch up. This is why I encourage entrepreneurs to evaluate their competitive landscape from a broader range of variables—not just product features and benefits.

The added value of conducting a thorough assessment of your competition is to check off a major requirement of business plans written for lenders and investors, which is the subject of the companion book, *Business Plans on Purpose*.

Your next action steps:

☐ **Explore market loser weaknesses**
Research and identify at least one competitor who is vulnerable or losing market share in your industry or geographic region. What are the reasons for customer defections? Poor product or service performance? An uncool brand? Changing management? Bad press? Loss of key distributors or retail partners? Patent expiration? Other factors? Once you know your weakest competitors, think through how you can entice them to shift loyalty to your company.

☐ **Highlight brand differences**
One of the most overlooked opportunities for competitive differentiation is brand messaging. Do all of your competitors look the same and say the same things? It's hard for a ncw markct cntrant to stand out on a store shelf or online if consumers confuse your brand with others. Compare your competition's tag lines, brand claims, packaging, website color schemes and brand positioning. Look for opportunities to communicate with customers in a fresh and distinctive way.

☐ **Explore strategic weaknesses**
No competitive landscape ever stands still. This is especially true of technology-oriented companies in which product features can become obsolete or copied quickly in the marketplace. Instead of just looking at your competition's product or service features, evaluate issues or roadblocks that would make it difficult for them to update or adjust their business model, production methods or distribution alliances.

Extra Startup Intelligence ······································

Larger companies that are losing market share may want to one day license or private label your company's technology advantage or buy your company. Explore the opportunities with your board members and other advisors.

··

☐ **Compare pricing and loyalty**

Create a list of your company's competitors by pricing and, if relevant, promotional practices. You can gain a higher purpose understanding of your competitive landscape by exploring why one or more price leaders are able to maintain their price advantage. Is it because of genuine product superiority and brand loyalty? Or are their "sticky" customers somewhat complacent or unaware of better value alternatives?

☐ **Brainstorm potential competitors**

Entrepreneurs often underestimate how fast smart business concepts are copied in the marketplace. They say, "We have no competition" or "No one offers a similar product or service in the marketplace." Even if you truly believe you don't have any competition, the situation won't last forever once your hot idea catches on. Eventually even the most staid industry competitor who seems locked into doing business an old school way, will wake up to marketplace realities.

Consider the following two questions: What competitors have the most to lose by your success? What competitors might logically enter the market in the future? Make a list of companies that may follow your lead or copy your most lucrative business initiatives. Don't be shy. Again, the upside of listing potential big name competitors is the strong likelihood that they can become lucrative piggyback partners in the future or the ultimate buyer for your business.

☐ **Compare distribution strategies**

Another way to evaluate the competitive landscape of an industry or region is to analyze how products or services are distributed to end-customers. While the Internet can provide direct sales opportunities for entrepreneurial companies, not all startups can thrive without securing key distributors or industry alliances. If relevant, how do your primary competitors deliver their products or services to end-customers? Are there certain distribution paths that are already contractually secured by competitors? Are there emerging partners who can help your company reach a broader base of customers? Think through the opportunities and road blocks.

☐ **Pull it all together**

Review the results of your multidimensional competitive analysis. Where can you compete in the marketplace with the least amount of competitive resistance? Once you identify these opportunities you are ready to test the appeal of your products or services with target customers.

FAQs

Q. **I like your idea about working with partners. Am I better off approaching big companies or small companies?**

A. Partnership proposals that are most likely to get serious consideration by corporations offer meaningful economic and strategic benefits to *both* parties. Think carefully about a list of partners that might benefit most from your technology, product or market idea. Also consider the size of the opportunity in relationship to the size of your potential corporate partner. Approaching a Fortune 500 company with a billion dollar revenue base with an idea that may, at best, generate $10 million in revenues won't get any return phone calls.

Here are a few other tips to soliciting corporate partners. If your idea's primary value to a corporate partner is cost savings, identify the names of general managers and senior finance officers for first solicitations; otherwise target managers at the vice president level or higher in the corporate hierarchy. If you don't have specific contact names, seek out senior officers in "new business development" or "corporate strategic planning." Provided you are friendly, executive level administrative assistants can help guide you through a corporate maze. Lastly, always hold off on disclosing the details of important technologies to potential partner candidates until you have filed at least a provisional patent application at the U.S. Patent and Trademark office.

Q. **My wife is eager to start a new business with me using some bonus money we got from my last tour in the military. I'm still not sure people will pay us enough to cover our costs. What should we do—just start and see what happens?**

A. I bet it is extremely tempting to "just get going" and as you say, "see what happens." But if you have already tested your concept with prospective customers and can't layout a practical "path to profitability" you already know what will happen—you will lose money!

As a veteran, you can try to overcome any short fall in your company's initial working capital by taking out a loan through the Small Business Administration's Patriot Express Loan Program. The SBA makes it easy for veterans to obtain funds for startup research, equipment, inventory, business expansion and other general working capital needs. Plus, the SBA promises veterans fast loan processing and the lowest interest rates offered to business owners.

But just because you may be able to tap extra cash with relative ease from your savings or from the SBA, doesn't mean that it is worth doing. Many veterans and small business owners misunderstand the language of a "SBA-backed loan guarantee." Commercial banks that offer SBA-backed loans to small business owners can call on the federal government for loan payment if the small business borrower defaults. But that doesn't mean that borrowers are off the hook for loan repayment. SBA loans require borrowers and possibly their spouses to personally guarantee loan payment. It's a big obligation to pay personally if a business cannot generate enough cash flow to pay the loan interest and principal on time.

I assume that the purpose of your new business is to make money, not lose money. If your startup idea involves more cash than you can afford to lose, don't go forward. Go back to basic training and explore where you can improve your business strategies, products and pricing. The SBA and Veteran's Administration offer classes for veterans. I often teach pro bono classes for veterans so maybe I'll see you there!

Q. **I've done a lot of customer testing and have improved my product thanks to the feedback I received. But when I start out, I'll be the little guy against some monster size companies. Am I crazy to think that I can win?**

A. No you are not at all crazy to be ambitious. I firmly believe that within every new startup is another David and Goliath story. We all know the tale of how a fearless, seemingly puny challenger outsmarts the monster competitor. On the battlefield, David takes his sling and selects a pebble that will penetrate the one place where the mighty giant is most vulnerable. The pebble reaches its target and Goliath crashes to the ground in defeat.

Whenever you ever feel overmatched by the industry brute remember that your "monster" competitors have weaknesses. You can find them! Also, pay close attention to the action steps in Chapter 8 and Chapter 9. It's easier to fight a tough battle with capable "been-there done-that" advisors, board members, independent contractors and employees at your side.

Launch It!

How to Secure New Customers with Confidence

Does this chapter subject intimidate you? It shouldn't. Talking to customers should be the most enjoyable part of your work day. After all, you get to share information about what you love doing.

Even though I come from a finance background, I teach a lot of workshops on how to pursue new customer relationships. I don't call these workshops "sales training" because entrepreneurs don't identify at all with the prospect of "selling someone." I certainly don't! It diminishes the spirit of why entrepreneurs go into business in the first place—to serve, create, build, heal, solve, soothe, or help someone in a meaningful way.

I know that most first-time entrepreneurs worry about being perceived as pushy when talking to customers. But that's not possible when you talk about your company's accomplishments and capabilities in an honest and enthusiastic way. During my workshops, I provide a playful, supportive setting for entrepreneurs to practice talking about what they do best. Pretty soon workshop participants realize that there is nothing to dread about "evangelizing" their companies to individuals or businesses that can benefit from their innovations and expertise. Actually, it becomes a lot of fun.

In this chapter, you will learn how to focus your sales and marketing efforts on initiatives that are worth your attention as well as what types of initiatives usually slow down sales progress. Unfortunately, too many first-time entrepreneurs struggle because they don't approach their sales and marketing efforts with precision. And when sales don't come in as entrepreneurs expect, their knee-jerk reaction is to do two things: first, they expand their target market to appeal to more potential customers and second, they spend more money on marketing. The approach is flawed because marketing messaging to the masses becomes too vague—the opposite of what's required to encourage first customers to take fast action.

Your next action steps:

☐ **Ditch debilitating excuses**

"I'm afraid of being turned down." "I'm afraid he won't like my designs." "I'm afraid of failing at my dream." If you believe in the quality of your product or service, then you have nothing to fear. Success in business is not defined by obtaining orders from 100% of the individuals or businesses you target, but obtaining enough customer orders—perhaps just 5% to 10% of your total solicitations—to help you reach the 4 Milestones of Financial Safety.

☐ **Build customer relationships**

Look back at Chapter 3. Especially if you operate a service business, your company's financial valuation will be based on the nature of your company's customer *relationships*. Notice that I did not write "revenues" or "sales." Customer relationships represent far more than the numbers that are reported on a company's income statement. Relationships involve people and how they *feel* and what they *want*.

Can you create successful customer relationships? Sure you can. Just treat your customers the same way you treat your close friends. You listen, collaborate, adapt, and enjoy doing things together. You smile, ask questions, and care about the person's happiness and satisfaction. It's not rocket science.

☐ **Use "hard times" to your advantage**

As a business owner, you can't afford to think that there is ever a "bad time" to solicit new customer relationships. Actually, I think recessions are the very best time to solicit new business relationships. Why? Because while your competitors wait for "the market to turnaround" you can be out creating new opportunities with less competitive interference.

$$ ☐ **Prioritize customer targets**

To speed cash generation from new customer relationships, prioritize the kinds of customers that are "worth" targeting first, second and third. For example, is your objective to take customers away from existing competitors or capture customers at the point when they first buy into your product or service category? The answer to this basic question will affect your company's marketing initiatives, website content, customer solicitation strategies and pricing promotions.

Consider the following factors to help you prioritize and plan your customer solicitation efforts:

Prioritizing Your Customer Solicitation Efforts

Factors that make it easier for entrepreneurs to start a dialog with prospective customers:

1. High degree of customer "want"
2. High level of dissatisfaction with existing alternatives or industry competitors

Factors that speed cash generation:

1. Short length of time to make a purchase decision
2. Ability to pay on time

Factors that reduce ongoing cash outlays for marketing, advertising and customer solicitation:

1. Low average cost to solicit and acquire a target customer
2. High potential for repeat business
3. High potential for customers to communicate satisfaction to like-customers

---

☐ Target "customer communities"

Add precision to your solicitation efforts by grouping prospective customers into what I call "customer communities." Customer communities are groups of individuals who define themselves in terms of their favorite activities, life style, health status and family priorities. They say "I'm a cancer survivor," "I'm a grandmother," "I'm a horse owner," "I'm a scuba diver," or "I'm a business owner."

By targeting a customer community, you can adapt your talking points to community priorities, create more precise website landing pages, and explore ways to add extra services that will excite your target community audience. Over time, companies that target and serve customers in defined communities can gain a reputation for being "the best," "the favorite," or the "#1 provider." Pretty soon, the community generates business for the entrepreneur through enthusiastic referrals whenever someone asks, "Do you know someone who does…?"

During your first year in business, choose two or three specific customer communities to focus on. For example, a photographer could target business executives who need headshots, pregnant women who want to commemorate their pregnancies, engaged couples seeking wedding portraits, and ad agencies that want original photography for their clients.

Research can help the photographer choose which customer community is most representative of the fundamental attributes of valuable customer relationships

(Chapter 3) that are "worth" pursuing. After completing his research, the photographer strongly favors the executive community because of high local business demand for executive photos for websites, social network sites, brochures, annual reports, speaking engagement announcements and press kits. He also reasons that corporations are not price sensitive and are likely to be repeat customers. And he perceives that executives *want* more up-to-date, good-looking professional photos, but don't know a trusted resource that specializes in the service.

While the photographer's business may serve many other types of customers, all of the photographer's cash outlays and active customer solicitation efforts are geared to securing customers within the top priority target community. The photographer's weekly call list—discussed later in this chapter—consists of executive community targets. The photographer's local networking activities are more focused too—he attends events where he is likely to talk to business owners and business managers in larger corporations. He knows exactly what he will say to community members because he knows more about what they want and how they want to be served. This is the way the photographer will soon become #1 in the customer community—because no other photographer will deliver this service better or more often.

Extra Financial Empowerment ···

Certain types of businesses that sell innovative technologies can use customer community marketing to build a highly desirable "network effect." As highlighted in Chapter 3, businesses receive valuation bonus points when they build a network of customers or consumers that are inter-dependent on a product, a technology, a distribution service or other business attribute to function. Sometimes this dependence occurs simply because "everyone" in a community uses just one product or service supplier.

···

☐ **Consider credibility**

Is there a customer in your industry or region that would make it easier for you to develop other customer relationships because of their reputation or fan following? Think about it—who are they?

Extra Financial Empowerment ···

While securing a big name, highly influential customer may lead to easier future revenue generation, a startup can't survive if too many big name customers receive margin-killing discounts. Sometimes, it's better for startup entrepreneurs to secure several smaller, profitable customer relationships before going for the big-name customer.

···

☐ Dedicate time all the time

If your business does not yet have any customers, then you must devote the majority of your time—at least four full days a week—to soliciting new customer relationships. Entrepreneurs who struggle to generate sales tend to prioritize their work week the opposite way—they spend the majority of their time on PR, social media initiatives, Internet searches, or administrative tasks even though none of these activities represent the fastest way to cash-generating customer relationships.

Extra Financial Empowerment ···

Freelance workers, consultants, contractors and other types of project-oriented entrepreneurs make a big mistake every time they stop soliciting new business because they are "too busy serving existing customers." Business is about change. Projects end, budgets get cut, natural disasters interrupt everyday operations, and so on. Even if you think you have "enough business" today, you have to schedule time every week to solicit new customer relationships to ensure that you don't ever run out of customers.

··

☐ Develop a target customer contact list

Developing new customer relationships can mean making direct sales to end users or selling to other entities such as distributors or website partners who can connect you to end users. Start your target list by researching and organizing the names and contact information for 10 to 20 customers within your selected customer communities. If you sell to businesses, refer to social media, industry associations, websites, and company press releases to mine the names and titles of top managers.

Why 10 to 20? The absolutely least productive way to solicit new customer relationships is to research one target, then contact the target; research one target, then contact the target. A better way is to research 10, then call or contact 10. For investment banking work, I used this disciplined strategy to contact a lot of people within a short period of time to raise funds for businesses or sell businesses. More recently, I've used this approach to help raise funds for non-profits or other social enterprise development initiatives. After you've worked through your first target customer list, research and develop another one. Try it! You'll find that it's easy and will help you accomplish a lot each day.

Extra Startup Intelligence ···

Should you include the U.S. government on your target solicitation list? Possibly. By law, federal government agencies set aside billions in government contracts to award to small businesses.

Veterans, women and minorities who are U.S. citizens and own a majority (51%+) ownership stake in a small business get certain priorities in contract awards, provided that their ownership stake is "certified." There are certification services in every state plus national resources like the Women's Business Enterprise Council. No single certification agent covers every type of government contracting opportunity so it is important to choose a certification service that best matches the government agencies you want to sell to. For more information, visit www.SBA.gov.

···

☐ **Develop a referral contact list**

Create a list of 10 to 20 individuals who may be able to help you brainstorm new opportunities for new customer generation. Your purpose in talking to individuals for referral purposes should be genuine. Do not use these conversations as a backhand way to ask for orders. Also, avoid asking referral sources for new business opportunities just because your company is "desperate" for business. Give people a better reason to refer prospective customers to your company—like their friends and business colleagues will be delighted with your service.

☐ **Make the calls**

Start your daily routine by closing the door to your office and turning your phone and computer to mute. One by one, contact individuals on your direct customer contact list and your referral contact list. Don't stop for coffee breaks. Don't stop to look at text messages. And don't stop to look at email until you have contacted at least five target customers and five referrals every day. You will be amazed at how your solicitation efforts can produce exponential growth in your company's customer base. Your enthusiasm for pursuing new customer relationships will increase too.

I have a friend who implemented my daily call system to help turnaround his business. Once he prioritized his customer targets and made it a daily priority to contact them, he booked more new business. He called his success in soliciting new customers an "orgasmic high." When you focus on doing just a few things well, business can be a lot of fun…and satisfying.

☐ **Master project proposal writing**

The time to learn about customer preferences and potential areas of discord is not after you have done the work, but before you start the job. Detailed written proposals give prospective customers one more opportunity to give you valuable information about their product and service delivery preferences. Given the fast pace of everyone's workday, it's too easy for misunderstandings to occur during short telephone conversations and meetings. Create one basic work proposal that can be adapted with time-saving ease to different customer situations. Revisit Chapter 6 to make sure your work proposals include all the terms and conditions that can help you get paid on time.

☐ Phone and meet with purpose

Before calling, emailing, connecting or meeting with prospective customers, take a few minutes to write down the primary purpose of the interaction—one purpose only! What do you want to achieve? Is it to find the name of the key decision maker within an organization? Is it to schedule a demonstration? Is it to invite a decision maker to your booth at an upcoming industry trade show? Don't "wing it." When you define progress in logical steps, your phone calls, voice mail messages and meetings become more efficient and effective.

Extra Financial Empowerment ···

I get a lot of calls from entrepreneurs who talk and talk and talk without saying who they are or the reason for the call. Fortunately, I'm good natured about this. Every once in a while, an especially enthusiastic entrepreneur will straightaway ask me to invest in a company which is the equivalent of asking for someone's hand in marriage on a first date! Angel investors and VCs won't ever say "yes, I want to invest" on a first phone call, but they can say "yes" to giving you an email address so you can send them an executive summary or "yes" to telling you what time is most convenient for a meeting.

···

☐ Develop your communication style

If the process of new customer relationship building is new to you, carve out a few hours of uninterrupted time to skim through several books on customer solicitation, customer negotiation and cold calling at a library or book store. Select the books that offer time-saving strategies that resonate most with you. Here are some of my favorite tips from my workshop sessions:

- **Say it with precision.** The average individual's attention span is about 30 seconds or less. Don't move on to the next action step until you can answer each of the following questions in less than 30 seconds!

  Susan: What does your company do?
  You: We specialize in providing…
  Susan: Who buys from your company?

> You: Our customers are…
> Susan: How's business?
> You: Business is great. We were just named best new restaurant of the year by…

- **Get to the point.** The subject line and first sentence of an email are the most important part of any email communication. Challenge yourself to write short notes that customers can scan with ease on a cell phone, pad or notebook computer.

- **Share your enthusiasm.** Nothing is more contagious than listening to an upbeat person who enjoys her work day.

  > Susan: What do you do?
  > You: I design jewelry for retail stores and catalogs. Now is an exciting time because we…

  After you have said something positive about your business, stop talking. Allow the other person to comment or ask a question.

- **Avoid yes or no questions.** At the start of my business career, a highly successful investment banker gave me some good advice. He said, "Whatever you do, don't ask yes or no questions during a first meeting with a prospective client." Why? Because one-word replies make it too easy to shut down a conversation. A better approach is to ask questions that start with the words: who, what, where, when, why, which or how. "What didn't you like about your last service provider?" "Which day is better for our company to meet with your graphic designers—Wednesday or Thursday?" A clothing shop owner can ask a customer, "What's your favorite color?" instead of something unimaginative like, "Can I help you?"

- **Don't "sell" in social situations.** If you meet a strong candidate for a future business relationship in a social setting, focus on obtaining a business card and confirming the best way to follow up with the individual early in the conversation.

☐ Listen for clues to customer "want"

My grandfather used to tell me that "you can't learn anything while you are talking." His advice is especially worthwhile for startup entrepreneurs. Your job in soliciting new client relationships is not to "pitch" your products or your company, but to create a relaxed, two-way conversation.

Skilled sales professionals have a great "customer-side" manner. They ask about hopes, dreams, wishes and wants. They show an interest in people and their situation. They want to know how the customer feels, what makes the customer unhappy, and what their company can do to make the customer feel great about the relationship. Rethink your approach to your target customers, both online and offline. Do you invite two-way conversations or do you just tell customers what you want them to know about your company? Again, you can't learn anything about your customer if you are the only one talking.

☐ Embrace objections

Customer objections can seem like a scary, dead-end situation. But are they really? Customer objections help give clues to customer priorities as well as problems customers may have encountered with other similar product or service providers. For example, a customer's statement that "I don't need that!" can lead to questions about what a customer really wants.

To help take the initial sting out of objections, spend some time practicing how to keep a conversation going after hearing a negative response to one of your questions. Ask a friend or business colleague who has experience in sales to role-play discussions. Your objective is not to come up with a clever come back line to a prospective customer's objection, but to acknowledge an objection without disputing it.

Here are some common objections to practice during role-play sessions:

- "We don't have any budget right now."
- "I'm not interested."
- "That's not my job."
- "I have one of those at home."
- "I don't have any time right now."
- "You don't have what I really want."

☐ Write down notes

No one's memory is as sharp one hour, one day or one week after any meeting or phone call with a prospective or current customer. Don't drive away to a next appointment or go back to other desk work before taking detailed notes about what you learned and follow-up action steps.

☐ Understand "No!"

Not everyone will say "yes" on your time schedule. When a potential customer says "No," don't get angry or discouraged. A "no" today can just mean "not now."

☐ Incentivize sales generation

Developing a purposeful commission structure for sales employees requires thoughtful attention—and more than a five minute discussion with a sales rep. It's natural for new business owners to be overly generous with sales reps in terms of territory coverage or commission rates when the company is desperate for new customer relationships. However, these early agreements can cause personnel dissention and contractual conflicts as a company grows.

I believe that sales commission checks are the best checks to sign because the expenditure is tied to cash generation and building a company's customer base. Here are my recommendations for rewarding sales achievement:

- All sales that involve a commission payment must be profitable sales. If your sales reps have a degree of price quotation flexibility, then consider developing a reduced commission schedule for less profitable sales.

- Research commission practices in your industry. Don't rely on a sales rep to tell you the norm.

- Avoid indefinite promises and the word "exclusive." Create a flexible sales commission plan that can adapt to product line adjustments, new sales partnerships, and geographic or industry expansion.

- Pay sales commissions to employees only after customers pay the bill. This policy will motivate your sales reps to avoid selling to deadbeats and help collect payments from slow-payers.

- Create a basic company sales commission plan and stick to it. Changing commission plans every year or so is emotionally and operationally disruptive to sales staff.

- Set specific end dates to every sales or distribution contract with all independent contractors, distributors or other sales agents. For example, the standard notification period for discharging an independent grocery broker is just 30 days. Also, consider early termination clauses that include the right to end a sales relationship for lack of performance, marketing competitive products, fraud, and other issues that might damage your brand or company's reputation.

Making the Most of Your Marketing Dollars

Standard marketing advice and tactics that work for big corporations may not work for cash-starved startups because all "brand awareness" and no "sales" can put a young company out of business. Here's another thing that many marketing professionals don't appreciate about startups and most small businesses in America—they can't survive on one-time customer visits, especially if the visit involves selling products or services at a deep discount!

Your next action steps:

☐ **Rethink free samples**

There is nothing "free" about giving a free sample to prospective customers. It's true that freebies can boost traffic to a website, store or office. However, freebies tend to attract customers who have no intension of ever buying the product or service. Think about it. How many times do you accept free food, cosmetics, newspapers or other product samples? Did you really *want* them? Did you throw them away later? Were you hungry for something and ready to buy, but the freebie satisfied your craving enough to lose interest in making a purchase?

I have two exceptions to my no freebie rule. The first is to offer a freebie as part of a bonus gift with purchase. This ensures that the freebie gift always involves cash generation without lowering the perceived value of your primary product or service.

The second exception is when a prospective customer *expressly asks* to taste, smell, feel, or in some other way experience a product or service before committing to a purchase. When a customer asks for something, they usually really *want* something enough to commit to a purchase.

Extra Startup Intelligence ···

There is no such thing as "free PR." Public relations and online viral campaigns take time to plan and execute, even if you do all the work yourself without paid assistance from public relations professionals. Until your company reaches the third Milestone of Financial Safety (consistent positive cash flow), your publicity initiatives should be geared to attracting target customers in your target geographic area or customer community, not the general public. Also favor publicity opportunities that promote your product or service rather than you as a featured entrepreneur.

···

☐ **Up-sell and bundle special offers**

No matter what kind of business you operate, offer every customer an "up-sell" opportunity. You can ask each customer to buy one more thing at the time a customer requests your services, while you are actively delivering a service, or at "check-out." In general, the add-on purchase should be less than the cost of the first purchase and should not require customers to think about it too long. Brainstorm ways you can make a customer's experience extra special or extra convenient. For example, a gardening service can offer to clean a homeowner's gutters at the time it rakes autumn leaves. That's one trip which generates two fees instead of one.

Alternatively, the gardener could bundle the same two services into one special promotion. Bundled promotions help hide the price of individual services from comparison shoppers. Bundling also increases the dollar value of each customer transaction, which is crucial for startups that might not yet enjoy steady customer traffic.

☐ **Explore referral and re-order initiatives**

Statistically, it is easier to generate a new order from a current customer than from a first-time customer. As your company develops customer relationships, how will you incentivize re-order activity and referrals? Don't make these important marketing decisions "on the fly." Plan them with precision for best results.

☐ **Discount the value of discounts**

I'm not a fan of coupons as a tool for generating lasting customer relationships. Sure, coupons might temporarily boost traffic and sales but it's highly likely that you are spending money to attract customers who won't be loyal to your brand. These commodity shoppers may come back again, but only with another coupon in hand. Startups just can't afford this kind of promotion misfire!

So are there any times when price discounting can be good for a new business organization? Yes. Special discounts work best in companies with high fixed costs and excess capacity. My favorite coffee shop discounts prices during specific slow-traffic business hours. Another productive use for price discounts is to help convert slow-moving inventory into cash. Still, try to bundle or include excess inventory as part of a gift-with-purchase.

☐ **Insist on a positive return on marketing initiatives**

Start On Purpose entrepreneurs don't "spend" their company's cash, they "invest" it. If you invest $500 in online advertising, then your company had better reap far more than $500 in profitable sales activity. If it doesn't, don't sign up for another round of money loss.

$$ ☐ **Monitor "cost of customer acquisition"**

If you don't measure performance, you can't improve it. As emphasized in Chapter 3, companies that pay a consistently high cost to earn a new customer will be valued lower than a company that can attract new customers in an efficient, low-cost manner. One metric that every entrepreneur should track at least on an annual basis is their company's "cost of customer acquisition." This number represents the average cost of securing a new customer relationship.

Different industries can calculate the cost of customer acquisition differently. However, the easiest way is to simply divide your company's total marketing and advertising costs by the number of new customers secured during the same period of time. Ideally, your company's cost of customer acquisition will go down year after year as you improve the effectiveness of your promotions and solicitation efforts. You can use this same formula to measure the effectiveness of different advertising initiatives too. Of course, consider using your company's cost of new customer acquisition as a metric for marketing employee performance evaluations. Make it a "do or die" deliverable.

FAQs

Q. My bakery can't afford to match my competitor's pricing—especially grocery stores. What can I do? Should I keep my prices high but then offer coupons to attract new business?

A. Consumers and business customers are happy to pay a premium for brands they love and value. To the extent that you create a brand promise that exudes delicious satisfaction, happiness, reliability, exclusive status and more, your customers won't compare your prices to cheaper competitors. This is why product pricing is not just a financial challenge, but a marketing challenge too.

With coupons, you don't want to spend hard cash to attract opportunistic coupon clippers who will talk more about the amazing deal they got, rather than your amazing cakes. Your marketing dollar should be allocated to securing customers who are able and willing to pay a premium price for a "quality experience" over and over again.

Think about how you can differentiate what you deliver (not sell) to your target customers. What "extra" can you provide that matches your company's brand promise? Can you package it in an unusual but consistent way—like Tiffany's robin's egg blue box and white ribbon? Can you create a unique little signature icing swirl—like Vienna Hotel Sacher's distinctive "S" that is added to the world-famous chocolate torte?

Your ability to sell your cakes and pies at a premium price will be based on your customer's appetite for your company's brand. Notice that I said your "brand" not your "pie" or "cake." New Yorkers can buy brownies at a grocery store or they can buy "Greenberg's brownies" from William Greenberg's little Madison Avenue store. Upper East Side New Yorkers make a point of announcing when they serve *Greenberg's* brownies because they are something special and nostalgic.

Your branding objective is to add something delightful to the experience of buying from your bakery. It doesn't have to be expensive, just something consistent. In the same way that a box of Cracker Jack has a prize and Raggedy Ann and Andy dolls have a little "I love you" message printed over the doll's heart, you can add something special to your product line that your customers will always look for and enjoy.

After you have added something special to the experience of buying and enjoying your bakery treats, your next action step is to identify different customer community targets to jumpstart your customer solicitation efforts. Don't wait for business to just walk in your door! Think about the kinds of events that call for something extra special. Identify at least three target customer communities and the reasons why they will *want* to be loyal to your bakery. Then start building your daily call and referral lists.

Remember, *you* have to create initial sales momentum for your bakery. Try to personalize your outreach efforts too. I know that I am far more likely to visit a bakery after a friendly discussion with the owner than receiving a flier in the mail.

Q. **I can't get a buyer on the phone to schedule a first meeting, should I go over the person's head to a higher level boss?**

A. Maybe. As a business owner, you are empowered to talk about business opportunities, not sales opportunities. If you go over the buyer's head you have to be prepared to elevate the conversation to a higher business purpose that is worthy of the time and attention of the boss. You can do this. For example, can you ask the boss for ideas and feedback on a prototype product or service? Can you explore a special marketing partnership—something that can boost the prospective customer's revenue base and yours? Here's one last tip before going over the buyer's head. Don't complain to the boss about the poor response of the junior buyer. Remember, it won't help to criticize a target customer's organization in any way.

Conquer It!

How to Lead Your Company Through Emotional Setbacks and Cash Flow Challenges

You don't need a fancy MBA to build a valuable business. You don't need to be from the "right side of the tracks" to raise thousands or millions of dollars of investment capital. And you don't need to have the slickest presentation skills to attract and retain a loyal customer base. All you need to succeed is cash and confidence. And that's what this chapter is all about—preserving your cash and confidence as you confront challenging situations and demanding personalities.

Conquer Indecision and Bad Decisions

Why do so many first-time entrepreneurs make decisions that they know deep down are wrong at the time? Why don't they trust their better judgment? As a startup educator, it's sobering to hear about a decision—made in a matter of minutes—that took a hard working entrepreneur's business seriously off course.

When I ask business owners to tell me more about the specific circumstances and moments right before they made a whopper mistake, they often talk about feeling "pressured," "distracted," or intensely "angry and frustrated." They also say that at the time when something went extremely wrong, they felt compelled to *just do something* without much thought about what else could go wrong from the move. In other instances of fateful decisions, it often turns out that it wasn't so much the specific problem that was the catalyst for the bad decision, but interactions with people that rattled the business owners' confidence and ability to make the right call—on their own terms.

Here are some types of situations that contribute to bad decision-making:

- Feeling "caught off guard" by someone (employee, vendor, customer, competitor, or investor) pushing for a fast decision
- Just assuming because of title or bravado that the person pushing for an answer really "knew more" or was "smarter"

- Trusting that the person giving advice was representing the entrepreneur's best interests
- Caving in to threats of a lawsuit, without learning if there is a legal basis for a lawsuit
- Not asking questions when people were using unfamiliar or intimidating technical terms
- Not speaking up about concerns and misgivings

Your next action steps:

☐ **Adversity is not failure**

When big problems surface, entrepreneurs often mistake them as a sign of professional failure—which really means to the entrepreneurial soul "I'm a personal failure." Unfortunately, I've seen how feelings of helplessness and "failure" can sap the resiliency of once fearless entrepreneurs.

Adversity is not failure. I say this quite a bit when I meet with struggling business owners. Adversity is not failure. It's important to remind yourself of this (or have your spouse or trusted advisors remind you) before your confidence sinks into a debilitating funk. Temporary problems are just that, temporary.

Highly debilitating, lasting feelings of failure can creep into the mindset of your company's board and employees when you—as the leader of your company—lose the will to fight, improve, and prosper. This means, especially if you are a first-time entrepreneur that you shouldn't give up or give in too soon. Adversity is not at all the same thing as failure.

☐ **Expect adversity**

Years ago I had a running coach who taught me a memorable lesson about how to cope with (not get rid of) extreme muscle aches and fatigue. She said, "Don't allow pain to paralyze you, rather welcome it as just part of the challenge of running a marathon." I didn't appreciate her advice at first but over time her wisdom proved to be extremely worthwhile.

All business leaders and companies struggle. One day a hacker may shut down your website. Another day, one of your oldest customers may file bankruptcy before paying your company's bill. When nasty surprises occur, just say to yourself, "Hello adversity, I've been expecting you." You can maintain psychological advantage when you accept problems and setbacks as a normal part of business flow. Saying "Why me?" doesn't work. Instead, confront adversity and figure out what you will do first, second, and third to solve the problems presented to your company. It's all about not *allowing* adversity to gain the upper hand of your emotions and confidence, which you can certainly do.

☐ Decide before noon

When is the best time of the day to make important decisions? In the morning! As the work day progresses, your resistance to bad employee behavior, outlandish customer requests and pushy sales people goes down. It is at these times when we are more likely to "just give in" to make a problem or person go away. Entrepreneurs who work long hours have to be highly disciplined to avoid making big decisions in the afternoon or evening hours. It's far better to "sleep on it" and make a decision in the morning when you are more refreshed and confident.

☐ Clear the room

"Present bias" is the term behavioral scientists use to describe a situation in which a person's willpower or resistance is compromised by something or someone who is present at the time a decision is being made. Judges often leave a courtroom before making important decisions. You can too. Send all sales people and staff members out of your office so they don't have the opportunity to compromise your better judgment.

☐ Change the time line

There are not many decisions that really have to be made on the spot. Usually people who are pushing for a fast answer do so for convenience and negotiating advantage…to them, not to you.

There are many effective ways you can "buy time" when you feel stressed out, surprised, manipulated or uneasy about making long-term contract commitments. I'm not talking about ducking responsibility in a fearful way, but buying more time to gather facts, read the fine print of a contract, explore competitive options or improve your negotiating tactics. Here are a few talking point examples which demonstrate how to stand your ground:

- "I haven't had a chance to read the paperwork but will try to in the next day or two. I will send you an email with specific questions and issues."

- "It's clear that this contract was prepared by a lawyer, so I have to get this document in front of my attorney for review."

- "I am not prepared to agree to this proposal as it now stands. If I was forced to give you an answer today, it would be no. Perhaps you can take a few days and improve your proposal before we give you a final answer. Some of our sticking points are…"

- "I really appreciate how fast you got this proposal into our hands—actually it was faster than we expected. As a matter of course, our company always obtains at least three competing bids for any job. We will get back to you once we've talked to a few other vendors and compared everyone's pricing and capabilities."

- "We are not ready to make an offer of full-time employment to you. However, we do have a project coming up that will require some of your programming skills. Perhaps we can explore a short-term consulting assignment so we can evaluate your ability to program in C++ and Java."

- "The office properties you've shown us today don't meet our budget specifications. I'd rather wait to get what I want than accept something that will create problems for my company from day one."

- "I read the fine print of your lease proposal. I saw that you included a personal guarantee, which is a deal breaker for working with our company."

After you announce your decision, stop talking. Don't let an awkward silence unnerve you. Be friendly, but firm. You'll soon find that the easiest way to stop being pushed around by pushy people is simply to disrupt their rhythm and momentum. You do have a lot of choices in managing your company, including the choice not to be pushed into something you don't really want or need to do.

☐ Walk away from anger

When people don't get what they want, they can erupt, make disparaging comments, name call, yell, or threaten an attack on social media. What should you do when someone attacks you in a hurtful, unprofessional way? Leave the room. Nothing good can come from talking to someone who is unable to reason or listen to your point of view. Here's one more tip. Don't agree to meet with the person until enough time has passed for reason to prevail. And when you do meet, consider inviting a third person to the meeting to temper more angry flare-ups.

☐ "Phone a friend"

When you have to make one or more critical decisions on matters that are relatively new to you, solicit at least one business colleague, advisor or board member for an independent perspective. You should never be too proud to ask for help, especially when you need it most. Failed entrepreneurs have told me over and over again, that they let their ego become the boss of their business.

☐ Share leadership

The more you want to grow your business, the more you must let go of the notion that you are the only—or even the most important—decision maker in your company. You can't always be there to tell employees what to do, but you can teach them how to make decisions that represent your leadership priorities.

If your employees are too dependent on you for direction then your company will struggle to move forward at a productive pace. Further, it's hard to consistently make really good decisions if you are overwhelmed by having to make too many decisions every day.

☐ Decide to be a "change agent"

It's ironic. Entrepreneurs are very good at recognizing what in the world needs improvement, but they often resist changing the very issues that cause the most grief and money loss to their beloved companies.

It's not hard to find businesses that keep selling products or services that just don't make any cents. Einstein said it best. Insanity is "endlessly repeating the same process and hoping for a different result." I do appreciate why entrepreneurs avoid making decisions to improve their companies. Most often the decisions involve letting go of some employees or favorite products. Nothing I can say will ever make these decisions any easier, but your greater purpose has to be to constantly adapt to changing markets. If you are uneasy about discussing changes with reluctant staff members, vendors or partners, substitute the word "improve" for the word "change."

Conquer Cash Challenges

"If you could do it all over again, how would you manage your company differently?" This is the question I pose to every struggling or bankrupt business owner I've ever interviewed. In one way or another, the answers always involve how the founder spent the company's cash. They say if they could do it again, they would be "smarter," "less trusting," "less wasteful," "more cautious," or "more practical" about how they spent their company's cash.

There is a lot you can learn from the mistakes of other business owners. If an idea or initiative is not directly related to generating cash or obtaining cash, then try to renegotiate it or skip it entirely.

I do recognize that this advice is easy to say, but harder for entrepreneurs to do. In the real world, the pressure on startup entrepreneurs and small business owners to spend money is intense and unrelenting. While you are soliciting your target customers, other business owners have YOU on their target list!

The secret to saying "no" or "not now" to persistent sales people, employees and colleagues, is putting a very high value on your company's cash. Cash is your company's life line. When you fully buy-into the close connection between your company's lasting health and its cash resources, then it will become easy to do the right thing in any situation.

Your next action steps:

☐ **Reset workday priorities**

Whenever you feel overwhelmed by a long list of "to do's," shorten your workday list to activities that will most directly and quickly bring cash to your organization. For startup companies, this usually involves soliciting new customers, pursuing investors for investment capital or calling delinquent customers for faster payments. At the start of each day ask, "What can I do today that will bring more cash to my company? Teach your employees to prioritize their workday in cash-generating terms too.

☐ **Evaluate spending opportunities in terms of purpose**

Every bill that you incur or pay can be grouped into one of four different types of business expenditures. Two of these expenditures are purposeful and can lead to a positive return on invested cash. The other two produce a negative return on invested cash. If too much of your company's cash is allocated to cash-losing initiatives, then someday soon your company's logo will appear on a tombstone in the dead business graveyard! Here are the four options:

How to Spend Your Company's Cash

Most Desirable:
1. Spend cash to generate revenues
2. Spend cash to buy or build valuable assets

Least Desirable:
3. Spend cash to support Uncle Sam
4. Spend cash down the drain

1. Spend cash to generate revenues

My favorite kind of cash expenditure directly builds a company's revenues and ultimately, it's "free cash flow" from operations. It's a matter of spending money on initiatives that have the best chance of bringing back even more cash to your company. Spending cash on first-class airfares may feel good for a few hours but I'd much rather allocate the cash to more purposeful uses such as hiring a new sales rep.

2. Spend cash to buy or build valuable assets

Company assets can include equipment, patents, inventory, customer lists, real estate, cars, computers and more. The value of a company's assets are totaled up on a company's balance sheet and help establish a company's "worth" to lenders and investors.

However, most assets like equipment, inventory, cars and computers lose their cash value over time due to technical obsolescence or age. Other assets, like intellectual property and real estate can grow in value and even kick off extra cash in the form of rent or licensing income, which of course I love most.

The best way to think about asset purchases is to be realistic about the value of the asset for your company's current operations. From a tactical standpoint, you want to avoid overpaying for assets that may lose their functional and financial value quickly. You can buy them; just don't break the bank to do it!

3. Spend cash to support Uncle Sam

Like it or not, your business will have to share its cash resources with city, state and federal government agencies every year you are in business. Some of these cash expenditures will be tied to your company's level of revenues, profits or payroll while other government obligations relate to annual business licenses, import tariffs, sales taxes or other fees that are relevant to your type of business. Will your business benefit as you write checks to the IRS and other government agencies? Certainly not on a direct basis, but paying taxes in a timely way can keep your business out of trouble or you out of jail. As long as you own your business, it will be up to you to seek out every legal tax loop hole and deduction you can use to pay the least amount possible to Uncle Sam.

4. Spend cash down the drain

Companies that spend their cash on initiatives that don't either build assets or revenues are what I call wasteful, business-killing "draino-dollar" expenses. These expenses can't be covered up or forgotten easily because they will show up on your company's financial statements in the form of bills to pay and red ink losses for prospective investors, lenders and business buyers to see.

What are some common draino-dollar debacles for startups? Check out my short list of no-good no-no's.

- Buying or manufacturing too much inventory that sits in a warehouse for months or years (Most auditors, lenders and business buyers "write down" the value of unsold goods to zero after 12 months.)

- Providing unclear or vague project specifications to software developers, contract manufacturers and other vendors, which lead to incomplete or unacceptable work, costly "change" orders, or an entire "do over" by another more qualified vendor

- Providing services or shipping products to customers who have no ability or intention to pay
- Hiring more people in administration and marketing than sales
- Spending more on administration and marketing than sales
- Missing errors in printed marketing literature, product packaging, business cards, etc. that end up in the trash
- Failing to obtain basic business liability insurance coverage to cover the unthinkable
- Hiring friends and other employees on a whim without considering their qualifications to improve your company's operating position and value
- Overpaying for anything

Whenever someone approaches you to buy something for your business, use this simple framework to help you carefully weigh the value of the initiative. Will the initiative directly build revenues or assets? Or, is it just another well-disguised draino-dollar expense? Whenever you uncover a draino-dollar expense in your organization, don't stop to blame yourself for the error. Just take fast steps to stop the flow of dollars down the drain.

☐ Perfect make-do management

Do you really need to buy brand-new office furniture or can you "make-do" with lower priced used desks and office chairs? Do you really need to dedicate a phone line for fax transmissions or can you test to see how much your business needs a fax machine before making a purchase?

When you have cash in your company's checking account, treat it like gold. Teach your employees to do the same. It's not a matter of being stingy, but purposeful.

Extra Financial Empowerment ··

Whenever a company has serious cash flow problems, vendors who complain the most often get paid first. This reality is rarely in the best interests of your company or you! During a prolonged cash crisis, pay bills in the following order:

1. Payroll taxes, income taxes and other tax-related interest and penalty obligations that can become the personal obligation of company officers and directors if the business defaults

2. Employee salaries and employee-related healthcare or other benefit programs including retirement contributions

3. Obligations that are backed by a personal payment guarantee such as business credit cards, small business loans, or leases

....

Conquer Doubt

Whenever I am asked to talk about an unusually inspirational entrepreneur, my thoughts always turn to a 60-something grandmother who repairs mud huts in rural South Africa. When I first met Iris, she did this backbreaking work, in the hot sunshine, with her baby grandson strapped to her back. Imagine that! She had many factors working against her: AIDS in her family, poverty, crime, lack of education. She could have let fear of failure, her age, or any other excuse discourage her from starting a business, but she didn't. With the help of a micro-loan to buy a wheelbarrow, cement and trowels, she was able to get her business off the ground and persevere in a very profitable way. She's a star.

As you start and build your business, know that I am your biggest fan. What you are about to do can be transformational for you, your family, and your local community. Your new company might soon put dozens or hundreds of people to work. Your company's innovations may solve a major problem for our nation or our planet. Or, like Iris, your new company may provide a better lifestyle for your family.

Along your entrepreneurial journey, whenever you feel like you are out of ideas, flip through the pages of this book for a few fresh ideas. Let them give you a renewed sense of confidence in your ability to build a lucrative business that someday will be worth two, four or ten times your cash investment. How do I know you can do it? Because, just like Iris, you have what it takes to achieve your purpose!

FAQs

Q. **Can I send you my business plan and get your feedback before sending it to investors?**

A. Outside of my workshops, venture finance activities and business plan competitions, it's hard to squeeze in several hours to read business plans cover-to-cover. For this reason, you should *not* want my help. Remember from Chapter 9—accept feedback from individuals who are knowledgeable about your industry *and* can give your business plan the thoughtful attention it deserves. Don't settle for anything less! Still, you can send me a specific question by email or through Twitter. Each week I spend a couple of hours replying to as many questions and letters as I can. Write to: questions-for-susan@StartOnPurpose.com

Acknowledgement

Start On Purpose has had a long incubation period. It began with Don Smith, the former business editor of Hearst Corporation's *Seattle Post-Intelligencer*. Years ago, Don took a chance on me—a finance person with an idea but no professional journalism credentials. Each week, Don, Margaret Santjer and John Cook made sure that my work was up to their high standards. No rookie newspaper columnist could ever have better guidance and role models. Thank you.

I am especially grateful to the business owners around the country who shared their stories of money loss with me. It's easy to talk about business success, but much harder to talk about dashed dreams and disappointment. They allowed me to ask tough questions, open old wounds and talk about their businesses in deeply personal ways. Their experiences have brought a higher purpose to my work today.

Start On Purpose is a better book because of Steven B. Winters, senior intellectual property attorney at Lane Powell. Steve is a perfect partner for entrepreneurs who want to achieve great things.

I'd also like to thank all the highly dedicated managers and executive directors of SCORE, the Small Business Administration, micro-finance organizations, veterans' assistance programs, and incubators who have given me an open door to test new ways to teach entrepreneurship and sustainable small business management.

Over the years of writing print and online articles, I have relied on the insights and expertise of many professionals from BDO, Davis Wright Tremaine, Colabella & Company, Deloitte, DLA Piper LLP, Grant Thornton, Ernst & Young, Fenwick and West LLP, Fish & Richardson, KLA Gates, KPMG, Lane Powell, Orrick, Perkins Cuie, PriceWatershouseCoopers, and Wilson Sonsini. These firms are generous sponsors of business plan competitions, angel investment forums and entrepreneurial education events around the country. I am also grateful to Steven Saide, a valued friend and master talent in securities law who taught me early on how to be more precise and thoughtful about issues that can affect a young company many years down the road.

Taking on new career challenges is always easier when you are surrounded by determined trailblazers who work with a strong sense of community. Julia Bolz, Janine deZarn, Lisa Indovino, Lauren Lazin, Cheryl Nixon, Mary Ostien, Susan Petty, Pamela Ottaviano Rhodes, and Anne Zeiser each helped me stay the course from the moment of inspiration and forward. Thanks for all your smiles and support.

I am grateful to my editor Waverly Fitzgerald and book designer Bob Lanphear for enhancing every page of *Start On Purpose*. They understood the spirit of the book and never tired of looking at check lists and offering suggestions. I admire their perseverance and creativity.

And lastly thank you to my beloved husband Dan, whose patience and good humor is unending.

Index

About the Author

Susan A. Schreter's background in finance covers the life cycle of starting, building and selling a business in America through investment banking, angel investing, lower middle market buyout fund investing and commercial banking. She is a National Association of Corporate Directors fellow and active board member for emerging growth companies.

Susan is a MBA-level instructor in entrepreneurship with a special focus on social enterprise development and startup sustainability. She is a regular contributor to MSN, Yahoo! Small Business and Fox Business and featured writer in business and entrepreneurship magazines. She is a popular speaker and workshop presenter to micro-finance organizations, incubators, colleges, and the Small Business Administration as well as a non-partisan television commentator on public policy issues that affect small business.

SOMETHING I'VE BEEN TOLD TO CHANGE.
o

WHAT WILL I DO TO MAKE THE CHANGE?
o